LONG DAYS AND SHORT PAYS

THE ADVENTURES OF A SMALL-TIME PRO WRESTLER

Duke West

LONG DAYS AND SHORT PAYS

THE ADVENTURES OF A SMALL-TIME PRO WRESTLER

BY

H.E. "DUKE" WEST

EDITED BY SCOTT TEAL

CROWBAR
PRESS
Gallatin, Tennessee

LONG DAYS AND SHORT PAYS

THE ADVENTURES OF A SMALL-TIME PRO WRESTLER

Published by Crowbar Press
106 Tattnall Court
Gallatin, Tennessee.

www.crowbarpress.com

Book layout and cover design by Scott Teal
Cover photo courtesy of Harold West

Library of Congress Cataloging-in-Publication Data

West, Harold
Long Days and Short Pays / by H.E. West — 1st ed.

1. West, H.E. 2. Sports—United States—Biography. 3. Wrestling—United States—Biography. I. West, H.E. II. Title.

Printed in the United States of America
ISBN 978-0-9844090-0-6

First Edition / February 2010

TABLE OF CONTENTS

This book is dedicated to the memory of Robert "Bobby" Golden. He was a true friend who taught me so much about wrestling, life, and loyalty.

Acknowledgements

To my wife, Tenna, who encourages me and inspires me every day.

To my editor, Scott Teal, for making it possible for me to put these memories in print.

To all my friends and loved ones who have stood by me for so many years, through good times and bad.

Foreword

About a year ago, I was flipping through the TV channels and came across professional wrestling. It was one of the big national cable promotions. I hadn't watched any wrestling on the tube for a while, so I thought I would check it out. I witnessed about 25 minutes of promos, cheesy skits, and ridiculous "over the top" costumes. I thought I had accidentally flipped onto the cartoon channel! When they finally got around to showing about a three-minute snippet of ring action, it looked like a Chinese acrobat act at the circus.

Two guys were taking turns doing all sorts of spectacular aerial work. I saw back flips, cartwheels, somersaults, and other things I can't even describe. They did just about everything but wrestle! They made contact with each other and one of them wound up on his back in the middle of the ring. The other guy ran across the ring, climbed the turnbuckles like a ladder, and did a back flip onto his opponent. Finally, the referee appeared to make the three count. Up until then, he had stood in one of the corners and hardly moved at all. I guess his only function was to be there when it was time to count.

I had to wonder if either of those guys knew what an arm bar was. I was sure they had no idea what a "figure four leg lock" or a "full nelson" might be. I don't think I saw them "lock up" at any point! It was all fluff and no substance.

I could only stomach about 30 minutes of the stuff and switched to something more entertaining, like reruns of infomercials for making a fortune in real estate without a down payment.

I wondered if this was what wrestling had really come to. Has it gone from the time when guys like my uncle, Leaping Louie Allman, began their careers in a carnival sideshow to being a cable TV sideshow? It made me think about the wrestling I grew up with — the wrestling that I was a part of. My mind wandered back to the "old days."

Wrestling, or as some called it, 'rasslin', was an important part of my life while I was growing up. There were fans and there were non-fans. Part of what made that era interesting was the "mystery." There was always the big debate over whether or not wrestling was "for real," fake, or something in-between. I really believe that most on either side of the issue were never really one hundred percent sure.

The debate went on at the assembly line in the plant where my father worked. It was discussed around the water cooler at the newspaper office where my mother worked. And, of course, it went on in the schoolyard and playgrounds where I spent my youth. The non-fans talked about the "pulled" punches, and the foot stomp, which was where the power of the punch went, instead of to the opponent's face. And, of course, the infamous blood capsules they swore they saw the guy smash on his head.

As a kid, I must say I found some of these things to be quite possible. However, having been to a live show and having seen one of those guys bleed up close, I knew blood capsules could only produce so much blood. Once a wrestler busted a capsule on their head and the small amount of blood ran out, where was the rest coming from? I saw the blood oozing from a guy's head! Also, what happened to the broken capsules? Did they just vanish into thin air? None of the non-believers could produce a broken capsule from around or in the ring. If I pressed the issue with my schoolmates, they would back off and say the guy I saw bleed probably got cut accidentally, but it was really all fake!

Since they weren't fans and never watched it on television, I often wondered how they all became such experts in the wrestling business. As I grew older, I began to watch wrestling with a more skeptical eye. I was still drawn to the sport. I loved it. My family loved it. Even with those lingering doubts about the "validity" of the wresting game, we couldn't wait for that next TV show, or the next time they had a house [arena] show in our town. The mystery was part of the reality and the reality was part of the mystery.

Like most of the fans, I knew deep down inside that there was something suspicious about a guy getting beat down until he was barely conscious, and then two seconds later, he was well enough to come back and whip his opponent. Still, when the announcer would talk about the resiliency of wrestlers, their toughness, their ability to rebound, we all sat nodding our heads in agreement. If you wanted to believe, you were a fan. If not, there was nothing anyone could do to make you change your mind. Even if we saw a really bad match where it was blatantly obvious that a guy missed a punch or a kick, and his opponent sold it like he was really hurt, we dismissed it. We would simply say, *"Well, it isn't all faked!"*

When I got an opportunity to get into wrestling myself, I remained a fan. To this day, I love to watch "old-school" wrestling. And, I dismiss those critics who imply that my involvement in wrestling made me somewhat of a con man. I know a little something about con men. Con men only want your money. Con men really don't care if you get anything of value from them. I have received a great deal from wrestling — both as a fan, and as a wrestler and referee. As a wrestler, I wanted to leave the fans with something they would remember. When I strutted to the ring as "The Canadian Rose," I saw excitement and joy when I looked into the faces of the fans. It was the same look I saw on the faces of my parents and grandparents. Sometimes, I would see a young lad look at me with the awe and wonder that I had when I was a child attending the matches. I was a heel [bad guy], and when I was getting my dues from the babyface [good guy], I would often look out and see the glee the fans were feeling. For those few moments, I was the bully at their school, their unreasonable boss at the office, or the nasty neighbor down the street. They were experiencing the joy of seeing justice served, just like when the cavalry rode in to save the day in the old westerns. That was exactly what I wanted to give them for their money, and I got that from being a wrestling fan.

Most con men make a lot of money. I didn't. In fact, I probably lost money when everything was said and done. Most of the promoters I worked for claimed they didn't make a lot of money, either. I can't tell you how many times I heard them say they had lost money when it came time for the payoff. And yet, we continued to do it week after week. Once the wrestling game got into our blood, there was no turning back.

We loved doing what we did and the fans loved to watch, which meant we were both winners. We gave them a good product for a good price. You could call it an athletic event, entertainment, an exhibition, or a combination of all three. I rarely heard of anyone leaving one of our shows unhappy. Disappointed, perhaps, if their hero got beat, but I never heard a complaint from someone who felt they did not get a good show!

What I saw in the new cable wrestling show, however, was very disappointing. For the first time in my life, I was not only upset with the show, but I was embarrassed for the wrestlers ... and for myself for having once been associated with the business.

As I began to reflect on the "old-school" wrestling I knew and loved, I decided to write down some of the stories. This is the story of guys who loved the business and were dedicated to it. It's the tale of a hack wrestler and his friends. It's the story of how wrestling used to be and (I hope) will be again.

Chapter 1

The Dark Period

In the 1950s and 1960s, people had only a few reasons to own a television set. After all, we could only get five channels, and that was if we had a really good, outdoor antenna. Some of the reasons we had a television were *The Ed Sullivan Show*, *The Red Skelton Show*, *Bonanza*, *The Wonderful World of Disney*, and, most importantly, pro wrestling, or as we knew it back then, 'rasslin'. In the earliest days, TV wrestling aired from of Chicago and the broadcast times and dates weren't always consistent. Eventually, we got the shows out of Indianapolis on WTTV, Channel 4. Those shows brought us names like Dick the Bruiser, Wilbur Snyder, Bobo Brazil, the Sheik, Bobby Heenan, and many more that we loved to cheer or hate.

Like everyone else at the time, we had a black-and-white television set. We never dreamed of a day when we wouldn't look down the street and see those big TV antennas on the roofs of every home. Looking like giant metal trees, they emerged from every rooftop and had to be pointed south towards Indianapolis, which was where four out of the five channels were broadcast: ABC, CBS, NBC, and WTTV. We could also get WLBC, the local channel, but it was more like a forerunner to PBS. At any rate, I saw wrestling and all the heroes of the ring in black and white. I knew the wrestlers were real people, but it was hard to picture them in color. Even my fertile, young imagination couldn't begin to prepare me for the first time I saw wrestling live.

Years later, Grandpa bought one of the first color TV sets when they came out. On the first Sunday night after he got the set, we went over to his house to watch *Bonanza*, one of the few shows broadcast in color. We all sat around, eagerly waiting for the show to begin. When it did, it was as if a rainbow of colors exploded in front of our eyes. We were amazed and awestruck.

Today's technology is so advanced, and changes come so quickly, that it seems our young people are barely impressed by the advancements. They can't imagine a world without color TV, and I doubt they can imagine a world without cable TV. Back then, the leap from black-and-white to color was a miracle of sorts.

We lived in a typical, middle-class neighborhood in Muncie, Indiana, a blue-collar community with typical mid-America values. My dad worked at an automotive plant in Anderson, Indiana, while Mom was a writer for the local newspaper. My grandfather was a greenskeeper at the local country club. The one thing we all learned to share and love was professional wrestling, and in our house, plans always revolved around being sure we were home on Saturday afternoon to watch wrestling. We could depend on that being the cleaning day and we had hamburgers for dinner ... and we always made sure we finished our chores in time to watch wrestling on Channel 4. If, for some reason, we weren't at home to watch, we were at Grandma and Grandpa West's house. Grandpa *really* got into 'rasslin'. I can still picture Grandpa in his recliner. As the action got hot and heavy in the ring, Grandpa got a death grip on the arms of his chair. He would tense up and the veins would stand out in his neck as he began rolling and bouncing around in the chair. At times, he would voice a loud "boom!" with each punch landed by the "good guys." If the good guy was victorious, Grandpa's applause could be heard throughout the house. If the bad guy won, there was the obligatory conversation about how the "ref" was paid off or just plain blind. The conversation continued for some time after the show ended. You could tell just how good the show was by how long the conversation continued afterwards.

Then there was my Uncle Taylor. He was not as animated as Grandpa when he watched wrestling, but he sure was intense. Uncle Taylor was known for his propensity for the use of profanity. During the matches, he usually sat still, staring at the television. I can still picture him leaning forward, with his arms on his legs, staring intently at the tube. He hardly moved a muscle until the match was over. If the bad guy won, he would let loose with a string of cuss words to describe the bad guy and/or the referee. We all cracked up the day Aunt Lena snapped at him after one of those tirades. *"Taylor West. Can't you say even one sentence without cussing!"* Uncle Taylor's immediate response was, "Oh, the hell I can't!" Grandma even had to move her parakeets to the spare bedroom when Uncle Taylor was around. It seems they were quite adept at picking up the colorful phrases used by Uncle Taylor. They sometimes would repeat them in mixed company, which caused great embarrassment (especially when the preacher would call unexpectedly).

Uncle Taylor was not one for smiling or laughing. He did love his wrestling, though. I never saw any indications of affection from him for anything else. The closest thing I ever got from him in the way of affection was when he squeezed my shoulder as he passed me on the way to the living room from Grandma's dining room. Oh, and there was the one time when he asked me to pull his finger. I never did that again!

He really did love his 'rasslin'. Uncle Taylor attended a live show at the Muncie Fieldhouse. At that time, the top heels in the area were Ray and Roy, the Shire brothers. One of the prelims [preliminary matches] on the card was a ladies match. The villainess sported bleached-blonde hair, just like the Shires. At one point during her match, she wound up outside the ring. As she passed Uncle Taylor, he called her "Grandma Shire." He swore that was all he said to her, but who really knows the truth. At any rate, she spun around and slapped him across the face. He said he had a ringing in his ears for days. After that incident, when we all went to one of the live shows, Uncle Taylor would watch with the same intensity he did when it was on TV. However, he never said a word to anyone, especially the wrestlers!

When Uncle Taylor passed away, I was really surprised to learn that he had requested my brother and me to be pallbearers at his funeral. I guess that ornery old coot liked me after all … or, maybe, it was because I was a wrestler by that time. I hadn't seen much of him for a few years before his death. They said he had changed a lot. He was going to church and had cleaned up his language. Still, at that funeral, I had to keep from chuckling as the minister was speaking. I thought about the "Grandma Shire" incident and pictured him leaning in towards the TV set, as if he was in a trance. He never expressed any emotions or told us he cared about us. I guess when all was said and done, the things he did care about were the important things — family and wrestling. He just wouldn't admit to the family part.

When talking about the fans who interacted with the wrestlers, there was an elderly lady named Anna Buckalew, popularly known as Ringside Rosie, at the matches in Pittsburgh, Pennsylvania, who really got into the action. She sat in the front row every Saturday at the Pittsburgh TV studio matches. She was continuously standing up and sitting down, and she yelled at the bad guys throughout the matches. Often, when the heel [bad guy] was getting the better of the babyface [good guy], the camera would cut from the ring to see her reaction to whatever the heel was doing to the babyface at the time. She was even known to swing her umbrella at one of the wrestlers. I remember one time when she nailed Gorgeous George on the back of his legs as he stood on the apron of the ring. The photo of that incident wound up in magazines and newspapers.

Ringside Rosie inspired me to pursue one of my earliest dreams as a teenager. I wanted to open a bar-and-grill type of operation, which would be centered around a ring on a lower level where I would present boxing and wrestling matches on a regular basis. Tiers of seating would go up to the main level. I pictured the establishment as one decorated with posters and photos of all the great boxers and wrestlers. I wanted it to be a place where they could train by day and work by night, all in the presence of the patrons. I even dreamed that a well-known boxer might use it as his training camp to prepare for an upcoming bout. The place would have been called "Ringside Rosie's," in honor of the lady I considered to be wrestling's greatest fan. Of course, some folks would swear I wanted to name it after the Canadian Rose (my future ring persona), but I had that dream long before I ever dreamed of being in the wrestling business. It was just a way for me to be close to the business when I became an adult. I dreamed that boxing and wrestling fans would flock to Ringside Rosie's from all over the country and I could live every day with my love of the ring sports. I imagined the great ring stars of past eras stopping in to check things out and how we would all become great friends. Unfortunately, it was a dream which never came to fruition, but a fellow can dream, can't he? When I did get into the wrestling business, I soon discovered how tough it was to make big money. I invite anyone to steal my idea, but if you do, I ask is that you build it close enough to me that I can be there regularly. And, I had better be invited to the grand opening. I'll send you a Canadian Rose photo for the wall.

On Mondays, the conversation at both work and school often revolved around wrestling. The fans talked about that weekend's wrestling show, while those who weren't fans just shook their heads and walked away. This might be hard for the younger generation to believe, but *nobody* in that day (fan or not) could say they had never heard of Dick the Bruiser or Wilbur Snyder. Some of the kids at school would make fun of those of us who watched wrestling, and yet, if we growled something in a "gravelly" voice, they knew we were imitating the Bruiser.

Then there was the "Dark Period." There came a time when the powers that be had the audacity to move *Championship Wrestling* from the Saturday afternoon time slot to one o'clock a.m. on Sunday morning. Of course, that was a time before VCRs and DVD recorders had been invented. If we missed a show, we missed it, unless, of course, there was a repeat of the show at a later date. By then, however, someone had already told us all about it and spoiled the whole thing. Anyway, that put an end to watching wrestling in our household. Dad wouldn't allow me to stay up that late (or get up that early) and he sure wasn't going to.

Now, Grandpa was a different story. He still went to bed at his normal ten o'clock, but he set the alarm to wake him in time to watch wrestling, and afterwards, he went right back to bed. Grandma declined to get up with him. She did have to get up one night when she heard Grandpa clapping and cheering loudly, followed by a huge "thump!" She rushed out to discover that while he was bouncing around in his recliner, he lost his death grip on the arms of the chair, toppled the recliner backwards, and unceremoniously dumped himself out onto the floor. Grandpa wasn't hurt, but he was the subject of family ribbing for the rest of his life.

The only thing we knew about wrestling during that time was from the briefing we got from Grandpa on Sunday evening. If something really exciting happened, we would get a call in the mid-afternoon, but it was usually late in the day unless my Dad called him first. For me, the wait was torture, and even after hearing about it, the idea that I hadn't been able to see it was murder. Fortunately, the "Dark Period" didn't last too long and 'rasslin' once again began airing on Saturday afternoon where it belonged. All was right with the world again.

Occasionally, we would even get a bonus. Once in a while, one of the stations would broadcast one of the west coast wrestling promotions and we got to see the likes of Hard Boiled Haggerty and Skull Murphy. It didn't happen often enough for us to really get into the story lines, or to pick a favorite, but it was 'rasslin' and that was all we needed to know in order to watch.

One of the things I learned growing up was that Muncie, Indiana was not the entertainment capital of the world. Most of the shows which hit Indiana in those days took place in Indianapolis. Ball State University was still Ball State Teachers College, and few dreamed it would become the big university it is today. I never imagined it would someday boast a beautiful campus auditorium where first class-acts would perform. Indianapolis wasn't close to what it is today, either. It was large and dirty. My dad hated it when he had to go there for any reason. He would take us there for the state fair every year, but that was about it. There was no interstate highway then and it took almost an hour to get there. As a result, kids in Muncie had only a few things to which they could look forward. The biggest events in Muncie were the Muncie Central Bearcat high school basketball games, the annual pancake supper at the Masonic Temple, the circus, Soap Box Derby races on the street by McCulloch Park, harness racing, and outdoor wrestling shows in the summer at the Delaware County fair grounds or the Muncie Fieldhouse.

The fairground sat on the north side of Muncie and hosted a large county fair every summer. It was a good-sized place with lots of buildings and exhibit areas. On site was a grandstand with a quarter-mile track for harness racing, occasional midget race cars, and (of course) professional wrestling. For many years, wrestling was a staple at the county fair. That was where I had my first experience with live wrestling shows.

Every month, I would scrape up enough money to go across the street to the Haag Drug Store and get my copies of *Wrestling Illustrated* and *The Ring, Wrestling*. I read them both faithfully and many of the photos of my favorite stars wound up adorning the walls of my bedroom. I loved a lot of sports: boxing, racing, basketball, baseball, and especially football. However, my real passion was for wrestling. If you are a real wrestling fan, it gets in your blood and stays there. Even today, I love reading about the old stars of the past, and get me a ticket to some old-fashioned 'rasslin' action and I am a happy camper!

In the 1960s, the heroes were guys we could relate to. They weren't pumped up artificially with steroids. You could easily differentiate between the good guys and the bad guys. There was no grey area whatsoever. When Dick the Bruiser "flipped" and went from being the worst of the bad guys to being a "good guy," his style never changed, but the fans always knew which side he was on. Fritz von Erich, Baron von Raschke, and Mitsu Arakawa represented the dreaded Nazi and Japanese empires that our parents and grandparents fought against. And then there was The Sheik [Ed Farhat].

Long before terrorism became a huge issue in this country, the Sheik was able to capitalize on our ignorance of the culture of the Middle East. Long before we were ever directly attacked or threatened by radical Muslims, the Sheik was bringing his prayer rug into the ring. He couldn't begin a match without saying his prayers to Allah. His "camel walk" had him strutting around the ring with his head bobbing and exaggerated arm movements. He let his tongue hang out of the side of his mouth and he occasionally roared out, *"Wayy-ohhh-wayy ohhh! Too-Too!"*

As a youngster, I often entertained my family with my imitation of the Sheik. It was all quite humorous until I passed along my act to my younger nephew. Unfortunately, he chose to show off this new talent in the middle of a nice hotel when my sister and brother-in-law were on vacation. After that, I was sternly advised to give up, or at the very least, to severely curtail my impressions of the Sheik. I imitated many of the other wrestlers, but none were as much fun as the Sheik. We loved to mimic and mock the villains of wrestling, and we would entertain ourselves for days after the shows. However, our parents weren't too happy when we would play wrestling. When we did, we usually broke something. Since my bed was our makeshift ring, I must confess to having cracked a few bed slats as a youngster as I pretended to "bulldog drop" a bad guy. When we outgrew my bed, we pretended to do interviews, using one of my mother's egg beaters as a makeshift microphone. I usually imitated the Bruiser.

In those days, I had my own version of backyard wrestling. I didn't look at what I was doing as pretending. In my eyes, I was a wrestler in training. I was the youngest of my family by seven years and there were few playmates my age in the immediate neighborhood, so much of the time, I entertained myself with my imagination and whatever props I could lay my hands on. My sister Janet, who I am told made it her mission to spoil me as a baby, got married when I was quite young. My sister Betty was busy with her activities and was soon off to nursing school in Fort Wayne. The closest to me in age was my brother Wayne, but he was usually playing with the Yoakum boys next door who were closer to his age.

Some of the kids built makeshift soap box cars and took turns pushing each other down the alley behind our house. The alley had a nice little downgrade and dumped them out onto Elm Street. They always had a spotter stationed at the bottom of the hill who would give the "all clear" signal when no cars were in sight. The car was pushed down the alley to speed across Elm and up the alley on the other side, where it coasted to a stop. One time, after convincing me it was perfectly safe, they gave me a turn. Just as I began to roll down the incline, the spotter yelled, *"Car!"* I was certain I was about to be splattered all over Elm Street, but worst of all, I worried about who was going to explain it to Dad. Fortunately, the car was quite a ways off and I survived the trip. They didn't have to worry about me asking to participate in that activity again.

There also was the time my brother chased me around the yard with a "snake" that was actually a piece of rope. I made my way into the house and locked myself in the bathroom. To my horror, Wayne decided to throw the "snake" through the open transom over the bathroom door. I yanked the door open so quickly that the hinges came loose, which got me into trouble with my parents.

Oh yeah. And then there was the lake incident. We had just arrived at the lake for summer vacation when Wayne and I raced down to the dock to check things out. At one moment, I was standing on the dock looking down at the water, and in the next, I was in the lake ... fully clothed and going under. I have to give Wayne credit for reaching down and dragging me out by my collar. To this day, he claims he had nothing to do with me winding up in the water, but I still refuse to be convinced.

Until I was old enough to wander across the street and venture off of my block, it was up to me to entertain myself. To that end, I often wrestled imaginary opponents on the front porch or in the back yard of our home at 421 East 7th Street. In order re-enact the matches I watched on TV, I had to create my own ring and arena out of whatever was available at the time. The top railing of our front porch was about three feet off the ground, so it became my top rope. Of course, the corner post became ... the corner post. I became fairly accomplished at "going over the top rope" [porch railing] and landing on the ground below. I could flip myself around the porch in mock arm drags and hip tosses. I ran my head into the imaginary turnbuckle on the corner post of the porch. I had some pretty good matches against all the great heels of the day.

As I grew, the porch could no longer handle my matches. Not only was it too small, but I feared the trouble I would be in if I managed to break one of the boards on the porch floor. Additionally, I became aware of the passing traffic on the highway near our house, and embarrassment forced me to move my venue to the back yard. The large tree became the corner post into which I whipped myself or my head. The thick bark made it rather uncomfortable, but it was a better option than the hard wood of the porch. The siding on the house was like sandpaper, and when I was careless, I would lose a few layers of skin. Occasionally, I would throw myself onto a stone or a twig, and the matches would be cut short. If the errant debris caused a bruise or obvious discomfort, I never told anyone what really happened.

My faithful dog Trixie often became the audience. She didn't get excited about the ring action. Rather, she looked somewhat bewildered at the sight of me crashing into the tree and flopping about like a freshly-caught mackerel. When I laid on the ground, selling a bodyslam or an arm drag that my imaginary foe had inflicted on me, she would walk over and carefully sniff me, before licking my face to be sure that I was really okay. She was a smart dog. If only I could have taught her to count, she would have made a great ref. She stayed out of the way until I was on my back on the ground.

With my brother Wayne's track record of terrorizing me, I wasn't about to invite him to participate in my wrestling matches. No doubt, I would be on the losing side. Inspired by watching *Friday Night Fights* on television, he would sometimes convince me to put on some mittens and box him. He always volunteered to get down on his knees and wear the mittens which had the most padding. He also swore he would, in his words, "go easy" with me. And yet, I always ended up with a bloody nose or a black eye. I guess Wayne was my first encounter with a "crowbar," as tough guys were known in the wrestling business. I figured it was much wiser, and ultimately safer, for me to give myself backdrops, arm-drags, dropkicks, and the like.

Practicing and learning those flops and flips on the hard ground at home made the landings I later made on a padded ring floor a little easier. I learned to go with the moves and get high into the air for a "good" bump. I guess that is a good example of play preparing me for life. I was in training for my future venture into wrestling, even though I didn't realize it at the time. I am sure some of those who observed my backyard antics thought I must be crazy. Probably so, but man, was it ever great fun!

The fantasy matches helped me pass many a long summer day and they became my wrestling fix until Saturday afternoon once again rolled around. Eventually, I outgrew the backyard wrestling, but it continued much later in my years than anyone would imagine. I became friends with two other kids in the area, Jack Bragg and Don Eplin, and we began to hang around together. We became known as the "Three Musketeers." I don't think they ever shared my zeal for professional wrestling, but we shared many other interests, like playing football, going to the movies, and, of course, girls!

I desperately wanted to become a wrestler, but how would a less-than-athletic guy like me get his foot in the door and find someone willing to train me. Well, there was my Uncle Louie. "Leaping Louie" Allman boxed and wrestled in the 1920-1930 era. I was twelve years old when I met him for the first time, but I had heard many stories about the exploits of that tough old bird. My grandparents lived about two blocks from the railroad yards in Muncie, so he would often stay with them when he passed through the area. It was quite common back then for hobos to hop on and off the many freight trains which passed through.

The story goes that Uncle Louie would go out for a long run every morning. One morning, while Grandpa was outside tending his garden, he saw Uncle Louie running along the street by the railroad yard. Two hobos were sitting on the curb. As Uncle Louie runs by, they said something and laughed. Uncle Louie promptly turned around and thrashed both of them, leaving them on the sidewalk like two bags of discarded trash. He then jogged off as if nothing had happened. It turns out that Uncle Louie sported the trademark of boxers and wrestlers of that day: cauliflower ears. The hobos thought his ears looked quite funny and felt compelled to tell him so as he passed. I guess they learned a lesson in manners that day.

In 1961, when I was twelve years old, the summers weren't as exciting as they had been in the past. Wayne was off in the Air Force, my sisters had their own families, and I had a limited circle of friends who (unlike my brother) were not obligated to keep me entertained all day while my folks were at work. Then came the announcement that Uncle Louie was coming to town. He would be staying with my grandparents for a month or so. I could hardly wait. On the first Saturday that he was in town, we were invited to Grandma and Grandpa's for a family dinner.

I have to admit that when I met my uncle face to face for the first time, I was a little disappointed. For all the stories about his feats of strength, both in and out of the ring, I was taken aback to see that he was not a big man, much less the giant I had expected. Even so, it took me a while to warm up to him as I was in awe of being in the presence of a real wrestler. I walked to my grandparent's home several times before I felt comfortable enough to talk about wrestling and boxing. I was surprised to find that he didn't have the same enthusiasm that I had about it. He was very matter of fact, answering all my questions, but volunteering little information.

By the time I met Uncle Louie, he was up in years and he walked with a cane. I have never been a small guy by any means. I began to tease him about the fact that he was up in years and I thought he was old enough that I could "take him." Uncle Louie just grinned as he switched his cane to his left hand, telling me to grab his arm. I took hold of his arm and held on tightly, thinking it was a strength contest. I couldn't have been more wrong. There *was* no contest. Without a pause, he lifted me completely off the ground, carried me to the other side of the room, and set me down. *"You still think you can whip your old uncle?"*

"Uhh, no, sir!" I guess I learned a lesson that day myself.

Uncle Louis would never talk much about his earliest experiences as a wrestler. The story that ran through the family at that time was that he originally boxed and wrestled as part of a carnival sideshow. They would roll into a town and there would be a challenge for anyone who could beat him or stay with him for "X" amount of minutes. A couple of "set up" guys [also known as shills or plants] would take up the challenge and put up money to take him on. The locals would see these guys "beat" Uncle Louie and get "paid" a nice reward. That, of course, was to motivate the "towners" to get up the courage to try it for themselves. They would put up money for the opportunity and other carnies in the crowd would make bets with the spectators. Naturally, Uncle Louie would dispatch the challengers with alacrity. I don't know the reason why, but he would never confirm or deny that story when I asked him about it.

I read a lot of books about wrestling and was fascinated when I could get him to talk about the days after he went to "legit" wrestling. He mentioned names like Strangler Lewis, Wladek Zbyszko, Frank Gotch, and other legendary grapplers which I had read about. They competed in the years before Gorgeous George and others ushered in the "new era" of showmanship in wrestling. Uncle Louie told me about wrestling on a house show in front of 100 people. He and his opponent would lock up and roll around for five or ten minutes before one of them would break loose and make another move. He would laugh and say that by the time the match was over, there might be 20 people left in the audience.

By the time I broke into the wrestling business, Uncle Louie was long deceased. He never knew that he had a part in that. It wasn't only that he inspired me to go into wrestling, but his name opened doors for me. Watching wrestling on TV, reading about wrestling in books and magazines, and hearing stories about or from Uncle "Leaping Louis" Allman — all those things enhanced my love of the game. Those were great times in my life. People can make fun of 'rasslin' and its' fans, but it gave emphasis to the values my parents tried to give me. The good guys eventually won out over the bad guys.

The first live show I ever attended was held at the Delaware County Fairgrounds. I remember as Grandpa, Grandma and I walked through the gate and to the grandstand, my first sight of the magnificent thing that had been so much a part of my life ... the ring. And for the first time, it was in living color! I was mesmerized by the red, white, and blue bunting around the ring. The mat looked like the brightest, glowing white I had ever seen. It was a visual experience, much like the one I had during my first trip to the circus, and there was going to be triple the excitement of watching it on the tube. I can remember my first smell of the popcorn, the buzz of the crowd, and the vendors who walked up and down the grandstand selling hot dogs and cokes.

Finally, at bell time, the wrestlers for the first match emerged from the tents in the middle of the track and made their way to the ring. They looked enormous to me. In fact, they seemed to be so much bigger than they were on TV. Seeing their tan, powerful bodies, and colorful robes, trunks, and jackets, was like one of my favorite comic books coming to life in front of my eyes. In the semi-main event that night, Wilbur Snyder took a pounding from Mitsu Arakawa, one of the top heels of that day, before winning with his famous "abdominal stretch." And then it was time for the main event. I remember thinking at the time that I was glad we were sitting up in the grandstand and not at ringside. Walking down the aisle were Dick the Bruiser, billed as the "world's most dangerous man," and his opponent, the Sheik. In the eyes of an impressionable youngster, they were equally scary.

I was well aware of all of the hype and legendary stories of Bruiser's escapades. It's hard to say how many were true, but to a little kid like me, I believed them all! My dad often told a story that he had heard at work. During that time, Indiana had a law which prohibited patrons in a bar from walking around while drinking. They were supposed to remain seated. They could move to another table or location, but they could not drink while they were walking. It seems that Dick the Bruiser was walking around in a bar in central Indiana, visiting the different tables, and swigging his beer as he walked. The story goes that the bartender told him he needed to sit down. Dick looked around the bar and said, *"I don't see anyone here big enough to make me sit down!"* Supposedly, everyone in the bar fell silent and he finished his beer as he stood in the middle of the floor. There were many other stories about Bruiser, all of them involving bar fights and cops being thrown through glass windows. Those stories made the one Dad told seem to be mild. On that night, however, Dick the Bruiser was about to climb into the ring right in front of me, and I was shaking. In fact, I wanted to tell Grandpa that I was ready to go home. For my sake, he probably would have agreed to it, but I wouldn't have wanted him to miss a minute of wrestling. Besides, I would probably be in trouble at home when dad found out.

Bruiser looked every bit the man I heard about in those legendary stories. He had a scowl on his face and a growl in his voice as he made his way to the ring that night. Even though we were eight to ten rows up from ringside, I leaned in a little closer to Grandpa. Dick began chasing the Sheik around as soon as he got into the ring, and, of course, after they went back and forth, trading the advantage, he beat the Sheik in a brutal match which had the fans going wild with excitement. At one point, they wound up outside of the ring and Bruiser slammed the Sheik's head into the seats just below us. I thought I would pee my pants!

When it was all said and done, I left the fair grounds with an even stronger love for professional wrestling. I would never be the same. Whenever wrestling came to Muncie, I had to be there, and I saw many memorable matches there. One which stands out was a match between Bobby Heenan and Moose Cholak. About halfway through the match, someone threw a beer bottle which sailed right past Heenan's head and shattered against the corner post. Moose and Heenan hesitated just long enough to point out to the police the scofflaw who had thrown the bottle. As soon as the guy had been arrested and they began to escort him out, Heenan and Cholak went on with the match as if nothing had happened.

Then there was the night when Dick the Bruiser was led away by the police. I can't remember for sure who he was wrestling, but it was a much-hated heel like Fritz von Erich or the Sheik. It was the most heat I had ever witnessed in a match. They wound up outside the ring and continued to go after each other. Some of the ringside fans decided to put in their two cents and chairs began flying toward the wrestlers. Fists began flying among the spectators at ringside and the police rushed up to the ring.

One of the cops, Jack Mann, had the reputation of being the "biggest and baddest" cop in the Muncie Police Department. Jack stood about six-foot-six and easily weighed in the 270-pound range. He had as big a reputation for breaking up bar fights as the Bruiser had for being in them. Jack ran up behind the Bruiser and grabbed him. I think Bruiser thought it was one of the fans as he suddenly turned and punched Jack. I remember seeing Jack's hat fly off of his head. The next thing I knew, Jack's size fourteens could be seen sticking straight up in the air. Seeing one of their own in trouble, all the cops piled on, and the next thing you know, Dick was on his way to a ride in a police car.

The next morning, I was shocked to see Dick the Bruiser's mug shot on the front page of the *Muncie Star*, with headlines declaring that he had been charged with battery to a police officer. Subsequent reports said the charges were dropped, but he paid a hefty fine for disorderly conduct. Years later, I got to know Officer Mann pretty well, but he never would discuss the incident. From what I've heard, the same thing happened in other places, as well, leading me to believe his arrest had been a publicity gimmick. More than likely, Dick the Bruiser was driven around the block and dropped off at the back of the tents which served as dressing rooms. I never could substantiate that, but I strongly believe that's what happened.

The show at the fair grounds also gave me my first up-close encounter with a wrestler. One of the babyfaces was Cowboy Bob Ellis. My mother's maiden name was Ellis and he resembled the Ellis clan. We all noticed it right away. Even on our black and white TV set, we could clearly see the dimple in the middle of his chin which is an Ellis trademark. Every time we saw him wrestle on TV, someone would speculate that he very well could be related. Then came the day when he was scheduled to wrestle at the Delaware County Fair. As we shuffled in with the crowd, the first thing we noticed was that a booth had been set up just inside the gate. There were pictures, cowboy hats, and cowboy scarves, all bearing the name Cowboy Bob Ellis. I didn't notice it right away, but as I stared intently at the treasure trove of merchandise, I looked up ... and there he was! Cowboy Bob Ellis was sitting at the end of the table signing autographs. My first thought was that it was my opportunity to ask him if he might be related to my mom's family in some way. When I stood in front of him, I was sure that he was. He looked a lot like one of my uncles, and there, plain as day, was that dimple in the middle of his chin. It looked so much like the dimple on my own chin. However, being so awestruck, I shook his hand and walked on without saying a word.

Sometime later, I actually wrote him a letter and told him about his resemblance to our family, and gave him the names of my relatives on mom's side. I never got a return letter from him. However, one day, as I was looking out the front door of our house, I saw a car pull around the corner and park across the street alongside the furniture store. A man, a woman, and a little girl stepped out. He was wearing a cowboy hat and sure looked like Cowboy

Bob Ellis. He actually paused and looked down the street, stopping when his eyes settled on our house! He stood there for several long moments, just staring at our house, before they all moved and disappeared around the corner. When they reappeared sometime later, he opened his car door and leaned forward on it, once again staring right at our house. I was convinced it was him, but I didn't have the courage to approach him, and they finally left.

Cowboy Bob Ellis was one of my heroes of that day and time. By the time I got into wrestling, he was no longer wrestling. I was proud to have that dimple on my chin and I told my friends to look at Cowboy Bob because he had one which looked the same ... and I added that he was an Ellis, just like me.

Encountering my heroes at the Delaware County Fairgrounds bolstered my dream of one day getting into professional wrestling. I wanted to be a wrestler, but I would have settled on being an announcer, timekeeper, referee, or whatever. I just wanted an opportunity to one day step inside a ring.

From time to time when we were vacationing at Crooked Lake in Angola, Indiana, we would go to the matches at Buck Lake Ranch. Buck Lake was somewhat of a combination of a campground, museum, and amusement park all wrapped up into one. The grounds also boasted an outdoor theater where many big-name performers appeared. It was there that I first saw a wrestler named Leaping Larry Chene. He was the most exciting and dynamic wrestler I had ever laid eyes on. The ring at Buck Lake was set up in front of the stage so the wrestlers could walk from the dressing rooms, across the stage, and into the ring. There was also a cement slab in front of that stage where the ring was set up. I will never forget the night when Larry Chene was flying all over the ring. It was like he had drunk a gallon of coffee before the show. Suddenly, his opponent picked him up for a bodyslam. He was dropped over the top rope, without touching it, and landed flat on his back on the cement with a sickening *smack!* I was sure he was seriously hurt, but he soon bounced up and got right back into the ring. I had never seen a bump like that before or since.

For several days after, I re-enacted those matches. I would pretend that a heel was ramming my head into the corner post (where I discovered that if I wasn't careful, running my head into a wall can hurt like hell). I also threw myself all over the yard, simulating being the victim of "arm drags." Actually, that became the inspiration for what became my finishing move, the flying rollover. My kids and their friends always got a kick out of it when I would have them pull on my arm and I would fly over and land on my back. Or, I would have them push me and I would "crash" into the wall and pretend to be hurt. Sometimes, it would wind up being quite a workout as every kid on the street would be invited over to watch the other ones toss me around. As a youngster, though, I tore up a few pairs of jeans and left Mom with the challenge of getting rid of some serious grass stains. I also learned to patch up my own scrapes and bruises.

Of course, that wasn't something you wanted to tell your guidance counselor at school. Wrestling was still controversial and fans were often subject to a lot of ridicule. As a youngster, I had to learn to which of my friends I could talk about wrestling. I also learned that girls weren't usually impressed if you had expertise in the game. There were two girls I had a crush on at an early age. One was Charlotte O'Dell. She was a little older than me and I soon learned she was not a fan. Charlotte's family had been neighbors and was close friends with my parents. Whenever she was around, I stifled the wrestling talk. Another was a gal named Paula Jane Davis, who also was a few years older. She never paid any attention to me, but when I did have a few brief conversations with her, I knew she would not be a fan. Those were simply schoolboy crushes on older girls, and thank God it was never more than that. If I had been faced with making a choice between wrestling and the girl (or girls) I loved, it would have been gut wrenching. I would have hated to see them go!

Such was my life growing up in Muncie, Indiana. Of all the adventures and experiences which could influence a youngster growing up in the 1950s, there was nothing for me like wrestling. Of course, I didn't have a computer or TV in my room, and there was no cable, cell phones, or any of the other distractions of today. You had the limited (by today's standards) entertainment on television and your imagination. Wrestling fed my entertainment needs and provided inspiration for my vivid, youthful imagination. Week after week, that magnificent thing called 'rasslin' unfolded before my eyes on the tube. It wove itself through the very fabric of my life. It was only a dream when I was a kid, but somehow, someway, someday, I wanted to be a part of it. Many such childhood dreams fade away into the reality of life. Even the noblest of youthful dreams are lost to maturity and adulthood, and the responsibilities that come with them. My dream, however, would not go away. I knew the odds were against me making those dreams a reality, but I wasn't going to let them die without making an effort to make them come true.

I'm jumping ahead in my story, but my dream of becoming a wrestler did come true. Was it easy?
No.

Did I become a legend?
No.

Did I make a lot of money?
No.

Did I ever wear a championship belt?
No.

Was it worth every minute of it?
Absolutely.

Chapter 2

Homer, Bobby and Rick

By the time I began looking for ways to get into the wrestling game, Uncle Louie had passed away. My one hope was that someone out there in the wrestling world had known "Leaping Louie" and would give me a chance. I began to look around for promoters and wrestlers who might have come out of his era. I read every wrestling magazine and book I could get my hands on. After doing some research, I got a phone number for Vince McMahon, Sr. and gave him a call. In those days, the WWWF was a big wrestling promotion in the northeast, but they had not yet gone national. Mr. McMahon referred me to Louis Klein in Detroit, Michigan.

When I talked to Mr. Klein in mid 1973, he said he remembered my uncle and invited me to come to his gym in Detroit where he would work with me. When I met with Klein, I told him a few of my "Uncle Louie" stories. Klein just said, *"Kid, you should only believe about one-half the horsesh–t an old wrestler tells you. And don't believe a damn thing he told you about me."* He asked about Uncle Louie and I told him he had been dead for some time. He shook his head and grunted, *"Well, don't matter. You're gonna have to get in that ring and show me you got somethin'."* I was about as green as you could get, and I know that during that first session, I looked like crap, but, probably out of courtesy to my late uncle, Louis let me keep coming back.

I would arrive at Louis Klein's gym in Detroit on Saturday morning with only a "hope" that someone would be there to work with me. Lou was getting up in years and couldn't get in the ring to work with me. On a few occasions, it was a wasted trip as nobody was there to work with me. It wasn't always a total loss because I got to sit and listen to Lou tell stories, but stories weren't preparing me for a career in the wrestling business. In early 1974, after I made a few long trips to Detroit and suffered one concussion, Louis suggested I hook up with a guy in La Porte, Indiana, named Homer Miller.

La Porte was only 112 miles from Fort Wayne, where I lived at the time, which was about 36 miles closer than Detroit. While it was not exactly a great savings in time or gasoline, Miller had a small stable of wrestlers who worked together regularly. I took Louis' advice and it turned out to be a good decision because I got a lot of ring time with guys at different levels of expertise, including rookies like me. I often wondered if, perhaps, Louis just passed me off to get me out of his hair, but things turned out great for me.

Homer, a truck driver by trade, had wrestled and refereed when he was in his prime for Dick the Bruiser. His gym was in an old metal building which had no hot water. Miller was too cheap to keep the heat turned up, so the winter sessions were usually pretty rough. The cold showers weren't so bad in the summer, but it was a wonder we all didn't get pneumonia in the winter. Every Sunday afternoon, however, we got all the time we wanted in the ring.

One of the first people I met when I first arrived at Homer Miller's gym was Bobby Golden. I lived just an hour east of Bobby, and Miller's gym was another 1½ hours west of Bobby's house, so Miller decided the two of us should carpool. It worked out great as we soon discovered that we shared the same phobia. I hate being late for anything, and I think Bobby was even worse. Where I always tried to be at least one-half hour early for an appointment, Bobby liked to be there an hour or more before the scheduled time. If we had a four-hour drive and we had to be there at six o'clock, Bobby would want to leave by ten or eleven in the morning. That was fine with me. Traveling with Bobby was always a blast. Those road trips seemed so short. We listened to his collection of Richard Pryor tapes on every trip. Bobby had them memorized and would mimic his favorite parts. He would glance over at me and let out the roar of a laugh he had. After listening to the tapes, we would exchange the latest jokes we had heard. Occasionally, we would discuss our personal lives and share one another's problems and concerns. After a while, we grew to trust each other with our darkest secrets. Looking back, I wish we could have been on the road together even more than we were.

We rarely ate anything before getting to the gym. We would normally get to the gym at eight o'clock in the morning and train until one or two in the afternoon. After that, we hit whatever might be available along Route 30 between the gym and Bobby's house outside of Etna Green. We knew every fast-food joint, truck stop, and cafe along Route 30 pretty well. Thankfully, Bobby's wife or mother-in-law would occasionally have a meal ready for us when we got back to his house.

Miller was okay as a teacher. He gave us the basics, but we had to learn a lot of the more advanced things on our own. He was also a great guy and a lot of fun to be around, but he was what they call in the business a "crowbar," or someone who was difficult to work with. We all knew that when he got into the ring with us, someone was probably going to get hurt. Miller would get all fired up and forget we were there to learn — and not to get hurt. The longer Miller was in the ring, the more he got wound up. He would charge at us like a raging bull. He would thump on us, or get us into a hold and crank down on it until we wanted to scream. Miller was a short guy and up in years, but he was still as strong as an ox. Truth be told, we also thought he was about as bright as one.

In one session, we were having a tag team match. Miller, who was on the opposing team, threw me into the ropes. When I rebounded off, he nailed me right on the Adam's apple with a judo chop. I remember a bright flash and I promptly went to the mat with a sickening thud. I lost consciousness for a second or two, and then flopped around like a fish, trying to get my breath. I was sure I was going to die before I was able to get air again and it was nearly

Homer Miller wrestling as an Indian

a week before I could talk again without sounding like Dick the Bruiser. My throat was sore and felt like it was twice its' normal size.

When I returned to the gym, I told Miller that he was a "crowbar" and that I would kill him if he ever hit me like that again. Surprisingly, he didn't kick me out of the gym and he never charged me for training with him. Of course, he never did apologize for the incident. There were times when we would tell him to slow down a bit and relax, but our requests always fell on deaf ears. He would just laugh and tell us that if we couldn't take the heat, we needed to get out of the kitchen. It was funny, though. If we turned the tables and roughed him up a bit, he would be mad at us for weeks. More than once, I wondered if that was why Klein sent me there. Perhaps he figured Miller would kill me and I would be out of his hair.

Fortunately, Miller "the crowbar" turned over most of the training to Bobby. Bobby had been working with Miller for about six months before I got there. Bobby was a natural and an absolute breeze to work with. I learned more in the first five minutes with Bobby than I did in my first hour with Miller. Don't get me wrong. Miller was a great guy and I appreciate everything he did for me back then. I haven't said anything about him that we didn't tell him to his face. In fact, he gave a lot of "guff" back to us whenever he got the chance. Miller just loved wrestling and he put everything he could into it. The longer he was in the ring with us, the stiffer he got. When he would get carried away and give one of us a hard shot, we would tell him he needed to go sit down and chill out. He would cuss us out and call us "a bunch of pussies," and then laugh and go sit down. Miller knew his shortcomings and he never took it personally when we got onto his case. I think he turned me over to Bobby because he wanted Bobby to "size me up" and see if I had any talent. Miller was no fool. He knew it would be hard for him to be objective with a new guy. He was a little "old school" (more so than us) and he knew he had to step back a bit and let a new generation and style of wrestler take over.

When we really wanted to mess with Homer, we called him Humer Mueller. Most of the time, we just called him Miller, rather than Homer. I had an uncle named Homer. Miller wasn't like an uncle to me, so I had trouble calling him Homer.

After a few months, I was invited to work with Bobby and help train any new guys who showed up. I really enjoyed that part of it. I had so much fun and got so much satisfaction out of teaching and mentoring guys at the gym, that later on in life, I jumped at the chance to become an instructor at the police department. That led to me getting the opportunity to travel throughout the eastern United States, giving seminars and speeches to police agencies and conferences. For the small contribution I made to the wrestling business, it gave me back a lot. It goes to show that you never know what something you do might lead to. If I hadn't hooked up with (and got along with) Bobby and the guys at Homer Miller's gym, I would have missed out on so much in my life.

Bobby and his wife (at the time) live in a mobile home in the country on his in-laws' farm property near Etna Green, Indiana. They were preparing to build a house on the property, so there was quite a bit of area between their mobile home and the road. Now, when I say they were out in the country, I mean "way out" in the country. There was Bobby and Becky's mobile home, his in-laws house, and miles of nothing. Deep in the heart of Amish country, we could always tell if any of their neighbors were coming down the road. We heard, "Clip-clop, clip-clop."

Bobby and Becky would occasionally have us over for dinner (usually over at his in-laws). My daughter was close in age to their son, Jeremy, so they would play together while we enjoyed a nice visit. Bobby's in-laws were great people, too. They loved to joke around with us and we were always welcome in their home. One winter, when Bobby and I were going to leave his place early in the morning, his in-laws insisted I come up the night before and stay at their house. The idea of sleeping in and waking up to one of his mother-in-law's famous country breakfasts appealed to me, so I took them up on the offer. Besides, snow and ice would have made the early morning run from Fort Wayne a little dangerous.

That night, Bobby's in-laws put me up in one of their upstairs bedrooms. Bobby knew I had never been a person who enjoyed cold weather. However, what he failed to tell me was that his in-laws lived in a converted Amish farm house ... and there was no heat whatsoever upstairs!

The next morning, I took a steaming-hot shower and we all had breakfast together. I didn't want to be rude, so I didn't say a word about the fact that I had only slept about two hours due to bouts of uncontrollable shivering. As we loaded our gear into Bobby's car, he looked over at me with that twinkle in his eye and asked, *"Were you warm enough last night?"* Bobby laughed for the next ten minutes, which was about the same length of time that I spent cussing him out!

Homer Miller ran a few small shows around northern Indiana and often rented out one of his several rings. He had a permanent ring set up in the gym, a small ring mounted on a trailer which could be folded up and pulled away, and a "deluxe ring" that Miller rented out the most often. The ring in the gym was okay, but the ropes were kind of old and had to be tightened up after every match or workout. The "trailer ring" was rather small, was a real pain to get leveled up, and had way too much give in the flooring. We loved his "deluxe" ring. It had a steel frame and cross beams, with a large post which went across the middle to where the cross beams were connected. That post was braced in the center by a huge spring. The floor of the ring was solid and had very little give, unless you landed in the middle where the spring would give you a little extra bounce.

When we hauled that ring to a town for Miller, we made sure we were early enough to set it up and get in a workout before the show. We did that even when we were on the show later that night. Years later, Bobby tried to talk Miller into selling the ring to us, but Miller just wouldn't let it go. Knowing Miller, he probably would have tried to sell it to us for what he paid for it, if not more. Of course, he was more than willing to sell us his trailer ring, but we weren't at all interested. We could build our own ring and do better than that.

The Indianapolis promotion often used his deluxe ring when they had shows in northern Indiana. Miller had connections with some of their wrestlers and could occasionally book them onto his shows. That gave us exposure to some of the "name" wrestlers, who we all hoped would notice our work and, perhaps, put in a good word for us if a promoter was looking for guys to fill a card.

When we set up the ring for an Indianapolis show, we not only would get a workout, but we made sure we had our ring gear with us in case one of the wrestlers didn't show. We thought that, just maybe, that would give us an opportunity to getting a job with the Indianapolis promotion. We knew we not only had to learn the craft, but we had to get noticed in order to get the shot we wanted so badly. Homer Miller's little gym was a good place to begin.

When Miller rented out one of his rings, Bobby would haul it for him. One Saturday afternoon, Bobby called to invite me over for a visit. We usually went to Miller's gym on Sundays, so when I told Bobby I would see him on Sunday, he said he wasn't going to Miller's and that I should come up that day. He also told me to bring my workout clothes. I figured he had the gym keys and we were going to go workout, after which we would take one of Miller's rings to a Saturday night show somewhere. When I arrived at his house, however, I saw that Bobby had the ring set up in front of his mobile home. He had actually set up the ring earlier in the week.

After putting on our ring gear, Bobby and I began pushing each other around in the ring. After we wrestled for about 40 minutes or so, I looked up to see the whole road lined with Amish buggies. The people had stopped to watch us work out. When we finished, we broke down the ring and loaded it onto the trailer so he could deliver it to a venue that had rented it for that evening. His little ruse had given him an opportunity to work out with me, and then give him some help tearing it down and loading it up again.

Bobby Golden and Duke West entertain the Amish in Bobby's front yard

One wrestler who got his start at Miller's gym was Tom Lynch, a bodybuilder who won the "Mr. Indiana" bodybuilding contest. Tommy was a guy I thought might be able to make the leap to pro wrestling. He worked with the Bruiser and Snyder operation and he worked overseas. He also had a gym in South Bend, Indiana and would sometimes bring guys (like Lou Botka) over to train with us. Like Lou, Tommy vanished one day and I never saw or heard from him again. I've been in South Bend a few times since then, but I haven't been able to find any information on him or his gym. I called the number he had given me for the gym, but it had been disconnected. I hope he's still doing well. He taught me a lot when he worked with us.

Tommy became one of Bobby's favorite "rib" targets because he was pretty "easy." Shortly before Tommy left for a tour of Japan and Korea, one of the guys had warned him about not drinking the water or buying food from the street vendors (especially in Korea). When Tom got back, he was booked with us on an outdoor show. During the trip, he told us that he had been deathly ill throughout the tour with stomach cramps and diarrhea. When questioned, he swore he never drank any of the water and only ate at the hotels. Lynch insisted that he drank only beer. He matter-of-factly added that he couldn't find cold beer in Korea, so he put ice cubes in his beer. Bobby couldn't resist asking him repeatedly if he knew "what the hell ice cubes were made out of."

When we arrived at the fair grounds, we saw a line of cars at the front gate. Golden and I were heels and Lynch was a babyface, so Bobby told Tom we couldn't be seen coming in together, but he knew about a back gate right by the race track where the matches were going to be held. When Bobby suggested we drop him off there, Tommy quickly agreed. As soon as Tommy was out of the car, I saw "that look" on Bobby's face. Whenever he was up to something, or about to laugh, he would stick the tip of his tongue out through his teeth. No doubt, something was up. As we drove back around to the front gate, Bobby told me the gate where we had dropped off Lynch was the one which was the furthest from the race track. We were in the dressing room a good 20 minutes before Lynch strolled in, cussing and spitting. *"Here I am, lost in the damn fair grounds, tip-toeing through the god—mn daisies!"* Bobby roared with laughter and handed Tommy a glass of beer ... beer chilled with ice cubes.

Other guys came and went through Miller's gym but it was the three of us — Miller, Bobby, and me — who were there every week like clockwork. Sometimes, we were the only ones who showed up. Whenever that happened, we would do a quick work out. The rest of the time, we would just sit around and "shoot the bull" with Miller. We all liked a good joke and Miller would open with one that he had heard. We would take turns telling jokes and laughing heartily. Those were good days.

We did have a lot of fun, and after awhile, we would put on shows for the kids around the area. It gave us a chance to learn to work a crowd and try out different gimmicks. By the time I got to work my first real show, I felt quite comfortable in the ring. I had enough matches under my belt that I felt like an old veteran. Miller had a row of about 20 chairs along one side of the ring, so it wasn't unusual for guests or neighbors to come and watch. That helped us get used to working in front of people. Sometimes, the guys who weren't in the ring would sit in the audience and harass the guys who were working. It was great fun.

We also enjoyed turning the tables on Miller and getting him worked up. We would have backdrop competitions to see how high we could get up into the air. Invariably, we would push the limits and begin trying to see if we could get high enough to kick the lights which hung over the ring. If we were successful, we would break a bulb or two, spreading dust and light bulb fragments all over Miller's ring. He always watched our contests and never said a word until someone kicked a light. When we did, he would lose his cool and begin screaming at us. *"Damn you, guys! You're going to clean this sh— up and somebody is going to pay for the lights!"* The more we laughed about it, the madder he got. He would eventually threaten to kick us all out or charge us a fee to train, but he never followed through on his threats. Of course, Miller had a good thing going because we provided him with free labor around the gym. We swept and kept the gym clean. After I had been with him for some time, Bobby and I helped with the training. He also had us haul his ring to towns when he rented them out to other promotions. He told us that if the promoter had a "no show," he would put in a word for us and we would get to work. That never happened. Miller was really tight and never offered us a nickel for the work we did for him, but we were thrilled to be in the business and we were willing to do whatever we could to be close to it.

The guys who came to learn but didn't volunteer to help out around the gym paid something, but Miller never told us what he charged then. I think he was afraid we would want a cut. The rumor was that Miller charged other guys four or five hundred bucks for training, but he would never verify that. If we asked, he would just blow us off and say, *"I never make any money on my wrestling stuff. You should be thankful I'm not charging you for training."* A few times, when we wrestled on his shows, he would moan and claim that he lost money. Even then, he usually paid us $25 each. We went along with whatever he saw fit to give us. I don't doubt that he lost money. His gym was in Kingsford Heights, Indiana — just a bump in the road and a few miles from La Porte, where Homer lived.

Miller would often remind us that he was supposed to charge us for training, but as long as he liked you, you never saw a bill. He never discussed the fees he charged his students, but the guys he did charge were the guys who didn't have what it took (talent, athleticism, looks, etc.) to be a wrestler. If Miller didn't want them to be wrestlers, he didn't want them hanging around, so it became our job to "train" them. Actually, Miller told us to scare them to a point where they wouldn't come back for a second session. (Sorry, no refunds) Most of the time, we didn't even have to get into the ring with them. We would lecture them on pain thresholds and injuries, and they would beg to be allowed out of the gym without having to get into the ring with us. Most of them who came to us were convinced that wrestling was all fake, figuring we would let them in on the secret and put them right into the ring. After our little lectures, their beliefs flew right out the window as they ran right out the door!

But then, along came Rick.

One weekend, when we arrived at Miller's gym, he announced that a new student would be there later that day. Miller said he wasn't particularly happy about training the guy, but the guy had paid him $400 for wrestling lessons. Will Rogers, the legendary humorist and entertainer, once said, *"I never met a man I didn't like."* Miller's twist on the quote was that he never met a man (or woman, for that matter) he didn't like well enough to take money from them. Miller had his standards, but he could be bought. He made it clear that the guy didn't belong there, and he hadn't been successful in talking him out of pursuing a career in wrestling, but he expected us to take care of it. Of course, I'm reasonably sure the 400 bucks prevented Miller from working very hard to discourage him.

Within an hour or two, a young man named Rick walked into the gym. Miller had been correct in his assessment. Rick looked about as much like a wrestler as Dick the Bruiser looked like a ballet dancer. He was a real beanpole with a sunken chest. Not only could you count his ribs, but you could catalog every other bone in his upper body. He might have weighed 135 pounds soaking wet (which was about ten times the poor guy's IQ). I don't think he had ever been to a live wrestling show. The first thing he did was to walk around the ring, touching the mat and stroking the ring posts. He tugged on the ropes and patted the turnbuckle. As he walked around the outside of the ring, he ran his hand gently along the ring apron and the bottom ropes. He looked at the ring like he was looking into the eyes of his first love. I turned to Bobby and said, *"I think this guy's going to shoot his wad before he makes it to the dressing room!"*

We glanced at each other with a look that said, *"This will be easy. We'll scare off this guy in short order."* Rick, however, turned out to be a greater challenge than either of us ever could have imagined.

The usual lecture and questions about Rick's "pain threshold," health insurance, and whether or not his employer would hold his job for him if he was laid up for three to six months didn't seem to faze him. So, we moved on to teaching him some basics. Of course, we began by teaching him to take a bump [fall]. Usually, we had new prospects stand in the middle of the ring and fall backwards. The idea was to get them used to the feel of the bump, and to teach them to relax and not tense up on the landing. Eventually, we would teach them to fall backwards off the bottom rope, and then the middle rope. Finally, we would bodyslam or backdrop them repeatedly until taking the bump became natural to them.

Rick just couldn't get the hang of it. He would tense up while doing the basic standing flop to his back, and when he landed, he looked like a fish flopping around on a dock. We were sure Rick would hurt himself before any of us ever touched him. The more we made him repeat the drills, the more hilarious it became. Rick wasn't a train wreck waiting to happen. He was a train wreck that just kept happening, over and over. Whenever we took our bumps, there was a resounding "bang" that echoed throughout the gym. When Rick took the same fall, he barely wrinkled the canvas, and at the most, the only sound we heard was a mild "thud." We really did try to coach him through it. We would instruct him in what to do, and he would look at us, nod, and swear he understood. And yet, each time, he did it the same way he had done it the previous two hundred times.

When our efforts failed to elicit any improvement whatsoever, we thought a little hands-on training might do the trick. By this time, we had forgotten all about Miller's instructions to discourage Rick. He was so bad that it became our mission to see if we could teach him anything. It almost became a game to see which one of us would be the first to teach him something. Rick was body-slammed, back-dropped, and bounced off the mat in all sorts of ways. By the time our marathon session ended, Rick could barely catch his breath, and to tell the truth, Bobby and I were both exhausted, as well. It wasn't any surprise to us when Rick bypassed the shower door, got dressed, and walked out without saying so much as "goodbye" to anyone. When the door closed behind him, we all laughed and talked about how we wouldn't be seeing him again anytime soon. We were sure we had sufficiently abused and berated him so he would be thoroughly discouraged. We laughed with Miller when we told him that we had taken care of another one for him. We also suggested he ought to share whatever part of the 400 bucks he was planning to keep. Miller failed to see the humor in that. When it came to money, he had no sense of humor. None, whatsoever!

The next week, as usual, we gathered at the gym. Suddenly, the door opened and in strolled Rick with his gym bag in hand. He stopped, opened the bag, and showed us the trunks and wrestling boots he had ordered in anticipation of his future career. He was so proud because they arrived in the mail just in time for his second week of lessons. Somebody had given him the name of the company which supplied trunks, jackets, boots, and other gear for wrestlers that most of the boys used. I figured Miller was probably getting some kickback from the company for referring us. Rick held up his bright red trunks for all of us to see. It was like his badge of honor. He was a wrestler because he had the trunks and the boots. Somebody said, *"Jesus Christ! I didn't know they made trunks in size B.A."*

"B.A.?"

"Yeah. Boney ass!"

Everybody got a good laugh out of that. Everybody, that is, except for Rick.

When Rick went to the dressing area in the back of the gym to change, we devised a plan. We would have a tag team match. Rick would be partnered up with Miller against Bobby Golden and me. Bobby and I both weighed around 265 pounds. Rick was told Miller and Bobby would start out and I would tag in later. He was to stand in the corner and watch the action. If Miller got tired, he would tag Rick in for a short time. Shortly after Bobby and Miller began wrestling, Miller feigned an arm injury and tagged Rick in. The plan was that we would then "shoot" on Rick [go at him for real with everything we had]. Miller jumped down off the apron of the ring and sat in the corner, rocking and holding his arm like it was broken or badly sprained.

Rick climbed into the ring to face Bobby and began jumping around and circling him. He had his arms wide open like he was about to hug a 400-pound woman and his eyes were as big as saucers. Rick must have circled

Bobby 30 times. I think he was trying to decide whether he really wanted to make contact with him or to run for safety. I was yelling at Bobby to *"squash him like a bug"* and Miller was yelling at Rick to *"get in there and show him what you've got."* The problem was, the poor guy didn't have anything to show us.

Rick suddenly stopped bouncing around and froze in place with his arms wide open. Bobby walked up and planted a dropkick which caught Rick solidly in the middle of his chest. Rick cart wheeled backwards across the ring and landed in the corner. Bobby grabbed him and, for the next three minutes, tossed him around like a rag doll. Bobby body-slammed Rick in the middle of the ring and dropped his 265-pound frame across Rick's chest. Instead of allowing our "ref" to count Rick out, Bobby got up and tagged me, saying, *"Your turn."*

As I climbed into the ring, Rick struggled to his feet and backpedaled to the opposite corner. His lips were trembling and his whole upper torso looked like a giant welt. I moved toward him with the meanest look I could possibly muster. Rick squatted down in the corner, looking up at me as if in a complete daze. I was actually feeling a bit sorry for him. *"I think tough guy here has had enough,"* I said as I began to turn away from him. Suddenly, I felt a blow to the side of my head, and the entire side of my face began to sting. It seems our boy Rick had, at some point, gotten some martial arts training and chose that moment to deliver a swift kick to the side of my head. For the most part, I'm a pretty easy-going guy, but I wasn't going to stand for that. I went off like a rocket. I drove Rick back into the corner and pounded him unmercifully. I punched and kicked him as hard and as fast as I could. He rolled up into a ball against the bottom turnbuckle and covered up in an attempt to prevent me from landing any more good shots. When I finally let up on him, he looked up and stammered, *"W-W-West! ... You're a f-f-f-fu—ng animal!"*

Miller quickly intervened and put an end to the match. I thought, *"Surely, this will be the end of Rick."* Rick told Miller he would never get in the ring with me again. Rick dressed (no shower again) and left. Once again, we all "high-fived" each other. We were thinking we had done the trick for sure this time. There was no way we would see that "Bozo" again.

The next week, we nearly fell out of our chairs when Rick strolled into the gym. This time, before he could go to the dressing room, Miller intercepted him and told him we were getting ready for a show (which was true) and there would be no time for lessons. He invited Rick to hang around and watch. We even decided to let him referee one of our training matches. We thought that might be our out. Perhaps if we made him a referee, he would forgo the idea of being a wrestler.

Unfortunately, he was equally bad as a referee. He was always in the way and did not have a clue about what he was supposed to do. If someone was pinned or outside the ring, we had to remind Rick that he was supposed to be counting that person out. Miller promised he would figure out some way to get Rick out of our hair. He finally decided to tell Rick he could get into the show for free the following week by helping them set up the ring. Rick showed up early to help set up.

When it was time for the show, Rick planted himself at front row ringside. Before the night was over, he managed to pull out the proverbial "straw that broke the camel's back." He not only showed up at the match wearing his wrestling boots, but he rolled up his pant legs to make sure everyone saw them. He then announced to everyone within ear shot that he was one of the wrestlers. He told them he might be called on if one of the other wrestlers didn't show up. To make matters worse, he began screwing with our "gimmicks" by proceeding to tell everyone our real names, where we lived, and what we did for a living when we weren't wrestling.

One of the hard-and-fast rules of the business is that you don't mess with a wrestler's gimmick. If your worst enemy in the wrestling game wanted to sell himself as Karl von Schpiel from Germany, and you knew he was really Bruce Dudley from Topeka, Kansas, you kept it to yourself. At the time, I was billed as "Mean Duke" West out of Windsor, Ontario. Only family and a few close friends knew about it. However, when I was home in Fort Wayne, Indiana, I was mild-mannered Harold West. I could take my girls to the zoo or the mall and no one knew or cared about my alter ego. I was a small-potatoes wrestler who worked small shows on the Midwest circuits. I was having fun and that was good enough for me. I had no illusions about being a superstar. I was a wrestler and I was getting to meet and work with the guys who gave so much entertainment to my family when I was growing up as a youngster. It was much more than I could have ever hoped for.

Years later, when I was wrestling as "The Canadian Rose," I would get some TV time, and yet, people at home hardly ever recognized me. Occasionally, folks would point or stare at me when I was out in public. I hope it wasn't because I looked funny. I'd like to think it was because my ring career was advancing and I was good at selling the "Canadian Rose."

At any rate, Miller finally decided that Rick had to go. He finally told him that he was just too small and he would have to bulk up to 200 pounds before he could come back. I'm also sure he had to refund a portion of Rick's money. I can just picture Miller trembling, shaking, and nearly in tears as he reached into his wallet. That was Miller. You would think he didn't have a dime to his name to hear him tell it. He always promised us big money when we worked one of his shows. When we could finally track him down after the match, we would be lucky to squeeze enough out of him to cover our gas.

Rick never returned to the gym. I'm sure he told his friends and family some fantastic story about his escapades in professional wrestling. We strongly suggested to Miller that he should do a more careful job of screening anyone who applied for wrestling lessons. Fortunately, there were no more "Ricks." After that experience, we never had anyone just pop in off the street. We picked up a few guys referred by people we knew. Tommy Lynch sent over some guys who trained at his bodybuilding gym in South Bend. Other than that, the gym was pretty much a closed society.

I felt somewhat bad for the way we treated Rick. We were all young and dumb back then. On the other hand, we may have saved him some misery down the road. He was never going to be even a small-time wrestler like me, and if he had revealed the gimmicks of some of the name wrestlers, they probably would have hurt him. People had to understand that there are some guys who just didn't belong in the business. Most were easily convinced. I guess I have to admire Rick's determination. We recruited some really good athletes who showed promise, and yet, after a few weeks of training, most of them never came back. No, wrestling isn't for everybody, especially the Ricks of the world. I'm sure there were a few people (even Miller when he was mad at me) who thought I wasn't cut out to be a wrestler. I was good enough to hang in there with some good wrestlers and put on a decent match. I was happy and I never got any complaints from promoters or 99.9 percent of the wrestlers I worked with. I guess that was good enough for me.

I truly hope Rick found another dream to pursue, and I sincerely hope he reached that dream. Wrestling was just not to be for him.

Homer Miller's operation was a much-less-than-formal training school. It was more of a "here's a ring and some guys who know what they're doing, go work out with them" kind of deal. I think Miller kept the gym open because he sincerely loved the wrestling business, and he never really intended it to be a training school. He could hand pick guys from his gym for the little shows he would promote from time to time. If he was serious about his "school," he would have had a formal structure and a screening process which would have kept out guys like Rick. Of course, there wouldn't have been any "freebies" and we all would have had to pay a set fee.

Regardless of Miller's intent, the system worked out great for us. There was a natural progression as older guys would break in the newer ones. As other "newbies" would come along, those guys would teach them. By teaching, we developed a critical eye. If there was a "screw-up" when we worked out together, we all got a good laugh out of it, but we learned from the error and tried not to repeat it. If we were charged with training a rookie, we wanted to make sure we set a good example. We knew we might wind up working with this guy someday, so we wanted him to get it right. I found that one of the best ways to learn the business was to teach it!

Most of the guys who came to that gym were good people and good students. A few stayed a long time, while other weren't there long at all. They either got bookings and decided the gym was no longer a necessity, or they came to realize their dreams of wrestling stardom were not going to happen right away (if at all) and they simply gave up.

One of the guys who came to Miller's from Tommy Lynch's gym was Brian Costello. He was a good worker, but his attitude was so serious that I thought he wasn't all that enthused about the business. He trained at the gym and worked a few shows with us, but he didn't come to the gym regularly after that. I was surprised to learn that he continued in wrestling and actually worked in the AWA, the WWF, and promoted his own shows as the IAW in South Bend.

I picture Brian as a promoter along the lines of "Big Jim" Lancaster. I worked shows for and with Jim Lancaster and found him to be a very serious guy when it came to the business. I remember working in a battle royal on one of Jim's shows. Jim was up against the ropes with two guys working him over. I was on the other side of the ring with someone else. When I glanced over, I could see Jim's eyes roaming all over the ring. Between selling what the guys were doing to him, he was keeping tabs on everybody else to make sure all was going according to plan.

I had a lot of respect for Big Jim. When I worked for him, his shows were always well organized. The payoffs weren't great, but they were fair and we didn't have to ask for them. That was a major improvement over many of the independent promoters of that day. Jim wasn't one to joke around or converse at the shows, but he did what promoters were expected to do, which was to make sure the program ran as planned and be sure the people go home feeling like they got value for their money. At first, due to his aloofness, I didn't think he liked me at all. However, I showed up, did my job, and went home. I kept getting bookings from him, so if I wasn't making him happy, I'm sure he would have told me or quit booking me. I guess it was one of those deals where, if you never see the boss, you're doing okay.

A handful of us made Homer Miller's gym our permanent base of operation. We were there week after week. We drove many miles each week for a few hours of ring time. As long as we had that, along with an occasional opportunity to work a real show, our dream was alive. For me, if Miller's place was as far as I got, that would have been okay, too. I had the experience of being in the ring. I got into pretty good shape. I developed friendships for a lifetime and a treasure trove of experiences I will always remember. The joy those memories bring to me is something which can never be taken away. When I find little to smile about, I can always go back to those experiences and memories. As I meet others who have shared similar experiences in the wrestling business, I see and hear the same joy in them as we tell "war stories." It is that zeal for the business which creates a special bond between us. That is one of the reasons why I wanted to write this book and share my stories and experiences with others. I hope it will make people smile and appreciate what the wrestling business was all about. In spite of Rick being so inept and far from being potential wrestling material, maybe, just maybe, he got a piece of his dream that he can remember with fondness. When he tells his children and grandchildren about his experience, I hope he feels a sense of pride about his brief exploration into the wrestling world. Knowing Rick, I am sure he will most likely embellish the story quite a bit. That's okay. As we used to say, *"As long as it's good for the business."*

Chapter 3

The Canadian Rose

About six months after I began training at Miller's gym, I was booked for my first match, which would take place in Plymouth, Indiana. I had to decide what gimmick would work for me. Naturally, when I was growing up, my heroes of the ring were all babyfaces. The dream of any kid who followed wrestling in those days was to be like Wilbur Snyder, Cowboy Bob Ellis, Pepper Gomez, or any of the other popular stars of the day. When I got into wrestling, I realized that my goal might have to be different. One of the first things I learned was that the heel plays a very important part in the whole picture. After all, who would Wilbur Snyder be if he didn't have someone on whom to put the abdominal stretch? Who would Cowboy Bob Ellis be if there was no one to bulldog drop? And Bobo Brazil had to have someone to cocoa butt.

It helped that as a youngster, my mother decided I needed to be introduced to "the arts." The first thing she did was make me take accordion lessons. I hated it, and I sucked at it. I also played the infamous "recorder" at school and flopped at that, as well. In high school, I made the show choir and we actually won the state choral championship. Other than that, it was obvious that music was not my strong suit.

When Mom finally gave up on the musical instrument thing, she found a lady who ran a drama and theater school in town. Mom said Ms. Secrest had been a Broadway performer in her day. I really didn't want to do it, but it turned out to be great fun. Having been the youngest in the family by many years (you could say I was an "oops"), I had no siblings and no kids in the neighborhood to play with. I had learned to use my imagination to entertain myself. I had re-enacted segments from many of the TV shows (including wrestling), so taking on a "role" was easy to me. Ms. Secrest's theater school was cool because she had the costumes, and she encouraged ad-libbing, so changing roles in wrestling was no big deal to me. In fact, I was so prepared for my first match that I had almost no jitters at all. It was like another day at the office. The only thing I really worried about before that first match was the state of Indiana.

Back in that day, we had to deal with the Indiana Boxing and Wrestling Commission. Anyone who boxed or wrestled for money had to have a license. Everybody told me it was no big deal, but it required a physical examination, and that physical took place on the night of the match. Now, I never liked doctors too much, and I really didn't like physicals. I always figured that, if I'm going to die, I want it to be a complete surprise to everybody — especially to me.

I had put in countless hours of training for that one big night and I could just see some doctor shaking his head and saying, *"Sorry. No license for you!"* I tried to convince myself that I would already be dead if there was something seriously wrong with me. I had wrestled hundreds of matches at Miller's gym for free and had never experienced any problems.

Sure enough, the first people I saw when I walked into the dressing room was the "suit" from the commission and a doctor with a stethoscope in hand making his way around to all of the guys. The suit was asking the guys for their real names and checking his list to make sure they had their yellow card (license). The doctor slapped his stethoscope on each guy's chest and listened for a few seconds before moving on to the next one. It seemed simple enough and I felt a little better about it, but it seemed as if all the other guys already had their cards. I envisioned him breaking out his black bag when he got to the new kid (me) and checking every orifice of my body.

I knew I had to get it behind me, so as soon as the suit got close, I told him I needed to get my license. He wrote down my information and called the doctor over. I was praying he didn't see the beads of perspiration which were beginning to pop out on my forehead. The doc listened to my heart for a minute or so and took my pulse.

"How are you feeling?"

"I feel great. Just fine!"

"Well, good luck."

That was all there was to it. My physical was over. The suit collected his ten bucks and assured me that my yellow card would soon be in the mail. It was official. I was a professional wrestler! At least, I was according to the state of Indiana.

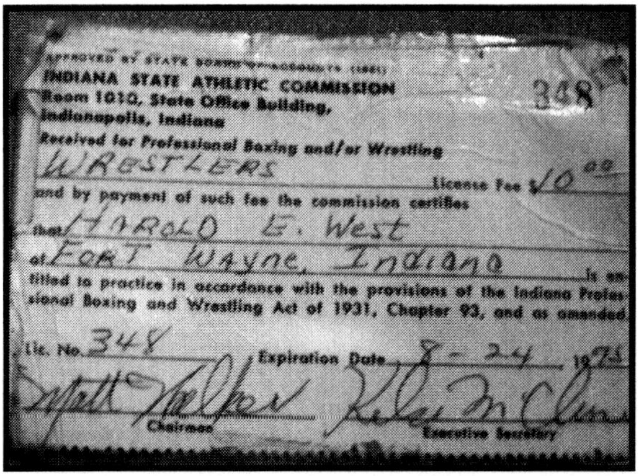

INDIANA STATE ATHLETIC COMMISSION
Room 1010, State Office Building,
Indianapolis, Indiana
348
Received for Professional Boxing and/or Wrestling
WRESTLERS
License Fee $10.00
and by payment of such fee the commission certifies
that HAROLD E. West
of FORT WAYNE, INDIANA
is entitled to practice in accordance with the provisions of the Indiana Professional Boxing and Wrestling Act of 1931, Chapter 93, and as amended
Lic. No. 348
Expiration Date 8-24
Chairman
Executive Secretary

Duke's first yellow card (wrestling license)

I don't remember much about the rest of that night. I don't even recall who I wrestled or what we did in the match. All I remember is that I was on "Cloud 9." Having that yellow card was all that mattered. A few weeks later, that precious yellow card arrived in the mail. I still have it in my box of memories.

The whole situation with the Boxing and Wrestling Commission was a joke. Professional boxing matches were rare in Indiana, and the doctors, who were supposed to hang around for the whole show, usually disappeared shortly after they had checked everybody. I can only recall one time when a doctor was going to stop a guy from wrestling. When one of the headliners was having a problem with high blood pressure, the doctor told him he would not be wrestling that night. The guy from the commission and the promoter discussed the situation and then met with the doctor. The doctor checked the guy's blood pressure every fifteen minutes for the next hour. Finally, he announced that the blood pressure was low enough that he would clear him to wrestle if it was still down when it was time for him to wrestle. He checked him again just before his match and gave him the "thumbs up."

I'm sure there were no special arrangements made between the promoter, doctor, and the bureaucrat. Stuff like that couldn't happen, could it?

A few years later, the state decided the commission was unnecessary. We no longer had to undergo physicals, or purchase annual licenses, but passing that first hurdle had given me the confidence to begin planning the role I wanted to play in the wrestling business.

The ring heroes of that day were usually handsome and they typically had lean, solid bodies. They also had a spectacular signature move they used to put away the bad guy. I didn't see myself fitting into any of those categories. I was just a big guy who could take big bumps. I felt I was pretty good at basic moves for a guy my size. At one point, I weighed 280 pounds, but I could still throw a dropkick and plant my feet right into a guy's face. Still, I had to find something which would help me stand out, something I could sell.

As a youngster, I was a big John Wayne fan, so some of the kids in middle school gave me the nickname "Duke." I tried babyfacing as "Big Duke" West, but neither the promoters nor the fans were particularly impressed. My next attempt was to wear a leather vest, grease my hair, and come to the ring with a cocky attitude as "Mean Duke West." Working as a heel got more of a reaction from the crowd than my "Duke" persona, but I still wasn't satisfied with my ring persona. For a short time, I wore a mask and became "The Creature." I absolutely hated it. When the weather is warm and I do any kind of physical activity, I sweat like a pig. That's a nightmare when your entire head is covered with a tight mask. I wore it when I was working around the house in an attempt to get used to it, but after a couple of months, I donated the mask to Homer Miller's gym. I told him to find somebody else to wear it.

One of the earliest memories I have of professional wrestling was watching Gorgeous George. That guy could build some heat! He really knew how to work the crowds. Back then, I hated that guy and looked forward to seeing him get trounced. When I got into wrestling, however, I learned to appreciate his skills. Gorgeous George was a wrestler who brought attention to wrestling to people who wouldn't normally give it a second thought. He appeared on non-wrestling magazine covers, national TV shows, and he was known all over the world. He was the pioneer of gimmicks in the wrestling world.

I heard a story about Gorgeous George meeting an up-and-coming boxer named Cassius Clay. George's advice to him was that, *"People either will pay to see you 'cause they love you, or, they will pay to see you get your ass kicked!"* Allegedly, Cassius Clay latched on to that advice, and became the arrogant, cocky, and much-despised Muhammad Ali. I do know that when I met Mr. Ali a few years ago, he wasn't the racist, radical, screaming maniac that he appeared to be during his days as the heavyweight champ. In fact, he was one of the nicest guys you would ever want to meet.

Duke, as the Creature, wrestles Bobby Golden in Homer Miller's gym [1975]

One day, I was flipping through a catalog from K&H Wrestling Wear [formerly known as Karl and Hildegarde], a company which sold wrestling trunks, costumes, jackets, boots, masks, and other ring gear. In the "clearance" section of the catalog, there was a pair of pink wrestling trunks on sale. Nobody in our little group of guys was doing the "gay" gimmick, so I thought, *"Why not?"* I didn't feel comfortable just wearing a pair of trunks on my fat body. The next thing I did was buy a pair of collegiate style, knee-length, grey wrestling tights (a singlet) at a local sporting goods store. On the way home, I stopped at a fabric store and bought an appliqué of a rose. I sewed the appliqué onto the front of the grey tights, slipped on the pink trunks, and ... ta-da! The Canadian Rose was born.

The next time I was booked, I strolled out to the ring in my new outfit. I stepped out from the dressing room with a somewhat effeminate and arrogant strut. Sure enough, before I took five steps, someone yelled, *"You faggot!"* Now, if you had said that to me at any other place and time, those would be "fightin' words," but at that time, it was exactly the response I wanted. I knew within the first few seconds that the gimmick would be one which would draw heat. Over the next few months, I was pelted with soft drink cups and cans. I was even smacked with a few purses. One old gentleman managed to give me a good swat with his cane. I went home with a good-sized welt on my thigh which served as a reminder of the incident for almost a week.

I wore a pair of sunglasses to the ring and made a production out of taking them off. I would loudly declare to the ring attendant, *"You take good care of those shades!"* I used nice sunglasses until a babyface decided to snatch them and crush them to tiny pieces beneath his boots. He wanted to build up a little heat before the match began, but he kind of forgot to let me in on it ahead of time. After that, I wore the cheapest sunglasses I could find.

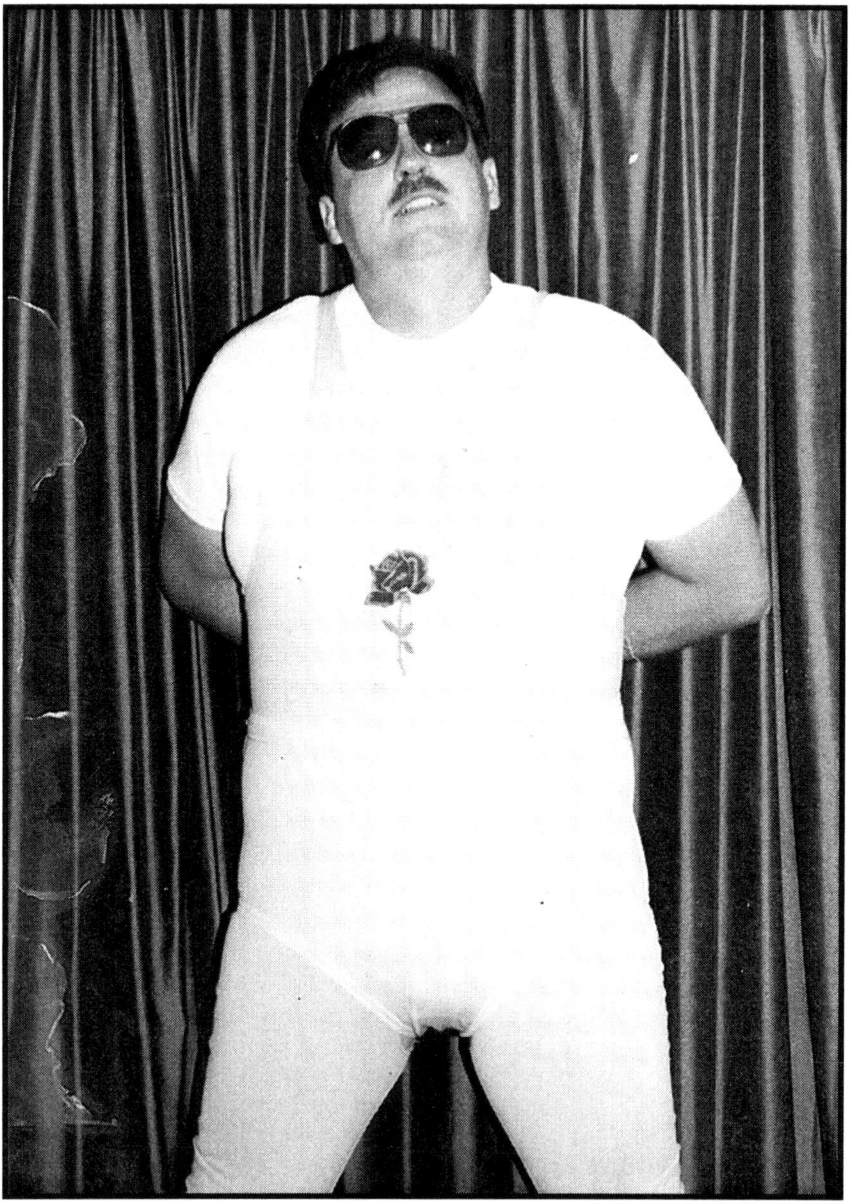

I also came up with the brilliant idea to carry roses to the ring and hand them out to a few of the ladies. Beside the problem of finding fresh flowers and keeping them that way on the road, I soon learned that an angry lady, a rose thorn, and my fat butt did not make a good combination. I had been hit many times with cups, beer cans, dirt, spit, and assorted other nasty things. I should have known better than to supply the weapon!

Someone suggested I let my hair grow and dye it an unnatural color. That might have been a good idea, but my full-time job was working as a cop. Department grooming standards were about the same as the military and I didn't think my command staff would give me an exemption because I wanted to be the "Canadian Rose" and wear pink on my days off. One of the great things about the character was that I could be the character on the road, but when I came home, I could be Harold West. I never was booked any closer than 30 miles from home. I never worried about wrestling fans finding out where I lived. I was more concerned that people I arrested would find out.

There was a time, though, when I was concerned for my safety. We were at a show in the hills of West Virginia where Bobby got "free" beer (you'll hear more about that later). During my match, I had the heat going pretty good. I suddenly heard a booming voice yelling at me. When I glanced over, a huge man in bib overalls stood up in the front row. He must have stood six-foot-five and weighed 350 pounds. He pointed his finger directly at me and said, *"I'm going to get you!"* I don't remember who I was wrestling that night, but I warned him that if I got tossed out on that side of the ring, I was going to kill him. That is ... if I survived long enough to get back into the ring.

The next night, we were wrestling somewhere around Dayton, Ohio, and I was working against Bobby. A few seconds after the bell rang to signal the start of our match, the same guy stood up in about the third row and pointed at me. *"I am going to get you!"* I gave Bobby the same warning I had given my opponent the night before. When the match was over, I bailed out on the opposite side of the ring. As we headed out of town, I kept a close eye in the rear view mirror. I never encountered that monster of a man again, and I can't say I'm disappointed about that. I can guarantee you that every time we were in the lower portion of Ohio, I kept a keen eye on the ringside seats.

Regardless of the potential dangers, I loved the Canadian Rose gimmick and I used it until I had to get out of the business. I still have the outfit, as well as the blue outfit I wore when I was a babyface. I suppose that someday, I'll have the outfit put into some kind of a frame. Perhaps my grandkids will get a kick out of it. Then again, they might want to have it destroyed. Not everyone in my family saw the humor of the gimmick. In fact, some didn't see any humor or honor in my being any kind of professional wrestler.

I think that if wrestlers were psychoanalyzed (and many of us should be), they would find some deep internal meaning to the characters we took on. I wasn't harboring an inner desire to be gay, by any means. To this day, when someone teases me about the pink tights, I respond by saying, *"I'm not gay, but I played one once on television!"* In reality, the Canadian Rose character acted more arrogant than effeminate. The Rose would often tell his hecklers that they had better shut up or he would take their women away from them so they could experience a real man. My goal wasn't necessarily to come across as being gay, but to leave the fans wondering.

There was only one wrestler (who shall remain anonymous) who gave me a bad time about the Canadian Rose gimmick. Whenever we were on a show together, he would make some comment. Finally, he looked over at me one night after I suited up and said, *"How do I know you're not really gay?"*

I said, *"I don't know. Maybe you should ask your wife."*

That was the end of that. Everybody got a good laugh and my point was made. Most of the guys were great. In my experience, nobody hassled anybody about their gimmick. Of course, there just has to be one in every crowd.

One of the things I've often thought about was that as a cop by day and a heel by night, I enjoyed being able to taste the "other side." Being a heel gave me the opportunity to break some rules without really hurting anyone. I also discovered that most of the heels I worked with were great guys, while many of the babyfaces were jerks. Looking at things from a different perspective, I spent my time enforcing laws and often felt the frustration of the bad guys seeming to win. Perhaps that's why I didn't mind doing a job [losing] for someone. Deep down, I wanted to see the bad guy lose … even if I was the bad guy! Then again, maybe I'm looking too deeply and trying to find psychological reasons for what I was doing. Maybe I just enjoyed playing both "cops and robbers" in order to get away from the pressure of the real world. Mean Duke West and the Canadian Rose were quite the opposite of who I really am. (I hope people don't see me that way), but it sure was fun being them for just a while.

I always found it amazing how a wrestler would "turn" and go from babyface to heel, or vice versa. I can remember when I first watched wrestling on TV and saw Dick the Bruiser. I still remember him wearing the long black tights on those shows out of the Chicago Amphitheater. At least, I think they were black. There was no color TV back then, so they looked black to me. The "heel" Bruiser was really scary. He would trounce the babyfaces and he seemed to be unstoppable. He struck fear into the hearts of many a fan just walking to and from the ring. I think he was responsible for more than one riot at the venues he worked. I sure wouldn't have wanted to cross his path in a dark alley … or for that matter, a light one. One day, out of the blue, Bruiser did a run-in and trounced one of his fellow heels. From that day on, he was one of the good guys. His style of wrestling didn't change one iota. He was still scary. He still went after the opponent with reckless ferocity, both before and after the bell rang. And yet, the fans all loved him.

Baron von Raschke had a great run as a heel with the Indianapolis promotion before he headed back to Minnesota and the AWA. His growling voice, sneers, and dreaded claw hold garnered a lot of heat with Indianapolis fans. I was surprised later to hear that he was beloved in Minnesota as a babyface, and he was enjoying the cheers of the crowd.

That was another lesson in life which wrestling taught us. There are times when people you consider to be your enemies will come through for you, and defend you when certain lines are crossed. In story lines where a heel turned, it was usually because another heel went way over the line in brutalizing the local hero, or his partner or another heel turned on him. Does that reflect real life? I think so. Just ask any cop what happens to child molesters or sex offenders who wind up in jail. I know a cop who owes his life to a fellow he had arrested many times. He was in a life and death struggle with a suspect when the other fellow intervened and helped him put the guy in cuffs. The fellow who jumped in to help the cop in trouble would be arrested many times more. However, assaulting a police officer was the one line he would never cross, and he refused to stand by while someone else did.

Other wrestlers work in one territory as a heel, and turn up in another territory as a babyface. Some could pull it off quite easily. As for me, I was never comfortable as a babyface. I liked being free to break the rules and to wrestle as I saw fit. I spent my time on the police department putting away the people who broke the rules, and yet, as the Canadian Rose, I knew no rules.

When Miller was booking me, one of the first decent shows I wrestled on was another show in Plymouth, Indiana, the same site on which I had my first wrestling match. It was 1975 and the show was a fund raiser for the local Boy Scouts program. They expected a good house [crowd]. On the card that night was a kid named Lanny Poffo. Lanny later went on to become "Leaping Lanny Poffo," and in the WWF, he achieved a degree of fame as "The Genius." I was excited because I had watched Lanny's father, Angelo Poffo, when I was a kid. Angelo had been one of our favorite heels. He always gave us a good laugh when he made a big production with his pre-match ritual of removing an extra pair of trunks he wore. He would shake his butt while he pulled down the trunks. Of course, he acted quite mortified and disgusted at the catcalls and hoots of the crowd as he wiggled his way out of those trunks. He would then kick them into the air and catch them in his hand.

I think Angelo was one of the inspirations for my persona as the Canadian Rose. My making a big deal about removing the sunglasses came from Angelo's trunk removal routine. Like Angelo, when the bell rang, the Canadian Rose became more like "Mean Duke" West. That is, until things began going south, and then Rose would beg and plead for mercy like a frightened little girl. Of course, he did that only long enough to regain the advantage.

I was booked to wrestle a guy named Ted. I don't remember his last name. We just called him "Teddy Bear Ted," or "Ted the Teddy Bear." At the time, I had no idea who he was. When I found out the guy used to do some wrestling and was now one of the local Scout leaders in Plymouth, I figured Miller was putting me up against him to be hamburger. Hamburger is what we called a wrestler who took a sound thrashing at the hands of another wrestler to make him look good or to build him up for a program. I wasn't sure if that was the case, but I wasn't too happy about having to let an ex-wrestler beat me when I was in the early stages of building up my career. I seriously considered telling Homer Miller to take his deal and shove it.

I shared my feelings about the situation with Bobby Golden, and he relayed them to Miller. He wasn't stooging, or carrying stories, but rather, he was in good graces with Miller and felt comfortable explaining the situation without hurting me. The next time I talked to Miller, he assured me that I wasn't going to be made to look bad. His plan was to get Ted back in the gym and get him back into shape. We would work out a situation where the match would end in a double disqualification and both of us would look strong during the finish. That sounded like a good plan to me.

As Miller had promised, Ted began coming to the gym and working with us. He was pretty rusty and his timing was way off, so I wasn't sure it was going to work out. Ted improved quickly, though, and he reached a level to where I was looking forward to the match. After all, the show was for a good cause and Ted was a decent guy. There was a lot of promotion work going on for the show and they were building me up as a big, tough heel. Miller invited the local press to the gym for interviews with Ted and me. The interviews were played on local TV and radio and the show was covered extensively in the local press.

One weekend, a few of the Scout executives showed up at the gym. They wanted to talk to me. I growled, grumbled, and stayed fully in character as I sat down with them. They told me they had heard of my reputation and wanted to talk to me before the match. They were concerned because they were planning a ceremony that would take place before the match. They planned to give Ted a certificate to show their appreciation for his work with the Scouts and for helping arrange the big fund-raising event. There would be a group of Cub Scouts and Boy Scouts in the ring for the presentation and their concern was that I might do something which might cause one of the boys to get hurt. I assured them that I didn't plan to kill their precious Ted until after the kids were out of the ring and the bell rang. It was tough to tell them that in a way which didn't show that I was actually touched by their plans and quite proud to be a part of it all.

When they left, the wheels began turning in my brain and I thought of an angle which would help put the show over. I couldn't wait to share my idea with Miller, so I pulled him aside the first chance I got. I told him to have the Scouts make up two certificates. Bring one to the ring to present to Ted and leave it on the timekeeper's table at ringside. During the match, I would eventually get frustrated over the fact that I wasn't able to whip a retired wrestler and I would bail out of the ring. After doing that several times, I would storm around the ring and go to the timekeeper's table. I would see the certificate on the table, pick it up, and rip it to shreds. The crowd would be upset and Ted would leave the ring to come get me. We would fight outside the ring until the other wrestlers came out of the dressing rooms to pull us apart. Of course, in the meantime, the referee would count us both out and order a double disqualification. The crowd would have seen a good show and everybody would go home happy. Miller thought it was a great idea and said he would take care of everything. I should have known better.

While I was talking to Miller, a newspaper reporter and photographer stopped by to interview us. When they finished the interview, the photographer (apparently a wannabe promoter) asked to speak with me. He told me he would be taking photos at ringside on the night of the match. He was going to bring an old camera and he would flash the bulb in my face. He told me I could then yank the camera away from him and smash it. He thought it would be great for the show. Now, I didn't know the guy from Adam. I figured he wanted me to go along with his deal so they could print a story in the newspaper about how the whole show had been staged. I just stared at him like he was some kind of a loony, shook my head, and walked away.

On the night of the show, I stood outside the dressing room and watched some of the preliminary matches. Sure enough, the photographer was taking pictures at ringside. He had an old-style camera around his neck which I had never seen him use. When I headed to the ring for my match, he switched cameras and stepped in front of me. He held it up to my face and depressed the flash button. I just glared at him and walked on by. The next thing I know, the jerk was poking me in the back with the camera! I spun around and said, *"Why, you son of a bitch!"* I lunged at him and a look of sheer panic crossed his face. He turned and ran up the aisle to the back of the ringside seats. During our match, he crouched in the aisle to take pictures, but never got past the front row. When I would get out of the ring, he would retreat to the back again. He never did ask me for any post-match pictures like he did the other guys.

Our plans for the match went off without a hitch. The scouts had their ceremony, which featured the kids getting into the ring with their flags. The match began and Ted and I traded the advantage back and forth. As planned, when I found myself in trouble, I rolled out of the ring and banged my fists on the ring apron in frustration. After repeating that scenario a few times I stormed around the ring and waited for the referee to get about halfway through his count. I ran to the timer's table and stepped up on it to climb back into the ring. When I looked down, I saw Ted's fancy certificate. I reached down and scooped it up, held it high in the air, and in dramatic fashion, slowly began tearing it into little pieces. The crowd went crazy! Unfortunately, so did Ted.

As soon as I began tearing up the certificate, I saw a look on Ted's face which immediately told me that he had no idea the certificate was a duplicate. Ted was balding, and his whole face and top of his head suddenly turned beet red. His eyes bulged out and the veins in his neck stood out like they were going to break through the skin. As he charged out of the ring, I began to back pedal, hoping to buy enough time to explain the whole plan to him. Unfortunately, the other wrestlers, who had been told to come to the ring to break us apart, arrived from both sides of the ring. Suddenly, my arms were pinned to my sides ... just as Ted hauled off and nailed me in the jaw with a right cross. I saw stars and my knees began to buckle. Luckily, they were able to drag us away from each other before Ted got in any more shots.

That damned Homer Miller had failed to tell Ted about the duplicate certificate. Ted thought I was upset because he was still a little rusty and had blown a few moves. At one point, I did tell him to loosen up and that he was too intense. He was convinced I deliberately destroyed the certificate which his little friends had presented him. When he got back to the dressing room, Ted was told the whole story and was given the original copy of the certificate. Once again, all was well. In fact, he even invited me to his house for a party he was hosting later that night. Everybody got a good laugh when we recalled the evening's events. I couldn't laugh too much because my jaw was pretty sore.

The event was a big success. The press in the area after the show was very positive. There were a lot of photos in the newspaper about the matches and the award ceremony.

Ted and I came to respect and like each other. We never socialized outside of the party at his house after that show, the gym, or in the dressing rooms at shows we both worked. He actually came back to Miller's several times and even worked a few more shows. Ted was a truck driver. When they changed his route, he was away from home a lot more. We never got to see him again. I came away from the event having learned another valuable lesson. From then on, if I changed something, or planned to pull an unusual gimmick on someone, I told them personally.

That was another good thing about old-school wrestling. Many of the small venues I worked were fundraisers for various charities. Regional promotions often partnered with community groups and organizations. The groups provided the venue and the promoters provided the wrestlers, ring, and a full evening of entertainment. With the small amount I got paid for those shows, I should have received a tax deduction for a contribution every time I worked one of those shows. Today, there are few such promotions. The big promotions have no use for the small venues or organizations for which we raised money in the past.

I think the story of Ted also speaks volumes on the true character of many of the wrestlers. His work with the local scout program is just one of many examples of the ways that many wrestlers and former wrestlers served their fellow man. I know of several who have been involved in many forms of community service. (Okay, there were a few who were involved in court-ordered community service, but that's another story)

People who weren't wrestling fans often thought that everyone involved in the business were con men. To them, wrestling was a cheap carnival act which duped people out of their money. They never saw the true side of the people in the business. As a cop who specialized in putting away con men, I can honestly say I never saw any of them devoting their time or talents for charity. The ones who did usually had another motive, such as using one con to lead into another, which led to them making even more money. I have been involved in crime prevention and safety programs for senior citizens. I know several guys who were worked regularly with volunteer fire departments, served as reserve police officers, and were active in civic organizations. Lanny Poffo has a crusade to discourage smoking, especially with young people. I have heard of many others who are involved in the Special Olympics, raising funds for cancer research, children's hospitals, the Leukemia Foundation, and many more causes.

I once thought about getting some of the guys together and doing one more show for a charity, but it wasn't to be. You'll read about that later. It wasn't to make any money for us. It was to have one more show together and to help others in the process. That is the wrestling business I remember. Those are the kind of wrestlers I remember.

Chapter 4

Sgt. Bobby Golden

Bobby Golden and I spent a lot of time together in the ring. Most of that time was at Miller's gym. We were there almost every Sunday. If we had a show coming up, or if had to go pick up one of the rings and take it somewhere for a show on Saturday, we would hit the gym early and work out before hauling the ring to the venue. If we had time after the ring was set up, we would work out again. In other words, our time at the gym took place mostly on Sundays. Saturdays were not too uncommon, but the distance made it difficult for us to be there on Saturday every week. Of course, after Bobby and I began working more, we didn't get to the gym as often because we were on the road every weekend. After working a Friday and/or Saturday night show, we weren't anxious to drive to the gym on Sunday.

If we worked a house show together, we usually tag teamed. We put in so many hours training together that all we needed was a time limit and a finish and we could work a great match. It was rare that we actually got booked to wrestle each other. There did come a time when we were booked against each other in a series of matches in northern Indiana and northwest Ohio. I was the heel and Bobby was the babyface. Bobby was well known in the area and he was very popular. We could stop at any restaurant or gas station within 30 miles of his home and, as soon as we walked in, someone would be yelling out, *"Hey, Bobby!"* He had friends everywhere he went, so being the babyface was perfect for him.

On the flip side, Bobby also had a knack for being a heel, but in many ways, even in that mode, he was still popular. It's hard to explain. Like Dick the Bruiser or Baron von Raschke, he could heel against a young babyface and the people still wanted to pat him on the back after a match. He had the type of personality which people just couldn't help but like. Of course, there were times when he heeled against a local hero and wasn't liked. For the most part, though, Bobby was a natural babyface because people liked him and he liked people. That seemed to always come through. When we appeared in his home area, the fans didn't care if he was the heel or the babyface. They knew the personable and friendly Bobby Golden as he appeared in his full-time occupation and other activities.

Those of you who are familiar with the way the wrestling business works might be asking yourselves, *"Why were these two guys traveling together?*

One of the hard-and-fast rules of the wrestling business was that babyfaces and heels were not allowed to travel together. It wasn't just a rule. It was good business. In our case, I was a heel and Bobby was a babyface, so in reality, it wasn't good for us to be seen together, especially since we often feuded *against* one another.

Sgt. Bobby Golden

Bobby and I went to great lengths to protect "kayfabe," which is the wrestling code of secrecy. Usually, we were the last car to leave the arena grounds. If any fans were still hanging around, Bobby would go out to sign autographs and talk to them, while I slipped out to the car. If necessary, I would leave and swing back later to pick up Bobby when things cleared out. I remember two occasions when he left with another babyface and we met up down the road. We also arrived at the shows long before anyone else, including the promoters. If, by chance, there were cars at an arena when we pulled up, we would leave and drive a few blocks away, where one of us would get out and walk back. Jim Lancaster was the only promoter who told us ahead of time to not ride together. Again, that was good business, and Lancaster was all about protecting the business.

I had managed to build a lot of heat in the area as a heel, and with all of our experience together, the promoters loved our matches. We worked together so often that we had complete trust in each other. When I critique young wrestlers, I always tell them, *"Don't sell it before you get it."* So many times I see young guys come off the ropes to take a clothesline, or a chop, and they slow down or even throw themselves back before contact is made. With most of the guys I worked with regularly, and especially with Bobby, I had enough confidence in them to trust running headlong into their chop or clothesline before I took the bump. If I was taking an elbow drop or knee drop, I never flinched and didn't react until contact was made. They trusted me, as well. When I did my finishing move, the flying rollover, I always told my opponents to lie completely still when I was ready to make the move. A few of them would see my big body somersaulting toward them and roll up on one side, or lift a shoulder and throw an arm across their chest. It was something they did instinctively, and yet, it was the wrong thing to do. If they stayed flat on the mat, I would roll over them and they wouldn't even know I had been there. I had practiced it for hours with Bobby and some of the other regulars at the gym. Those guys trusted me enough to know that I wasn't going to hurt them.

Bobby was like a brother to me. Many of the inhibitions we had when we worked with others were completely forgotten when we wrestled each other. Occasionally, we would try to throw each other off by changing up a move we had done a hundred times, or we would tell a hilarious joke while we were in the ring in order to get the other guy laughing. We were good enough that we were able to stifle our laughter, but in the dressing room after the match, we would yell at each other ... and laugh about it at the same time.

In the third match in our series, Bobby threw something at me which came completely out of the blue. If I didn't love the guy so much, I would have hurt him for doing it. When Bobby got tired during a match, he would give me an arm drag, or a hip toss, and then clamp a leg scissors on me. When I tried to kick out, he would clamp down on me and grumble, *"No, no, no, no!"* I knew that was the signal that he wanted some rest time. He would lean back on his elbows while I sold the move for him. When he was ready to go again, he would sit up on his hands and flex his knees to signal me to escape from the hold.

On that particular occasion, he hooked me with the leg scissors. We hadn't been working too long, so I figured he just wanted let me kick out and make a comeback by doing some dastardly deed to build more heat. Unbeknownst to me, he had his own malice in mind. When I tried to kick out, he tightened up. My head and neck were firmly locked between his legs just above his knees. I thought he might want me to turn and twist out, but every time I moved, he applied more pressure. I suddenly realized he was passing gas! I began thrashing about in an effort to get away from him, but he just locked me in more tightly. I felt a trembling in his legs and I could tell he was trying to suppress his laughter. In order to keep his composure, he let out an evil-sounding laugh and yelled, *"Ask him, ref. Ask him!"* The referee leaned in to ask if I was ready to concede the match. As he did, he caught "wind" of what was going on. He quickly backed away and shouted his question from the other side of the ring.

Eventually, Bobby decided he had inflicted a sufficient amount of suffering on me and released me from the hold. I had trouble keeping my composure during the rest of the match. I found myself torn between being angry enough to bash him and trying not to think about it so I didn't laugh. To add insult to injury, when we locked up, he asked me if I liked his new finishing move.

I was going to go over [win the match] that night with the flying rollover. When it was time to go home [end the match], I made my big comeback. I gave him a series of arm drags and a huge backdrop. I hit the ropes, did my somersault, and came down across his chest. As I said before, Bobby trusted me, so he never moved a muscle. On that occasion, however, as I rolled across him, I gave him a shot in the ribs with my elbow. When I covered him, he muttered, *"Crowbar bastard!"*

When we got back to the dressing room, he kept looking over at me and chuckling, and sticking the tip of his tongue out (which was his trademark when he was ready to laugh). He eventually told the story to everybody in the dressing room and had everyone in stitches.

Gas attacks happened occasionally when we were at the gym, which resulted in everyone but the offending party clearing out from the ring. The offending party would either be rolling around with laughter, or looking dumbfounded and asking, *"What's the problem?"* I had never heard of anyone doing that in an actual match, although I'm sure it happened on occasion.

For the final match of our series, Bobby would be winning and getting his revenge on "The Rose." We went at each other pretty fast and furious for awhile, until ... you got it. I found myself locked in a head scissors. It didn't immediately dawn on me that Bobby would repeat the reprehensible action he perpetrated during our previous match. I simply suspected he was tired and wanted to take a break. I sold the hold by grabbing at his knee and squirming around. Suddenly, he did it again, only this time I heard it. Once again, when I tried to do a kick out, he clamped down hard. I decided I wasn't going to let him hold me down again, so I grabbed the front of his leg and pulled it in ... and bit him right behind the knee. He let out a yell and jumped to his feet, rubbing the back of his leg and saying, *"Son of a bitch!"* I locked up with him and backed him towards the corner as we exchanged derogatory comments

The fans went crazy when Bobby polished me off. Like brothers, all was forgiven by the time we got back to the dressing room, and nobody but the wrestlers on the card knew anything about the impromptu drama which had played out in the ring. We had completed a great series of matches which the crowds and the promoters loved. Bobby and I both loved them, as well. We laughed about the match all the way home. When we worked out in the gym during the weeks that followed, he would threaten me with a repeat performance. After a month or so, he never mentioned it again. In his mind, it was as good as forgotten.

Several months later, Bobby called me to confirm that I would be coming to Homer Miller's gym to work out on Sunday. He told me the other guys were appearing on shows, or had other plans, so nobody would be there but Miller. He didn't want to work with Miller because of his tendency to "crowbar." I assured him I would be there. What I didn't tell him was that I would have a surprise for him.

Saturday night's dinner called for a generous helping of pork and beans, followed by a Sunday morning breakfast of hard-boiled eggs. It was a special, scientific, training diet I had developed for that specific occasion.

On Sunday afternoon, we had a few warm-up matches and we worked out a few new moves. As usual, we planned to end the day's training with a full-blown practice match. I was saving up for that match.

After we slammed each other around for a few minutes, I gave Bobby a backdrop. When he sat up, I dropped behind him, grabbed his hair, and pulled him down into a head scissors. With his head firmly planted between my knees, I let go with a window-rattling, earth-shattering, tears-in-your-eyes detonation. Bobby began to violently flop around and dragged me across the ring in an effort to break free. I wanted him to suffer for a while, but I couldn't control my laughter. I lost the strength in my legs and had to let him go. By the time I sat up and wiped the tears from my eyes, I looked around to see

Miller crouched down in one corner of the gym, holding his stomach in laughter. Bobby was pacing back and forth across the back of the gym, flailing his arms and saying, *"Dammit, West, you son of a bitch!"* Our session ended early that day.

For the next few weeks, I took every opportunity to remind Bobby that revenge was sweet, and "what goes around comes around." He may have gone over in most of our matches, but in the end, I won the war.

Road trips with Bobby were always an adventure. I never knew where I might wind up, or what might come out of his mouth. One night around midnight, while we were coming back from a show in Ohio, Bobby decided he was hungry. *"Just where in the hell do you think we'll find a place to eat, Golden?"* I tried to remind him that there were no major highways on the route home, and the small towns we would pass through all rolled up their sidewalks at ten o'clock. Bobby insisted we were going to eat before he took me home.

1975 tag team action at Miller's gym; Duke's big fanny blocks the camera

Sure enough, Bobby was correct. While driving through a small town about 20 minutes outside of Fort Wayne, we saw a pizza place that was all lit up. When we walked inside, we were greeted by the manager, who asked us if we had reservations. Bobby's eyes lit up. He bellowed, *"Hell, yes, we have reservations! We had reservations at the burger joint down the road, but we got there too late, but we want to eat here, anyway. Reservations for a fu—ing pizza joint? You gotta be kidding me!"* The manager looked like he was in shock, but he recovered quickly and showed us to a table. Bobby couldn't resist making one more shot as we sat down. *"Reservations? Did we take a wrong turn or what? Are we in frickin' Paris, France, or Bumfu—, Ohio?"*

Later, after we got our food, Bobby began to joke with the manager and staff. He told them who we were and about our road trip. He soon had the place in stitches. We left on a friendly note and gave our server a good tip. I think the manager and staff were Bobby Golden fans from that point on. Bobby had a way of making people believe he was a total jerk, and then turning things around and making them best friends. I always stayed on guard because more than once, I thought we were going to have to fight our way out of a situation in which Bobby had placed us. But, he never failed to turn on the charm and make it work to our advantage.

Bobby was quite the jokester, and you never know what might happen when you were with him. Total strangers didn't stay strangers to Bobby for very long. If you knew him for more than 30 minutes, you would probably be the object of one of his pranks. Bobby was a big guy with a barrel chest who could talk gruffly, but he was as nice a guy as you could ever meet. He always had a twinkle in his eye and a great laugh that drew you in. You just couldn't help but like him.

Bobby also was quite a smooth-talker with the ladies. It was that "talent" which nearly got us both into a lot of trouble on a long road trip. In the middle of a long, hot summer, we were scheduled to wrestle at a fair grounds show in the hills of West Virginia. After that, we were scheduled to go to Columbus, Ohio, before heading back to Indiana. We got to the fair grounds very early (of course) and set up the ring, along with a large tent which served as a dressing room. Bobby and I were the only people there and we were afraid to leave. We decided to hang around because we had no idea where or how far away the next town was, not to mention being afraid that we would never find our way back again. We went ahead and changed into our trunks because they were much cooler than our street clothes. It must have been about a hundred degrees inside that tent and not much cooler outside. We sat inside the tent, sweating like pigs. There was a concession trailer outside on the other side of the ring, but, of course, no one was around it. After a while, Bobby told me he needed some beer and was going to go out and scout around to see if he could get some. I wasn't a drinker, so I asked him to see if he could find a soft drink or some ice water. I would stay and guard our stuff. I was a heel and didn't particularly want to get caught out in the middle of a bunch of rednecks who might want to get vengeance for something I did to one of their heroes.

Bobby headed out of the tent and began walking toward the front of the fair grounds. He was gone for a long time, while I sat by myself in that big tent, drenched in sweat. I finally decided I was going to go out and find my own drink. As I peeked out of the tent flaps, I saw Bobby standing at the corner of the ring, talking with two young ladies. One of them outweighed both of us. She was wearing cutoff bib overalls over a white (actually, used to be white) t-shirt. She had long, stringy, brown hair with curly ribbons hanging down on both sides of her head. Her friend, who was only slightly smaller, wore spandex pants (that were at least two sizes too small) and a t-shirt. Bobby was chatting away when he glanced over and saw me. When he directed their attention towards me, they both turned and waved. I knew it wasn't going to be good.

I quickly ducked back into the tent and retreated to a corner bench. I thought, *"Surely he won't bring them in here,"* and yet, a few seconds later, Bobby strolled into the tent and proudly announced that beer was on its way. He had conned the girls into getting him the beer in exchange for a date with "us" after the match. When I protested, Bobby assured me that we would disappear before the girls ever found us. I was scheduled to wrestle right before his match, so he told me to be sure I was dressed and ready to roll when he finished his match.

Sure enough, about 30 minutes later, a six-pack of cold beer slid under the wall of the tent. I grabbed the beer, handed it off to Bobby, and stood staring at the tent wall, waiting for a pop or bottle of water. Nothing! *"Oh great, pal! You made sure you got your stuff and left me high and dry!"*

Bobby grinned and said, *"You can have some of my beer and you get first pick of the girls!"*

He laughed. I didn't.

After my match, I dressed quickly, packed my bag, and waited for Bobby. As soon as his match ended, Bobby rushed in and changed quickly. We rushed to the tent door and, as we were heading out, Bobby stopped suddenly and pushed me back into the tent. The girls had positioned themselves between us and the path which led to the parking lot ... so we had to sit and wait.

We took turns peeking out of the tent but the girls were always there, about 30 feet away and gazing at the tent. After awhile, the show ended. Once again, Bobby and I were alone in the tent. In fact, the whole fair grounds were deserted again — except for the girls. *"Okay, Golden,"* I seethed. *"How in the hell are you going to get us out of this one?"* His first suggestion was that I go out and "service" the young ladies so they would go away. I told him that was his job since I had never agreed to his little contract with them. In fact, I didn't even get a cold drink out of it! Eventually, Bobby took a peek and exclaimed, *"Hey, they're gone! Let's get the hell out of here!"*

We grabbed out bags and ran for the parking lot. By now, only two cars remained in the parking lot. One was ours. The other belonged to ... the girls. And they were standing by ours. Bobby ran up and hugged the bigger gal, glancing around over his shoulders. *"Listen, the promoter will have our asses if he sees us leaving with local girls. Is there someplace around here we can meet up with you?"* She pointed down the road to the right and told us there was a gas station about three or four miles in that direction. Bobby told her to go ahead and that we would catch up with them. They jumped into their car and drove off the lot to the right. Bobby and I got into our car and drove off the lot to the left, and we never looked back. As we sped away, I looked at Bobby and said, *"Write down the name of this place and make sure we never get booked here, again!"*

From that time on, if we were headed for an outdoor show in the summer, I made sure we had a cooler full of cold beverages in the car. I also let Bobby know that unless I was warned ahead of time, I was not to be a part of any more deals he might make, especially if it involved members of the opposite sex.

Another incident took place when Bobby and I set up Miller's ring at Buck Lake Ranch in Angola. There were a couple of females on the card that night. One was an older lady who was somewhat attractive. Bobby immediately took a shine to her and began hitting on her backstage before her match. The ring was pushed up against the stage, so we could stand in the back and watch the show. Even during the girls' match, Bobby and the gal kept shooting remarks back and forth. Bobby was convinced he was going to get a little action that night. He went back the dressing room and tried to get more information on the gal from Tommy Lynch. He wasn't happy when he came back onstage. It turns out the two ladies were much more than just ring partners. Tommy told him she would most likely be more interested in her opponent than she would him. Of course, that gave me some great material with which I could rib Bobby. From that day on, whenever I saw him checking out a young lady, I would always remind him to check on her sexual orientation.

At one time, when I got into racquetball, I joined a local club where I played one or two times a week. During one of my regular phone conversations with Bobby, I mentioned my newly found hobby. I told him it was a great way to stay in shape and also was good for my timing. Bobby said it sounded interesting and that he would like to try it sometime. I told him I would be going to the club on Thursday and he was welcome to join me. On Tuesday, Bobby called and asked if he could bring a friend along who might be interested in the game. I agreed and told him I had a friend who would be glad to round out the foursome. For once, I would be teaching Bobby.

When Thursday arrived, Bobby showed up at my door with his friend. I told him I had a couple of extra racquets which we would take for him and his friend. He said he had already borrowed a couple of racquets and they would use them. That should have been my first clue that something was up.

As we drove to the club, I explained a little about the club, the court, and the basics of the game. Once there, we dressed, entered the court, and Bobby and his friend listened intently as we went over the rules and the basics. My friend and I started out slowly, lobbing the ball against the wall so Bobby and his friend had time to get a feel for the game and return it. They would take half-hearted swings. When we picked up the pace, they not only muffed some of the shots completely, but Bobby took a few belly dives onto the floor as he swung wildly at the ball.

After a while, they began connecting with some of the shots and said they thought they were getting the hang of it. They were ready to play the game. Well, after they beat us in two out of the three games, Bobby grinned, shook our hands, and invited us to come up to his club and play sometime. He really got me that time and he sure was a long time letting me forget it.

In the later years, Bobby ran his own shows around his home town of Warsaw, Indiana. He used me and some of the other guys from the gym. They weren't big shows, but Bobby always paid us. He would also get some of the big-name wrestlers to work his shows. It sure wasn't because of the money. It was because they all liked Bobby Golden. We always had fun working with or for him.

I had many other adventures with Bobby Golden, some of which will be told in a later chapter. After I left wrestling, we lost contact for quite a while. Bobby and his wife eventually divorced and he moved around a lot. I just couldn't keep up with him. After several years, he came into my mind. For several weeks, I kept thinking about Bobby and wondering where he was. I kept telling myself that we should get together with some of the guys and do one more show — a reunion show for charity. I made up my mind to find Bobby and make that suggestion. Less than a month later, I got a phone call from a young lady who told me she was Bobby's fiancée. Bobby was in a hospital in South Bend. He had cancer and wanted to see me. She said things didn't look too good for him.

The next day, I walked into the hospital room to see Bobby. I was shocked by what I saw. He had whittled away to half his normal size and he was in obvious discomfort. He was bathed in sweat and squirming around on the bed. He held up his hand, and as I took it, he said, *"Hey, Duke. Think we could get in one more show?"* It was all I could do to keep my composure. We had a nice visit. A few days later, I helped carry him to his final resting place.

Bobby's funeral was just the send-off that he would have loved. The pall bearers were all wrestlers. The minister talked about Bobby's love of wrestling and the camaraderie he had with his fellow wrestlers. I had to grin as the preacher spoke. Only Bobby Golden would have a conversation about wrestling in church. I had a mental picture of the preacher asking Bobby what he thought of his sermon about David and Goliath, and Bobby saying, *"Yeah, it's cool. It reminded me of the time I wrestled Andre the Giant!"*

Every time I drive through Etna Green, Indiana, on Highway 30, I glance toward the cemetery and say, *"Hi, Bobby. Someday, we're going to do that last show together."*

I still get chills when I think about that whole "one more show" thing. Some might say it was just a strange coincidence. For me, I know I was blessed to have a connection with another human being which few people ever experience. We had a real connection. Bobby was much more than a good friend. He was closer to me than a brother. In those many hours we spent on the road all over the Midwest, we shared not only our love for the business, but our dreams and aspirations. We shared each other's joys and heartbreaks. In the end, I believe that even from a distance, we came to share that final dream —the dream of "one more show." That dream didn't die with Bobby. It was just postponed to be rescheduled at a new venue. I think Bobby has been awarded that shiny, gold belt. He earned it. Bobby touched the lives of many people while he was with us. All of us, especially me, are richer for it. I miss him greatly.

Here's to you, Bobby. When we do that one last show, it's going to be a dandy!

"Mean Duke" West, ready for action [1974]

Chapter 5

Moose Cholak and the Caddy Salesman

I was really excited when I got a call that I was being booked for a show at a place called the Horse Palace. It was located in the upper northwest corner of Indiana, not too far from Chicago near a town called Bass Lake. I had never heard of it, but I was finally going to get an opportunity to work with some of the wrestlers from the WWA promotion that I had watched when I was younger. Paul Christy, Tommy Lynch, and Moose Cholak were all on the card. I could hardly wait to get there.

It turned out that the Horse Palace was just that. It was a huge arena where they had horse shows and auctions. Our dressing rooms were horse stalls in which a folding chair had been placed. Actually, the stalls were much cleaner than some of the other places in which I had dressed. They smelled fresh and clean, and if you didn't see a few bales of hay here and there, you would have never known you were in a barn. I was thrilled to learn that I was sharing my stall with none other than Yukon Moose Cholak himself. Moose came in shortly after I arrived and sat down. We chatted a bit and exchanged small talk. Paul Christy popped in to say hello, as well as Tommy Lynch. Lynch had been to Miller's gym a few times to work out, so I already knew him.

I think Lynch must have told Moose that I was okay. Lynch and I had worked out together at Miller's and he knew what I was capable of doing. I had worked a few other shows where well-known wrestlers had been booked and some of them looked down their noses at those of us who were there solely to fill in. In their eyes, we were the rookies who, apparently, hadn't yet paid our dues. Some acted like we didn't exist, while others were just plain jerks. To my surprise, some of the rudest wrestlers were the babyfaces I had admired when I was growing up. After I actually met them, I began to admire the heels a lot more. It was another lesson in life which I learned from the wrestling game. Never take yourself too seriously. I pledged that no matter what success I might achieve in any facet of my life, I would always try to encourage and inspire others.

Moose Cholak was a babyface, but he was an exception to the statement I just made. When I met Moose, he shook my hand, looked me in the eye, and said, *"Nice to meet you."* Except for what Lynch or Bobby might have told him, I know he had never heard of me. He didn't turn his back to me, or launch into a long speech about his wrestling success. He just sat down and talked like any other friendly person who was meeting someone for the first time. He never asked me how many shows I had worked, or who I had worked with. Believe me; I had been the subject of that kind of interrogation before from some so-called "superstars." Obviously, Moose was not a "legend in his own mind." He had never forgotten where he came from. Everybody begins somewhere. In wrestling, unless you crossed over from some other sport where you had a big name, or you had some special characteristic like Andre the Giant, you were a rookie like everyone else. Moose seemed to understand that. He was popular and well known, especially throughout the Midwest, and yet, he was still one of the guys.

Later that night, Moose told everyone about his new Cadillac. I guess he always drove "Caddys" and the new one was his pride and joy. At some point, I told him I once rode in one of my old bosses' Cadillacs and that I was really impressed. He told me he could get me a great deal on one if I was interested. I laughed and said it would be a long time (if ever) that a cop and small-time wrestler like me could afford a new Cadillac. When he later asked me where I was from, I told him I lived in Fort Wayne. He didn't say too much, but he did ask me if I was familiar with one of the local Cadillac dealers. I told him I knew where it was, but I had never been in the dealership. That was pretty much the end of the conversation. We shook hands after the show and we went our separate ways.

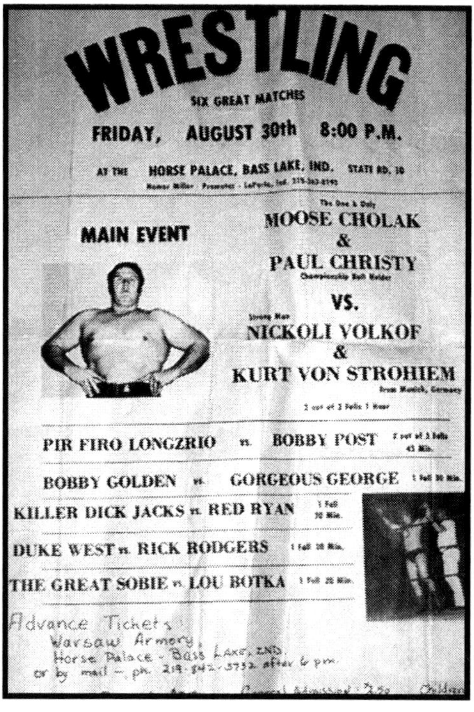

I had no idea that Moose had a connection to Fort Wayne. I don't know if he had lived there at some point, still lived there, or had family in town. Since we were only acquaintances and had only made friendly conversation, I certainly wasn't going to be so bold as to ask for his address and phone number. He never asked for mine. However, somehow, he did get mine. Only two people had that information: Bobby Golden and Homer Miller. My money would be on Bobby.

At the time, I was working the night shift on my regular job. I absolutely hated nights because my body refuses to rest if there is daylight outside. I had to struggle to get any sleep during the daytime. Ringing phones, kids playing outside my window, and the neighbors mowing their lawns constantly interrupted my attempts to get any rest.

Three days after the Horse Palace event, things got a lot crazier. I began to get telephone calls day and night from nearly every Cadillac dealer from Chicago to Indianapolis. They all mentioned Moose Cholak. He had told them I was looking for a good deal on a new Caddy. Not only that, but he also told them I wanted a cash deal. That sweetened the pot for the salesmen, who not only called, but sent letters and brochures which jammed my mailbox daily.

The next time I worked a show with Moose, he walked into the dressing room and roared out, *"Hey, West! Get that new Caddy, yet?"* He laughed, walked away, and never said another word to me all night. I told Bobby how strange I thought it was that I would be a subject of his prank when he hardly knew me. Bobby just shrugged his shoulders and told me he guessed Moose really liked me. He would know. Bobby was one of the master pranksters. It was a great feeling to know that Moose had accepted me as one of the guys when we had just met.

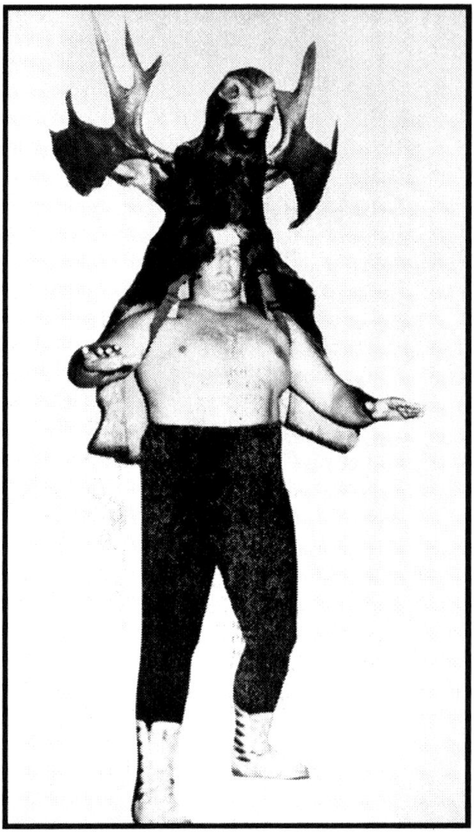

Moose Cholak

In late December a few years later, when I was still a uniform cop, I was directing traffic in the freezing cold outside the mall on the north side of Fort Wayne. All of a sudden, a big Cadillac roared up beside me with the horn blaring. I looked inside to see none other than Moose Cholak. He waved and laughed as he pulled into the mall parking lot. I guess Moose did like me, although I thought he could have come back and offered me a hot cup of coffee that night. Occasionally, folks would feel sorry for us standing outside, shivering in the below-freezing temperatures, and bring us coffee or hot chocolate. Being a cop, I was a little hesitant to accept food or beverage from a stranger. I would think someone like Moose, who actually knew me, would go out of his way to bring me something. On the other hand, since he was "Yukon" Moose Cholak, perhaps he thought I was happy to be standing in the middle of an intersection with snow blowing in my face.

Once in a while, Bobby would call and say he saw Moose someplace, and Moose had asked about me. He also said Moose had smiled and asked if I had that new Caddy yet. I finally told Bobby to tell Moose that "if he wasn't so damn big, I would come to his house and kick his ass." Bobby said Moose got a big kick out of my "threat." I also told Bobby to let Moose know that if I ever saw him out in the cold like that, I wasn't going to bring him a damn thing, either.

I never found out what connection Moose had to Fort Wayne. The next time I heard anything about him, I was reading his obituary in the newspaper. We had lost another good guy.

In 1976, Bobby and I got hooked up with a promoter who filmed a television wrestling show in Tam O'Shanter arena in Sylvania, Ohio, a suburb located on the outskirts of Toledo. He was a well-known Hispanic wrestler who had wrestled for the WWA in Indianapolis when I was a teenager. He would have us come up to Sylvania once a month where we would wrestle on a TV taping which would later air over most of northern Ohio, including Cleveland. He had a good deal. The TV taping was a house show and it promoted the next show. We always had a good house, so it should have been a good payday for all of us. I believe the arena seated 7,000 to 8,000 people. We usually filled at least half the seats and sometimes the place was almost full.

When Bobby told me about the opportunity, I was excited about it. Here was a veteran wrestler who was setting up a promotion and who liked us enough to ask us to be a part of it. He seemed like a nice guy and we looked forward to it. Not only that, but we would be appearing on television in the region and wrestling in a real arena, not a high school gym or armory.

For our first appearance, we wanted to get there early. We made it to Sylvania and the area of the arena. Whenever we went to Toledo, I let Bobby drive because I had a knock for *always* getting lost when I get there. I had better luck getting through Chicago. I usually drove when we went east of my home, and Bobby drove if we were going west, but he always took over when we got anywhere near Toledo.

We hadn't stopped to eat because we wanted to be sure we were there in time to find the place. Trying to find a restaurant in that area turned out to be a real challenge. After driving around for 30 minutes, we had to settle for a place that only sold bagels and lox. Now, bagels and lox just didn't cut it for two big wrestlers. After the show, we couldn't wait to get back on the road and find some real food. From then on, we planned our trips to Sylvania so we could get a meal as far away from that area as we could.

In Sylvania, I missed all the red flags, beginning with the fact that each of the wrestlers was shown to their own private dressing room. When Bobby and I walked into the building, we were ushered into a room which was actually the visitors' locker room for the hockey teams. I didn't think too much about it. After all, the Tam O'Shanter Arena was a big building and probably had dressing rooms for most of the guys. Our room was quite large and it had a huge shower. Most of all, it was squeaky clean. It was a setup which we seldom saw. Our wrestler-turned-promoter friend popped in to thank us for coming and introduce us to his "assistant" who would be giving us the run down. I thought, *"Okay, maybe this is going to be a high-class operation."*

I thought it was strange when I had never heard of the guy the "assistant" told me I would be wrestling. He told me they wanted me to go over and how they wanted the finish. No problem. It sounded great. Here I was at my first show in what looked to be a first-class operation and I was going to win. Then I asked the "assistant" a question: *"Okay. Can I get together with the guy so we can work out the details?"*

"Uh ... just a minute." The "assistant" walked out. I thought he was going to get the guy. A few minutes later, he came back alone and said, *"Just give me your high spots and the finishing move you want to use. I'll give them to him and bring back what he wants to do."*

In the past, even if I had worked with someone regularly, we usually got together beforehand and worked out the details. It wasn't that I felt like I couldn't do it without meeting the guy I was working with, but I felt more comfortable meeting him face to face before we went to the ring. I thought that perhaps this was how the guys did it in the "big leagues." I was going to have to wing it with a total stranger.

I got through the match just fine and everything worked out well. When I got back to the dressing room, I sat down and began telling Bobby about the match and the crowd response. After a few minutes, I began to undress so I could take a shower. When the "assistant" came to get Bobby, he asked me what I was doing. He then let us in on the fact that they were taping four shows and I would be wrestling two more times that night. Bobby and I just looked at each other and shrugged our shoulders. Bobby went out for his match, while I toweled off and sat down on the bench to wait. While I waited, I began thinking, *"Four shows! This is going to be a good payday."* While neither Bobby nor I had never asked the promoter what he was going to pay, I had made some assumptions and was multiplying those amounts times three.

I had fun in my next two matches. There was a large crowd in attendance, and with each subsequent match, I was able to build more heat. By the third match, the people all wanted to see me get a good beating.

At the end of the night, Bobby and I showered, got dressed, and prepared to go home. We were used to wrestling multiple matches at the gym, but we could also take breaks whenever we wanted, or stop to work on a new move or fix a mistake before continuing. The Sylvania show, however, had been a marathon. Working a live show takes more out of you than wrestling in a gym, and working two to four matches in a six-hour period was exhausting.

We sat on the bench in great anticipation of the promoter showing up with a fat pay envelope. We told jokes and laughed about some of the crowd reactions and unexpected incidents which happened during the matches. After we sat there for an hour and nobody came by, Bobby said he was going to go get our pay. A few minutes later, Bobby returned empty handed. He said they hadn't cleared the books yet and the promoter was going to mail us our checks. I was disappointed, but Bobby told me the promoter had assured us that he was happy with our work and he already had us booked for the next month's taping.

Later that week, Bobby called to ask if I had received my check. I told him I hadn't and he said he would call me right back. An hour or so later, he called back. *"The promoter said we were booked on the next taping and we would probably wrestle on all four programs. He'll have our money ready for us when we get there."* I was a little uneasy with the situation. Something about it just didn't sound right, but Bobby said the promoter also offered us free copies of the tapes of the shows so we could send them to other promoters.

Independent wrestlers trying to make it in the business have to perform a bit of a balancing act. Back then, there were a lot of small regional promotions and a lot of would-be promoters. We had to work for promoters who would pay us, but we also had to get exposure. We figured if we could break even until we could make a name for ourselves, we were doing well. There were plenty of promoters who would book us, but the trick was getting our pay from them. That was the case with the Sylvania promotion.

I once hit a real dry spell in my wrestling run because I couldn't maintain the balancing act. Fred Curry promoted shows in Ohio and gave us some good bookings, but after a while, he treated me like I was a full-time wrestler that he had under contract. He would call and tell me he had me booked for a show without confirming it with me ahead of time. Normally, that wasn't a problem because most of the shows were held on the weekend. One night, while we were at a show in Columbus, he told Bobby and me that we were booked on a show in Cleveland *"a week from Tuesday."* That wasn't an issue for Golden because he was a self-employed TV repairman. On the other hand, I had a full-time job, I had a family to feed, and I had used up my vacation and personal time. When I told Fred I wouldn't be able to make it, he told me he had already published my name on the posters and in the advertising. He went on to say that if I didn't go, I would never work for him again. I didn't go to Cleveland. After that, I didn't hear from him or any other promoter for a long time. I guess he "blackballed" me. It wasn't fair, but that was the nature of the business back then.

As promised, we worked the second Sylvania show, but when the promoter was nowhere to be found after the show, I was sure something was up. I suppose it was my "cop sense" that kicked in, but common sense alone would have told me that something just wasn't right. Once again, he called and promised a big check at the next show, but again, he disappeared when the show was over. It wasn't just us young guys. Even the headliners were getting stiffed on their payoffs. His whole operation came to a halt when one of the main event performers called the police when he didn't get his money.

Before the police arrived, the workers all gathered in the lounge, where one of the guys insisted the promoter come to pay us. It was there that we realized why the promoter kept us all in separate dressing rooms. If we had talked to each other sooner, the rebellion would have happened much sooner than it did. We would have learned that the big name guys who had worked the shows were complaining about advance and expense checks which were bouncing. We also would have known about the other broken promises, like the tapes we had been promised. No, we never saw them, either. We all agreed that we either get a fat cash envelope, or we would walk and never wrestle for him again.

When the police arrived, they had to drag him up to the lounge, where they pressured him to pay what he owed us. He agreed to pay everybody in cash.

For my efforts of driving 100 miles (each way) from Fort Wayne to Sylvania on five different occasions, and working two to four matches each time, I was paid a whopping 20 dollars. No, not 20 dollars a match ... 20 dollars for the whole gig! It probably worked out to about a dollar a match. Not only that, but he paid us in Canadian money. We gave that guy three months worth of TV, good houses, and some damned good matches. For that, we got a royal screwing. At any rate, that was the end of the Sylvania promotion.

Somebody told me later that the guy went to prison when he was found guilty of another scam. I wouldn't be a bit surprised if it were true. I have to give the guy credit. Even after the cops came and he handed Bobby and me our 20 dollars Canadian, he asked if we could come back next month. He promised he would, "take care of us." We told him he had already taken care of us.

It was a real shame. The guy had a good thing going. He had a lot of wrestlers coming up every month who worked multiple matches to give him a whole month's worth of TV shows. We always had a decent house in the arena in Sylvania and he drew some good houses at his other shows. I figured that, like a lot of promoters, he was paying off the headliners and we little guys would get the scraps which were left over. Of course, he wasn't paying off the headliners, and that was something the top guys wouldn't stand for. As for us underneath guys, all he had to do was pay us enough to help cover our expenses and we would have been thrilled, but he couldn't even do that!

In his heyday, the guy had been a fairly decent worker, so he knew what life was like on the road. It made me wonder whether or not he was really hard-pressed to come up with the money or if he was just trying to rip us off. We had worked with start-up promoters before. They always told us up front that we wouldn't get much money until the promotion got off the ground, but they also promised to do what they could. Most of them gave us a few bucks each show, so we worked with them. In subsequent weeks, however, if the houses went up and the payoffs didn't, we would move on. Regardless, we had fun and got a lot of experience at those shows, but the bottom line was that fun and experience didn't cover our expenses.

The one benefit of the Sylvania shows was that we got some good TV exposure, which helped me get more work in the months that followed. I also got to work with some great talent and I learned a lot from them.

On one of our trips, Bobby and I were sitting in the dressing room when one of the arena employees came in and opened the garage doors at the back of the room. We looked at each other, wondering if they were going to drive a vehicle into the middle of the dressing room. Instead, in walked the two biggest guys I had ever seen — the McGuire brothers, Billy and Benny. They were the world's largest twins and weighed 720 pounds and 680 pounds, respectively. They plopped down on the bench across from us and we began to engage in conversation. I remembered seeing their names in the *Guinness Book of World Records*, and there I was talking with them face to face.

Billy and Benny were a couple of really great guys and they were a lot of fun to talk with. Benny was very talkative and came across as one of those "good ole boys" who grew up in the country. The conversation ended with an invitation to visit them on their farm. Benny told us they had a stocked pond in which we would love to fish. He told us that earlier in the week, they had caught 18 bass. The smallest one was about 2½ pounds. *"They were good eatin', too. We 'et' them all in one settin'.* Bobby and I tried to look serious and fought the urge to break out in laughter. I wish we had taken them up on their offer and made that trip to the farm. I'm sure it would have been a blast. And, no doubt, we would have been treated to some genuine southern hospitality, not to mention some darn good fishin'.

Our conversation was interrupted when the promoter walked in to tell me I would be wrestling Billy. I think I broke the record for the shortest match in history (about fifteen seconds). When the bell rang for our match, I charged across the ring, jumped up, and threw myself right into Billy's chest. I flopped back hard onto the canvas with a thud. The next thing I knew, his huge butt was coming down towards me. It was like a total eclipse had just blacked out the sun. Billy just grabbed the top rope and sat down on me. (Lightly, thank God!) I couldn't move, and that was no work, either. I couldn't have moved if I had wanted to. The referee dropped down beside me and said, *"Get up! It's only been eight seconds."* I told him he was talking to the wrong guy. When he asked Billy if he was going to let me up, Billy shook his head and said, *"No."* The ref told me he had to count me out. 1-2-3 and it was over. As I walked back into the dressing room, Benny sat where I had left him. He shook his head and said, *"That's Billy. When he gits tarred, he just won't do nothin'."*

I worked a couple of shows in Sylvania with a guy who called himself the Pink Panther. The guy took a lot of his gimmick from Gorgeous George and his antics really got the crowd fired up. He would wiggle his butt and prance around the ring while the crowd booed and cried, *"You fag!"* Their cries got louder and louder as the match went on. He made such an impression that after a few shows, the yelling and booing began long before he reached the ring. I was also impressed with some of the moves he made in the ring. I would like to have had an opportunity to sit down and talk with him. However, we were all kept in separate dressing rooms and we never got a chance to interact with each other. I didn't know why at the time, but I found out later why they didn't want us talking to each other.

One of the things I really liked about that arena in Sylvania was that it had a lounge on one end which overlooked the arena floor. One night, I had finished with my matches and had some time to kill before Bobby would be done. I told him I was going up to the lounge to grab a sandwich and a drink and he agreed to meet me there when he finished. I found a table and sat back to relax and enjoy my refreshments. After a few minutes, I noticed an older, black gentleman at the bar who kept glancing over at me. He said something to the guy next to him, who then looked over and nodded his head. I was a heel and worried that they might be talking about administering some justice to me. I didn't look forward to fighting my way out of the arena. I looked around the room to see if any of the other wrestlers were there who might assist me, but there was nobody in sight. I realized that nobody would be coming to my rescue if things went south. I would just have to stand my ground.

Within a few minutes, the black man was walking towards me. As he got closer, I could see he was quite a bit older than I had originally thought. He also had a big smile on his face. I wanted to maintain my heel image, but in an attempt to defuse what might be a dangerous situation, I smiled back at him. As I looked into his eyes, I saw the same excitement I saw in my Grandpa's eyes when we went to a live show and he got close to one of the wrestlers. I decided that if he asked for an autograph, I was going to break my usual policy and give him one. How could I turn him down?

"I know you. You're one of those 'rasslers, ain't you"

"Yeah."

"I seen you on TV and seen you 'rassle down there a while ago, didn't I?"

"Yep."

"You guys are gladiators, man! Gladiators! My boy is downstairs watchin' the matches now. Can I go get him so he can meet you?"

"Sure."

I assumed I would be signing an autograph for a little kid, but then again, I was sure that even in Sylvania, they weren't going to let a little kid in the bar. A few minutes later, the old man came back with a young man in tow. He was a good-looking kid, maybe 21 years old. He had soft features and obviously was not the athletic type. He held out his hand cautiously and told me in a soft voice that he was glad to meet me. It was obvious he thought "The Canadian Rose" was going to turn on him at any minute. When I took his hand in mine and began to shake it, his eyes got wide. His dad began talking again. *"I want my boy to be a 'rassler. I want him to be a gladiator. Can you teach him to 'rassle?"*

His son's eyes widened even further and he said, *"Uhhh ... no, Daddy!"*

"You could take him with you and make a 'rassler out of him."

His son began to visibly get upset. *"No, Daddy! I really don't want to."*

I decided I needed to do something to help the young man (and me) get out of the predicament in which he found himself. Dad had obviously had a bit too much to drink and he wasn't going to take no for an answer. Not from me ... and not from his son.

"Have you ever boxed or wrestled before, kid?"

"No, sir."

"Played football?"

"No, sir."

"How much do you weigh?"

"About 180, sir."

"Hmm-mm. How's your pain threshold?"

"I don't know what you mean, sir."

"How much pain can you tolerate?" By this time, the poor kid's eyes were like saucers.

"Uh, Daddy. I don't think this is such a good idea."

I then turned my attention to his father. *"You know, he really has to want this. Not only that, but he needs to bulk up and put on at least another twenty solid pounds. As soon as you think he's ready, I'll be glad to work with him. Here's the number of the gym where we train. You can reach me there."*

Dad seemed satisfied with that response and took the number to Miller's gym. His boy seemed to breathe a huge sigh of relief. Miller never heard from Dad or his son, and neither did I. I guess Dad sobered up enough that the kid talked him out of it. Or, perhaps the boy decided it was a good time to run away from home.

Every road trip with Bobby Golden wound up being a bit of an adventure. Sylvania was no different. The Tam O'Shanter Arena was also the home of the local minor league hockey team, which competed in the same league as the team from Fort Wayne, where I lived. One Saturday, we arrived at the arena about five hours early, expecting the ring to be set up. Our plan was to have a workout, go out and grab a bite to eat, and then get back to the arena in time for the show. We often did that because we never turned down an opportunity to get in the ring and throw each other around. After stowing our bags in the dressing room, we walked out to see if the ring was up. To our surprise, the hockey team was in the middle of a practice. They were leaving on a road trip and were getting in one final practice before loading up the bus. I assured Bobby that they would soon be out of there. I occasionally worked security for the hockey games at the Fort Wayne Memorial Coliseum, so I knew how quickly they could transform a hockey venue to another event, but I also knew that by the time the floor was covered and the ring set up, there wouldn't be time for us to get in a workout.

As we stood watching at the glass on the side of the rink, the players began skating laps. Bobby decided to encourage them to give up the arena floor by banging on the glass as the players skated by. *"Hey! Don't you guys know there is wrestling in here tonight? Why don't you pussies get off the floor and let some real men get in there?"*

At first, all we got were some ugly glances as they skated by. "Bobby," I said, "you do realize there are two of us and a whole bunch of them, don't you?"

I just wanted to go get something to eat and then come back to get ready for the show. Bobby got that silly grin on his face and asked me, *"What's the name of that hockey team in Fort Wayne?"*

"The Komets."

Bobby began pounding on the glass again. *"Hey! You girls ever heard of the Fort Wayne Komets? I hear they kick your ass!"*

By now, the players were skating by and pounding on the glass in front of us with their sticks. Some even stopped and tried to stare us down. Of course, Bobby was challenging them to *"come on out of there."* Bobby was just being

Bobby. They didn't know him, though, and I was sure they weren't onto his sense of humor. All I could think was that we were about to be killed.

As the practice drew to a close, some of the players began exiting the ice on the other side of the rink. Several of them glanced back at us and talked back and forth, as if they were contemplating whether or not to take up Bobby's challenge. I grabbed Bobby by the arm and began to drag him away. He complied, but he couldn't do it without leaving them with his favorite "up yours" gesture with his arms. As we sat in the dressing room, I was sure about a half a dozen of those guys were going to come busting in and "clean our clocks." When I ventured outside later, I found the crew covering the ice and I saw the team filing onto the bus outside the door. I could breathe again.

The Sylvania show was an exhausting schedule. We did get a lot of good TV time and exposure. Financially, however, it was a disaster. We loved to wrestle and probably would have done it for nothing. However, when we couldn't make expenses, we had to do a lot of explaining when we got home. Our wives began to look at it as nothing more than an expensive hobby and things got a little tense on the home front. On the occasions when we did make a little money, Mama expected to get a little something out of it, and it had better be something more than flowers! It wasn't easy being a cop's wife, and it wasn't much better being the wife of a wrestler. My wife had the distinct displeasure of being both.

An old school mate of mine, Billy Wiseman, was a teacher in Toledo. In high school, Billy and I were practicing amateur wrestling moves in gym class. We were working on escape moves when your opponent was behind you in a standing position. We would grab each other from behind and practice dropping and spinning to escape. I got behind him and got a good grip around his waist. Suddenly, Billy grabbed my wrists, and as he tried to drop out of my grip, he threw his head back and smacked me squarely in the nose. I heard a loud "crack" and my nose began to bleed like crazy. That was the first of several broken noses I had over the years. Billy felt badly about it, and each time we saw each other after that, he mentioned the incident. I haven't talked to Billy in years, but I often wondered if he ever saw the Canadian Rose on TV and recognized me. If he did, I'm sure that if I ever run into him again, he will be bragging about being the guy who broke the nose of the Canadian Rose. He might have been the first, but he certainly wasn't the last.

When I wrestled, I would look out over the crowds and wonder if someone from my childhood days might be sitting in the audience. I wondered what they might think if they realized it was me. I did wind up working on my regular job with a guy from Defiance, Ohio. One day, some of the fellows got into a conversation about wrestling. Of course, someone had to bring up the fact that I was the Canadian Rose. All of a sudden, the guy said, *"No sh—! That was you?"* He went on and on about having seen me on TV and at a few live shows. He had attended shows in Toledo and Lima and remembered me, Golden, and Lancaster during the time when he was a big fan. We had worked together for two or three years, and he never figured out that seven or eight years earlier, he had been booing me. I thought that was cool.

I wouldn't trade those days for anything, but, I must have been crazy!

Chapter 6

The "Real" Dick the Bruiser

I was having so much fun wrestling. I didn't care if I was wrestling on television, in a high school gym, a big coliseum, or even Homer Miller's gym. At first, I had some pretty lofty goals, but after a while, reality began to set in. It took more than talent and a good gimmick to make it "big." Sometimes, it was just a matter of being in the right place at the right time. It helped if you had a job where you could break away to make shows which weren't solely on your days off. Or you had to know somebody who knew somebody. Otherwise, you were considered to be just another bush leaguer who they threw in once and a while to fill a card. When we worked for small promotions like Homer Miller's, we worked high school gyms and small armories in front of a few hundred people, and nobody got a big payday. The bulk of the gate went to the promoter and any headliners he might have brought in to build up the show.

After being in the business for several months, I wanted just one time to step into the ring with some of the guys I had watched when I was growing up. Grandpa was gone by the time I began wrestling, but I was sure he would be proud of me if that happened.

Once in a while, one of those name guys would pop into Miller's gym and I would get to work with them. Tommy "Mr. Indiana" Lynch came around once in a while. Sailor Art Thomas dropped by a few times. Porfirio Longoria came once. I had never heard of him before or since, but he was supposedly a champion in Mexico. I do know that he was one heck of a worker. I don't know how he hooked up with Miller, but he worked a few shows with us before he left. I was thrilled to have been a part of the Horse Palace show because it had given me an opportunity to meet Moose Cholak and Paul Christy. However, I wrestled on one of the "prelims" against Rick Rogers, who was another guy out of Miller's stable. We were there simply to fill out the card. At another show, Bobo Brazil was on the card, but he was running late. I saw him run into the dressing room to get ready for his match. As soon as the show was over, he was out the door and back on the road. I did get to meet him years later and actually wrestled him.

The first time it really happened for me was in Columbus, Ohio. Bobby and I were booked there on a show with Bull and Fred Curry, the Flying Tigers, and Apache Luis Martinez, to name a few. I was sure we were just going to be "fillers" or hamburger for somebody. I arrived to discover that I was booked to wrestle Luis Martinez. I was blown away! For the first time since I began wrestling, I got really nervous. Bobby sensed my apprehension and told me to just go out there and do what I always do. I decided I was not going to blow that opportunity. I set my mind to the fact that Luis was a man just like me and that the Canadian Rose was ready.

Everything clicked. It was the best match I had ever been involved with. Of course, Luis came out on top, but we worked back and forth, giving and taking the advantage. Luis didn't try to make a fool out of me and he let me work my gimmick. He treated me like an old, respected ring veteran. I never once felt like I was any less than his equal in the ring. Back in the dressing room after the match, Luis shook my hand and said, *"Good match."* I thanked him, but still kind of wondered if he was just being nice. He went into the next dressing room and I could hear him going on and on about the match, but his heavy Mexican accent made it hard for me to tell what he was saying. Later that night, one of the guys came out and told me that Luis was talking about what a great match it was and that I was great to work with. *"Good job, guy!"*

I don't think my feet touched the ground again for a week. As far as I was concerned, I had made it! Anything after that was just gravy. I had wrestled Luis Martinez, the guy we admired when I was growing up. I think Grandpa smiled.

For any kid who grew up in the Midwest, the ultimate would be to meet Dick the Bruiser or Wilbur Snyder. My first opportunity to meet Bruiser came through Homer Miller. Miller had quite a collection of rings and other wrestling accessories at his gym, including a cage [chain link fencing]. When the Indianapolis office rented his cage, he asked Bobby and me to put together a crew to take the cage down to Indy and set it up. While there, I got to hang out in the dressing room where Bruiser held court and talked briefly with Ernie Ladd. Even though I was now an adult and a fledgling wrestler, it was still a thrill to me. Whether we admired Dick the Bruiser, Gene Autry, or Johnny Unitas when we were kids, I don't think we ever get over the feeling of awe they inspired in us.

Bobby later got booked onto a few shows for the Indianapolis promotion. When they came to Fort Wayne, Bobby invited me to meet him at the venue. While there, he introduced me formally to Bruiser and Snyder. Wow! Dick and I seemed to hit it off okay. Wilbur, however, was not so thrilled to meet me. He took great offense to Bobby inviting a stranger into the dressing room. Even though I was a "worker," he looked at me as being "kayfabe," and wanted nothing to do with me. Bobby didn't get many more bookings from them. I hoped it wasn't because of me. If it was, Bobby never said so.

Years later, somebody gave me Bruiser's phone number and we chatted a few times. He was always very cordial to me. I'll never forget one occasion when we were talking. I kept hearing loud noises of children playing in the room. Dick said, *"Just a minute, West."* He put down the phone and I heard him say in a soft, gentle voice, *"Come on, kids. Go on out there. Grandpa's on the phone."* When he came back to the phone, he growled in his usual

Bruiser voice, *"Go—amn rugrats!"* I wasn't about to bring up the fact that I had just heard the real Dick Afflis, a proud grandpa.

When I did shows for Big Jim Lancaster in Ohio, or with Bobby in Indiana, I got to work with guys like the Flying Tigers and Al Snow. Al went on to do well in the WWE. Of course, Flying Fred Curry and Bull Curry were icons in the Ohio territories. In Minnesota, I worked with Verne Gagne, Bobby Heenan, and "Black Jacks" Lanza and Mulligan.

I wasn't making much money. In fact, I was barely covering my expenses. However, I was meeting the heroes of my youth. What could be better?

Dick the Bruiser

Chapter 7

"Bo"

When I finally appeared on a card with Bobo Brazil again, I was able to spend some time talking with him. He asked me where I was from, about my family and job, and made plain small talk. We weren't wrestling together that night and our paths didn't cross again for almost a year. When I was booked on another show with Bobo, I was excited. I had never dreamed that the guy whom I had watched on television so many times as a kid would have remembered our previous meeting. "Bo" walked in and looked over at me. I was floored when he said, *"Hey, Wes. How are the girls doing?"* From that day on, he always called me "Wes," and he never failed to ask about my family. I once told him that if he was going to call me "Wes," I was going to call him "Bo." He just grinned and said, *"That's okay with me."*

When my eldest daughter, Ann, began going with me to some of the shows, she got to meet Bobo. He was great to her and any other kids that happened to be around. He occasionally set up a gimmick [souvenir] table where he sold pictures and signed autographs for the fans. He often invited Ann to sit with him at the table and she would sell pictures and greet the fans for him. She loved it. I think she wound up with the world's largest collection of Bobo Brazil autographs. He gave her one every time he saw her. Ann recently told me that the first job she ever got paid for was selling autographs and photos for Bobo. That was the first time I had heard he actually paid her. At first, I thought she hadn't told me because she didn't want to limit her access to the "First Bank of Dad." When I think about it now, however, I wonder if she did it to spare my feelings. After expenses, she probably made more money in the business than I did.

My first opportunity to get in the ring and wrestle the great Bobo Brazil was in Elkhart, Indiana. We had a great match (at least, in my opinion). It was a tag team match and Bobo, of course, was the star of the match. However, like Luis Martinez, he treated me as an equal and made sure I looked good in the ring. After the show, he came back to the dressing room and congratulated me on a good match. When he sat down and asked about Ann and Kris (my younger daughter), he made me feel like we were old buddies from way back. I will never forget how proud I was to later tell my Dad that I was now friends with Bobo Brazil.

I always hoped to get my Dad to a show so he could meet Bobo, and maybe even Moose Cholak. He would have been thrilled. He did meet Bobby Golden and Tommy Lynch, only because we stopped by my folk's house on a road trip. Unfortunately, Dad wasn't that thrilled that I was wrestling. He always warned me about getting hurt. He had enough trouble accepting the fact that I was a cop. If anything happened on the job, or I got banged up in a wrestling match, I never discussed it in front of Dad. One time, when Mom and Dad came up from Muncie for a visit, I took him with me on an errand. On the way back home, the radiator of my truck blew with a loud bang. The blood drained from Dad's face until he was as white as a ghost. I had to convince him that we were not being shot at.

I later learned that my younger daughter wasn't too keen on me being in wrestling, either. At a match I was refereeing when she was just old enough to go to the shows with me, I was supposed to take a bump. I was going to get knocked out of the ring and, of course, by the time I made it back to the ring, the heels would have done some dirty deed and the babyface would be pinned. I would count them out and then I would have to be helped back to the dressing room. It went well until a few minutes after I got to the dressing room. Bobby came in with Kris in tow. She was certain that Dad had been hurt and she refused to settle down until Bobby brought her in to see me.

Bobo Brazil

Kris was never the big wrestling fan that Ann was. As for Bobo, he was by far the biggest man she had ever seen. No matter how hard he tried, she never warmed up to him. She was around Bobby Golden and his family a lot, but she didn't have a lot to do with him, either, unless we were away from wrestling and hanging out at his house or mine.

When I reached a point in life where I could no longer wrestle, I refereed for a while. I got to ref a few of Bo's matches. He had been wrestling since I was a youngster and he was getting up in years by then. He was having a lot of problems with his knees and he was close to the end of his career. During the last match I refereed with him, Bo was taking some shots from the bad guy. Bo stumbled back into the corner and I noticed him gesturing for me to come over. Bo whispered to me that his knees were going out. He asked me to stand there while he leaned on me until he could get his legs back under him. I stood there, holding the big man upright, while acting as if I was listening to him complain about his opponent while he leaned on me with his big arm on my shoulder. It was kind of sad for me as I stood there realizing that this great man's ring career was nearly over.

After the show, Bo came over to thank me for helping him out. I really wish I could have put aside my manly pride and told him that I was honored to have him lean on me. It was the least I could do for the man who had entertained and excited my family for so many years. He was a wrestler of such caliber that he could have blown off a hack wrestler like myself, but he chose to treat me the same as he would a superstar with whom he was sharing the main event.

I didn't get to see Bo again after that show. On the day I went to South Bend to see Bobby Golden in the hospital for the last time, I just missed seeing Bo as he had been in to see Bobby a few minutes before my arrival. Later, however, I did meet a Benton Harbor, Michigan (the hometown of Bobo) policeman who was a friend of Bo's. We served together on the board of a Midwest police organization and we saw each other a few times a year. Through him, Bo and I exchanged greetings and I was able to keep up with how he was doing. When I learned Bo was having health issues, I thought about heading up to Benton Harbor to see him. Sadly, I never got around to doing that.

When Ann called to tell me that Bo had passed away on January 20, 1998, I was saddened, and yet, I felt a great sense of pride for having known him. By the time the news reached our local newspaper, the funeral was over. I am not one for funerals, but I would have been there. After reading the obituary, I looked up, said goodbye to Bobo, and wished him well in his new venue. I still kick myself for not taking the time to drive up to Benton Harbor to see him before he passed on. If there is any lesson to be learned from all of this, it is that we should never pass up an opportunity to be with the people we care about. We should never stop telling them that they are appreciated. We never know when our last chance to speak with them will come.

I believe Bo is in that big ring in the sky. He is probably still patting little kids on the head and giving them that big smile for which he was known. Best of all, he no longer needs to lean on anyone.

Someday, perhaps, I will make it to Benton Harbor, Michigan. If I do, I fully intend to find his final resting place and pay my proper respects. I want to say "goodbye" to him and tell him "thanks for the memories."

I heard Terry Bradshaw talk about winning Super Bowls and other awards throughout his career. He said that years from now, nobody will remember that a person had five Super Bowl rings, or won an Oscar. When you are gone, people will remember how you treated others. They will, however, remember you if you were a decent, honest guy. That is how "Bo" will be remembered. Bobo Brazil was a legend in wrestling. I knew him as also being a legend of a man. I was so fortunate to have had the privilege of standing in his shadow.

Chapter 8

The Chief

Several years prior to getting into wrestling, I worked for a vending company that was based in Fort Wayne. One of the accounts I serviced was a local hospital. I met a security guard there named Irvin "Irv" E. Lindsey. Irv was a big man and we spent some time chatting whenever I was there to service their equipment. We became good friends and Irv got me a part time job with the security company. Irv worked as a security guard for Joslyn Steel and Slater Steel for 26 years. He also served as a reserve officer for the Fort Wayne Police Department, so he helped me get into the police reserve, which turned out to be the beginning of my career in law enforcement. I had weekends off, so I could put in the required monthly time and still make it to the gym and take the few bookings I got.

Everybody referred to Irv as "Chief," but I didn't know why until several years after we became friends. When he invited me to his house one day, I saw some wrestling memorabilia. As amazing as it seems, it turned out that Irv had wrestled under the name Chief Lone Eagle. I was especially impressed to see a trophy for the tag team of Chief Lone Eagle and Don Eagle. Don Eagle was one of the most famous wrestlers during the 1940s through the early 1960s, and I remembered him from my youth. Irv and I had some great conversations about wrestling and he had some interesting stories about some of the old-time wrestlers of my day. I couldn't believe we had known each other as long as we did and had never discussed wrestling. I guess I thought they called him "Chief" because of something to do with the police department. If we had been good friends before, our friendship was now sealed by our association with the wrestling business, and between wrestling and law enforcement, we always had plenty of war stories to share with one another.

I made him promise that if he ever decided to get rid of the tag team trophy, he would give me first dibs to buy it from him.

Even though Chief and I became good friends, I limited my visits to his house, so it wasn't until later that I learned he also had a penchant for an unusual hobby. He got me started collecting police patches and invited me over one day to give me some "traders" from his collection. It was then that I learned of one of his other hobbies. After swapping patches and police "war stories" (he had been a cop, too), Chief asked me to stick around for a few minutes while he fed his snakes. He showed me a room full of reptiles. I am not deathly afraid of snakes, but I don't go looking for them or collecting them, either. Chief told me that one of them was quite poisonous and he liked to have someone around to take him to the hospital if he "accidentally" got bit while feeding him. I told him I would be happy to wait in the car and keep it warmed up while he fed the snakes. I also would be happy to drive him to the hospital if he ran out to the car. That is, as long as he didn't have any of those damned snakes attached to him.

I'm sure he was probably "yanking my chain," but I didn't want to take any chances. I didn't mind coming across a snake outdoors because one of us, or both of us, would go out of our way to avoid the other. On the other hand, I didn't (and still don't) have any desire to pick them up or be around when someone else does.

Duke in his "other" uniform [1976]

After that, I was always glad to have Chief stop by my place for a visit or to meet him somewhere for lunch or coffee. If I did go over to his house, I kept an eye out for any creatures that might be crawling around and made sure the door to his "snake room" was fully closed. Eventually, he called to tell me that he had to get rid of his collection. It was now safe for regular visits for patch exchanges and "war stories."

Only a few people in my regular life knew about my extracurricular activities as a wrestler (or so I thought) and I never mentioned it. Of course, as my friendship with Chief grew, my secret identity as the Canadian Rose soon came to light. It wasn't long before the entire police department knew about my pink trunks and grey tights with the rose on the front. In fact, when I applied to go from being a civilian police employee to a full-time commissioned officer, I had to appear before the Board of Captains for an interview.

When I strolled into the boardroom, I saw that every one of the department's top brass was in attendance. I was a little apprehensive as I looked around. They were all smiling, but it was not a "nice to see you" smile. It was something else. Immediately, Lieutenant Bob Alderman said, *"So, tell us about these pink tights we keep hearing about."* They all began laughing and that broke the ice. I didn't mention that I was still wrestling occasionally. By that time in my life, I had begun to slow down. I hadn't quit wrestling completely, but I didn't think wrestling was something that needed to be thoroughly discussed. I had injured my back during a match in Minneapolis and I hoped they wouldn't pick up on that during my physical. I downplayed the whole wrestling thing to the brass and nobody asked any more about it. I didn't lie, but I wasn't going to volunteer any unnecessary information. When it was all over, I got the job.

I'm jumping ahead in my story, but when I retired from police work 23 years later, they held a reception for me. When I came back from lunch, my Canadian Rose ring attire was hanging in the lobby of the police station.

For the most part, I was able to easily juggle my schedule so I could make shows on the weekends. More than once, I got home just in time to get dressed and go to work. There were times when, if a show was close enough to home, I would wrestle, leave immediately after my match, and show up in time for my night shift duties. Occasionally, I would swap days off with someone, or schedule a day off that would allow me to make a show. I was young enough that lack of sleep was not an issue for me. I sure couldn't do it now.

After a few years, I was promoted to Sergeant, and then to Lieutenant, and I was again able to be off on most weekends. However, there were times when we made a long weekend trip that I had to race back to make a Sunday evening or Monday morning shift.

Learning to function without a lot of sleep came in handy when I spent the last half of my career as a detective. I loved my work, but often found myself waking up in the middle of the night thinking about the cases I was working on. Thoughts and ideas would roll around in my head as I considered what I should do, or should have done, to solve certain cases. At least three or four times a year, I was on call for an entire week. I would spend sleepless nights in anticipation of the phone ringing. About the time I would wear down enough to fall into a deep sleep, the phone would ring. I would be off to work and on the job for many hours after.

Performing in the ring also gave me confidence when I was called upon to be an instructor, or when I was asked to give speeches to various organizations on crime prevention and gangs. If you can prance around a ring in pink trunks before an audience, speaking in front of large crowds is a breeze.

For several years, Chief and I went to different jobs and only kept in touch through an occasional phone call. When I got into wrestling and hooked up with Homer Miller, I made contact with Chief and invited him to come up to the gym to work with us. Chief soon became a regular passenger when I made my weekly trek to La Porte. Eventually, Chief shook off the rust and even took some bookings with us for Miller and some of the other small promotions.

On one occasion, we drove up to Bobby's house to leave on a road trip for a match in Illinois. Bobby told me that an acquaintance of his wanted to go with us. He set things up by telling the poor guy that Chief and I were rivals and he thought it would be best if he sat between us to keep the peace. He almost backed out of the trip, but Bobby convinced him he would be safe.

The skinny kid wound up in the back seat of Bobby's car, firmly wedged between Chief Lone Eagle and Mean Duke West. It was a long trip, and with a little encouragement from Bobby, the Chief and I began talking trash to each other before we were a few miles down the road. The kid was sweating and he was so nervous that he was shaking. Each time we reached around him to take an occasional swat at each other, his eyes would bug out of his head. I could see Bobby grinning in the rear view mirror as the kid pleaded with us to settle down and stay calm.

At the first gas stop, the guy told Bobby he wouldn't go any further unless he could ride up front. Bobby allowed him to complete the rest of the trip in the front seat, but that was the last time he wanted to ride to the wrestling matches with Bobby Golden.

There was another time when Chief and I were both booked for a show in Lima, Ohio. I believe Jim Lancaster was the promoter. Jim had been a successful wrestler and I remembered him from the time he spent with the Indianapolis promotion. We didn't have any details other than the two of us were supposed to be there. We hopped in Chief's car and headed for Lima. Just outside of Lima, we decided to stop at a small Mom-and-Pop diner for a hot meal before heading to the arena.

We had just put in our order and were enjoying some good conversation when I noticed Chief staring over my shoulder. *"Oh, Christ! Look behind you,"* Chief said, as I turned to see what was going on. Right there on the wall by the door was a huge poster for that night's show. The poster was complete with photos, and smack dab in the middle of it was ... Chief Lone Eagle vs. The Canadian Rose.

Chief had noticed some folks glancing at the huge poster and then taking a close look at the two strangers in the diner. Other people coming in stopped to look over the poster and then stared at us as they passed our booth. That wasn't going to look too good. Big Jim wasn't going to be happy if he found out we were traveling together, and he would really be pissed if he knew we had been seen together in a local establishment. I don't think Jim realized that since we both lived in Fort Wayne, we car pooled to the matches.

We figured our only option was to do the trash talk thing again. *"I'm gonna kick your ass!"* I roared at Chief.

"Yeah? Well, we'll see in a little bit, won't we?" he shot back.

"I can't believe they're making me waste my time and talent on a 'has-been' redskin like you!"

"Better to have been a 'has-been' than a damn 'never-was' like you!"

We figured we would let things go at that and just gulp down our meal and get out of there. Before we finished, the owner appeared by our table, and told us that our meal was on the house if we would just calm down and take our battle to the ring. We agreed and left an extra large tip for the poor waitress, who was obviously terrified by our table battle.

We snuck into the arena and never mentioned the incident to Big Jim. We did have a good laugh going home, though. After that, I insisted on knowing who I was booked against before I agreed to take a booking.

Chief was with us for a couple of years before his age caught up with him. His legs could no longer handle the rigors of wrestling, or even the long car rides. He eventually retired, but this time, it was for good.

Every time Chief and I got together after that, we shared some of the memories and laughs from those days on the road. One of his favorite stories was from the time when Bobby and I worked as a tag team against Chief and Homer Miller. They were working Bobby over pretty good in the middle of the ring. Of course, as his partner, "Mean Duke West," the heel, I was obliged to attempt to tag in and rescue him by any means. After making several tags between the ropes (which the ref always caught), I decided to stand on the bottom rope and lean over into the ring. After a few failed attempts at making the tag, I moved up to the middle rope. By now, nobody was paying attention to me. I leaned way out, only to lose my balance and flip over the top rope. I landed in the ring with a huge "bang!" No one expected it and the action came to a standstill as they all stared over at me. All I could do was roll out of the ring and stand back up in the corner. I was embarrassed, but I had the presence of mind to make light of it by saying, *"Hey, I just thought I'd drop in!"* I stared at them with a deadpan look and told them to "get back to work!" Miller began laughing and pointed at me, as if he was making fun of me. Chief fell in with him and was really cracked up by the whole thing. Bobby was my partner, so he simply buried his head in the mat so nobody could see his face. When we all got back to the dressing room, Miller yelled at me, *"West! You son-of-a-bitch! Don't ever do that sh— again!"* Then he began laughing. Bobby and the Chief were rolling. Every single time he saw me after that, Chief reminded me of that incident. Even when his health went bad and he wasn't feeling good, I could get a smile out of him by saying, *"Just thought I'd drop in."*

Irvin Lindsey as Chief Lone Eagle

A few years ago, Chief left us to get ready for that big show in the sky. He passed away at his home on November 24, 2005. He was 72 years old. He was a big guy with an equally big heart. He could also keep up with the best of them when it came to joking around and ribbing each other. Before he passed away, he asked me to stop by his house, where he presented me with two of his old wrestling trophies. One of them is the one with Don Eagle's name on it. They have been proudly displayed in my home ever since.

Chapter 9

A Bloody Mess

One of the guys we picked up at the gym was an acquaintance of Bobby's who called himself Johnny Dillinger. He was a little guy, but he turned out to be a good worker. Man, did he love to wrestle. He came to the gym regularly, and if someone was there to wrestle, he would stay all day long. It was a good thing he had a bond with Bobby because, for some reason, Miller wasn't particularly fond of the guy. If not for Bobby, Miller would have sent him packing. I think Johnny and Miller were too much alike. They were both extremely hyper.

Johnny was a lot of fun to be around. Once he got the hang of it, he was a lot of fun to wrestle. For a while, like Miller, he tended to "crowbar up" in the middle of a match or workout. He just got so excited about wrestling that he got carried away. He would help set up the ring, referee, or do whatever we asked. He just wanted to be around the business. When he got to go on the road with us, he was like a kid in a candy store. I thought he was going to explode when he actually got booked to do a show. I think he would have paid the promoter for the opportunity to be in that first match.

Even though Johnny was a little small for a wrestler, he was able to pull it off pretty well. He earned himself a spot in our little stable of wrestlers and worked with us on both Miller's and Jim Lancaster's promotions. It was at one of Lancaster's shows that Johnny caused quite a stir.

We were wrestling at a National Guard armory in a small Ohio town. Johnny and Bobby were in a tag team match. They went out to do their match and it seemed to be going really well. The crowd was so loud you could hear them all the way at the end of a long hall where the dressing room was located. After a few minutes had gone by, I heard a loud roar and a lot of cheering, so I assumed the match was over. I got up and looked down the hallway to see Johnny walking toward me. Johnny had gotten "juice" [blood] and I could see he had done a good job of it. Just as he got to the dressing room door, he stopped, put his hand on the wall, and leaned down. I could actually hear the blood splattering onto the floor. As a cop, I had been involved in many emergency situations, so I grabbed him and made him lie down. Johnny was so worked up that he got back to his feet and began pacing around, stopping every so often to lean over. Each time he did, a fresh wash of blood would pour out of his head.

I knew that Johnny had juiced before. He had done it at the gym. One day at the gym, I saw Bobby showing Johnny how to blade. They spent 30 minutes taping up his finger, and during the match, poor Johnny spent another 30 minutes trying to get the blade through the tape. Once he got through that part of it, the rest went fine. However, on this night, it had gone all wrong.

Bobby juiced a lot and had the early signs of a "roadmap" forehead, while I could hardly juice at all. If I got cut, I got a little dribble that stopped pretty quickly. One time on my police job, I got my eye cut open during a fight with a guy we were trying to handcuff. As my partner closed one cuff on the guy, he pulled his other arm loose. As we were trying to secure that arm, his cuffed hand got loose. As he swung back, the handcuffs nailed me right above the eye. We finally got the guy cuffed up and secured. A few minutes later, my partner looked over at me and said, *"Hey, your head is bleeding!"* I had a deep half inch gash on my eyebrow. It should have produced a lot of blood, but all I got was a steady drip that didn't even begin right away. All Johnny and Bobby needed was to give themselves a little nick with their blade and they bled like stuck hogs. However, I had never seen anyone bleed like Johnny bled that night.

When I finally convinced him to lie down, I grabbed a clean towel and told him to hold it to his head, and then asked someone to find a first-aid kit. Unfortunately, nobody could find the janitor who opened up the building. The best anyone could come up with was a couple of Band-Aids, and they were practically useless in this situation. When Bobby walked into the dressing room, he looked at Johnny and calmly said, *"He cut a little deep."*

All I could say was, *"No sh—, Bobby!"* and I sent him out to call an ambulance.

Before long, the ambulance showed up and the medics walked in to see a room with blood all over the walls and floors. Johnny was still lying on the floor and holding the towel to his head. By that time, the towel was almost useless. It was totally soaked with blood. Johnny was yelling and babbling about what a great match it had been. Most of the other wrestlers are going about their business, while Bobby and I stood over Johnny and smoked cigars. As the medics went to work, one of them looked up at me and said, *"Do you guys really like doing this stuff?"* I shrugged my shoulders as if I was indifferent to the whole situation. Then Johnny piped up, *"Hell, yes! I love this sh—!"* The two medics looked at each other as if they had found themselves lost in some strange world that was like nothing they had ever seen. I suppose that was true.

As the medics loaded Johnny onto a stretcher and wheeled him out, Bobby and I grabbed some of the gear they had brought in with them and followed along. In order to get Johnny out to the ambulance, we had to go back into the armory and out one of the side doors. The look of shock and disbelief on the faces of the crowd as Johnny was wheeled by was priceless.

Some of the fans trailed along and watched as Johnny was placed in the ambulance. When they left, we went back inside. Fifteen minutes or so later, I went out and stood by the bleachers to watch one of the matches. Two young guys ran in through the side door and joined their friends in the stands. One of them exclaimed, *"They actually took that guy to the hospital!"*

Apparently, the two had followed the ambulance. I guess they were expecting it to pull around the corner and stop so Johnny could jump out and walk back to the armory. I'll bet those fellows never called wrestling "fake" after that experience.

A short time later, the local National Guard commander showed up and he was all worked up. He was sure that Johnny was going to sue them for something. He went on and on about how the promoter had to sign a release. He had to write a report and get Johnny's personal information. We didn't know Johnny well enough to have any of that information. If we had ever heard that his real name was something besides Johnny Dillinger, we couldn't remember. We kept trying to assure him that he wasn't going to get sued by Johnny or anyone else. It was all a part of the game. We all accepted the fact that we were involved in a sport in which we could get injured. It wasn't a big deal to us. I did tell him that I wished we had access to a first-aid kit. He calmly told me where it was located, as if I should have known that.

After the last match, we got ready to leave, but we suddenly realized that we had no idea where Johnny was. Where was the local hospital? Of course, by the time we got showered, the fans were all gone, and the janitor was still missing in action. Bobby decided the town was small enough that we could drive around a bit and find the hospital. I said, "I hope they have a hospital and haven't taken him to another town." You have to remember that this was in the '70s when we didn't have cell phones. We couldn't call him and he had no way to call us. We finally decided to set out on a search for either the nearest hospital or a police station where they could track him down.

As we drove around, we discussed the options we had if Johnny had to stay overnight in the hospital. We were hours from home, so if he couldn't leave, we had to decide if we were staying or coming back for him the next day. Bobby eventually found an open gas station and got directions to the hospital. We arrived and discovered that Johnny was indeed there. In fact, when we walked into the emergency room, we could hear Johnny. He was still excited and was babbling about wrestling. When we told one of the nurses who we were there for, she excused herself and left the room.

A few seconds later, a doctor emerged and told us Johnny was okay to be released. The cut on his forehead had required numerous stitches, but otherwise, he seemed to be okay. He then looked at us and said, *"Does this kind of thing happen often?"* When we told him it did now and then, he said, *"I told your friend you fellows need to find yourselves another occupation."* When we told him we loved it as much as Johnny, the doctor turned around and walked away, shaking his head as he went.

I'll bet the next time those people hear someone say something about wrestlers using "blood capsules," they'll have an interesting story to share. When people learn that I was a wrestler, that's one of the questions I most often get. They either ask, *"Is the blood real?"* or *"Did you guys use blood capsules?"* Half of the time, I don't think they believe me when I say the blood is real and it comes from cuts. I do know that it gets their wheels turning.

I don't remember if we ever wrestled at that armory again. I kind of doubt it.

Johnny was a tough, little dude who loved the business. Like the rest of us, he was also a big fan of Bobby Golden. Johnny was at Bobby's funeral. He came in and immediately broke down as he stood in front of the casket. After a few seconds, he turned around and walked out. I never saw him again.

Chapter 10

Fixing the Ring

(and the promoter)

I was thrilled when Miller called to tell me a promoter wanted to use me and some of the other guys from the gym on his shows in northern Ohio, northeast Indiana, and southern Michigan. For about six months or so, he provided steady work for us. The shows weren't very big, held mostly in high school gyms and small auditoriums, but over time, the crowds grew in size and we developed a good following with the fans of the area.

I realize that I don't always provide names for some of the wrestlers and promoters I worked with and for. Many times, Bobby or Homer would call with a booking for a show and I never knew who the promoter really was. This was during a time when the WWA promotion was winding down and a lot of Bruiser and Snyder's guys were trying their hands at promoting. Moose Cholak, Johnny Gilbert, Paul Christy were a few of the wrestlers who set up those shows in small towns.

We didn't always talk to the promoters, either. At most of the shows, the referee would get the opponents together and tell us who was supposed to go over [win the match]. They would tell us to work out the actual nuts and bolts of the match for ourselves. After the show, someone would hand out the pay envelopes (if we were lucky). If I asked someone who was promoting the show, they would tell me, but most of the time, I really didn't care. So, even if I heard, I didn't remember the specifics unless I worked for them more than once or twice.

Like many other promoters I dealt with, his payoffs were usually one-fourth to one-half of what was originally promised. Even so, work was work. And, of course, there was always the promise at the end of each show that he would catch us up or "make it right at the next show." I always gave him the benefit of the doubt, but by that time, I had been around enough to know that the "next show" with the bigger payday would never happen.

On most of his shows, he wrestled the main events. Of course, he always built himself up and went over in some spectacular fashion. When I was growing up, he was one of the babyfaces who worked in the Bruiser's promotion. And yet, like so many other babyfaces, in the locker room, he was a real heel. He spent most of his time talking about his great exploits and making it clear as to what a great wrestler he was, and talked down to all of us who had not made it to his level. He also stood in the shadows by the dressing room door, watching every match. He never offered any compliments, but was quick to criticize anything he didn't think looked just right. Of course, anything that went wrong in any of his matches was the other guy's fault. "We" did not have his level of experience or "greatness," so it had to be us that screwed up.

Even so, I was happy when he told me I would be wrestling him at a show in southern Michigan. In spite of the fact that he was a real jerk, I looked forward to showing him what I could do. I still thought of him as one of the great wrestlers (although I wasn't as passionate about that as he was about himself) and I thought I could impress him, not to mention learning a lot in the process. As things turned out, I did learn a lot ... but not in the way you might think.

My first clue should have been when the referee came into the dressing room and gave me the finish that the promoter wanted him to pass along. He also passed along a few of the high spots the guy wanted to do. Before I could tell the ref what I would like to do, he turned and walked away from me. I blew it off as I had wrestled against guys like Luis Martinez without any prior planning whatsoever. Luis was such a pro that it was like working with one of the guys from the gym. Whenever I worked with those guys, we were so familiar with each other that we could work the whole match with little communication. All we needed to know was who was going over [winning]. I knew the finishes they used and the amount of time the match would run, and we just improvised the rest of it. That's the way it went with Luis and I expected the same this time.

That night, when I stepped into the ring, I knew I would be doing a job for the guy. I never expected that it was going to be a match where I was going to be hamburger that would be ground up and spit out.

As soon as the bell rang, we locked up. I immediately noticed that the guy was a little stiff. I didn't expect that from him. I had seen him wrestle on TV and he seemed to know what he was doing. For that matter, he bragged so much about his ability that I thought he could work snug, but not as stiffly as he was. After he pushed me back into the ropes, we made a clean break. We locked up again and I pushed him back to the ropes. That was the point where I would establish myself to the fans as the heel. I pretend to be making a clean break, and just before I backed away from him, I hit him with a forearm across his upper chest. It was a good shot that was just hard enough to let him feel it without me being labeled a crowbar. That was the end of any offense for me. He threw me into the corner and began pounding me over my left eye. I could feel the swelling and warmth around my eyebrow. My first thought was that he was trying to juice me the hard way [inflict a cut without the use of a razor blade]. Every punch, move, and kick he delivered after that was a flashback to working with Miller. The longer the match went on, the stiffer he got. He put an arm bar on me that I thought was going to pull my arm right out of my shoulder socket. I was happy when it came time for the referee to make the three-count.

Back in the dressing room, some of the guys were examining the mouse over my eye. The promoter walked in and said, *"Hey, a little potato is good for business."* I wanted to deck him, but decided to let it pass. I wanted to be paid and I wanted the work. I guess when you want to do anything to be in the wrestling business, you do things that you would never do in any other situation in life. Looking back, I'd say that was a pretty stupid way to look at things.

I did get an opportunity to get back at him. He was fond of working tag team matches. I think, as he was getting older, he liked to let his partner do all the work, and then he would come in to make a spectacular finish and get all the glory. In the singles matches (like mine), he never wanted to go more than five minutes. In the tags, he could spend most of his time on the outside and work the longer matches. Bobby was heeling for him, so we eventually were teamed up to work against him and another of his babyfaces.

At the time, we were getting work from other promoters and figured we were getting close to the end of that gig. The bookings were getting further and further apart and he no longer boasted about the TV deal on which he was supposedly working. Bobby and I decided that if we dealt out a little ring justice and he fired us, it would be no great loss. We decided that a few potatoes on his head would be "good for business," not to mention for our egos.

By the time we went to the ring for the match, we were ready to have some fun. Of course, he let his partner work the first seven or eight minutes against us. When he finally tagged in, I saw that twinkle in Bobby's eye when looked at me that told me now was the time. When he charged at Bobby, all set to make his big, exciting comeback, I jumped right into the ring. Bobby worked him around and threw him into the ropes. As he came off, I stepped in front of him and raised my leg, placing a hard kick right into his chest that sent him crashing back onto the mat. Bobby and I began stomping on him with some pretty good force behind our boots. We picked him up and took turns thumping on him. The whole time, he was swearing at us under his breath. Finally, he had enough and told us to go home [finish the match]. He made his big comeback (which we allowed this time), and after putting both of us down with dropkicks and punches, he pinned Bobby.

Back in the dressing room, he stormed in and shouted, *"What the fu— got into you guys!"* Bobby was quick to snap back, *"We wanted to make a good sell. Besides, a few potatoes are good for the business."* He stormed out of the room. We only got a few more bookings out of him, but neither of us worked against him again. It was no great loss because his promotion was going down the tubes as the crowds dwindled in size. Without TV, he had a hard time sustaining the crowds that we initially got at the house shows. A lot of the bigger names that were involved in the beginning had moved on to greener pastures. Many of them had complained about him being a crowbar when they had to work with him.

And then, there was his ring.

To be honest, the thumping we gave him was not the first time we had conspired against him. Not only were his payoffs cheap, but so was the ring in which he had us working. I think he built his ring from parts he salvaged from a junkyard. It was a fair-sized ring, but the canvas had several tears in it and looked like it had never been cleaned. The turnbuckle covers were covered with duct tape and the ropes were covered with plastic garden hose. Cracks and splits in the covering exposed the steel cable underneath. If we hit the ropes in the wrong place, we got a nice welt on our backs. The flooring also had its own set of problems. The padding was lumpy and uneven, and the boards of the ring floor were obviously bowed or broken in several places. If we didn't pick up our feet when we moved around the ring, we often stumbled on one of the many "lumps." Sometimes, when we would circle our opponent, our feet would drop into a hole and we nearly fell down.

Our complaints were always answered with promises that either a new floor, or even a new ring, would be ready in the near future. Of course, that didn't happen. Like his other promises about TV deals, payoffs, and everything else, the ring wasn't going to be fixed ... at least, not until we took matters into our own hands. We took a page from our old days at the gym where we would make high bumps and try to kick the lighting over the ring. We figured if we could really break the ring, he would have to fix it.

One week, he had a show booked in virgin territory. We had never been to the area, and with no television, we would not have to explain to the fans the reasons behind someone flipping. Bobby decided to convince the promoter that he wanted to babyface against me at the show. He called him and made up a story about family coming to the show and that we could work a good match together. The promoter agreed. He had no idea as to the devious minds he was dealing with.

Bobby and I made sure we were there as soon as the ring was set up, which was long before the doors were opened. We climbed into the ring and carefully mapped out the weak spots in the flooring. The rest of our plan would be relatively simple.

During the match, we made sure that it was full of backdrops, hip tosses, and bodyslams. All of them were aimed at the specific points in the ring that needed to be repaired. Two of the spots were near the center of the ring. They groaned in protest when we landed on them, but they refused to surrender to the abuse. We finally concentrated on a hole near one of the corners that we were always wary about stepping in. The hole seemed to get deeper with each bump. Finally, Bobby whipped me into the ropes and gave me a back flip right toward the hole. He pushed off of his knees, while I pushed hard off of his back to make sure I got way up into the air. Just like at Miller's place, we wanted to make a high, extra hard bump. I'm sure that was one of those bumps that came back to haunt me later in life when my back gave out.

I soared high into the air and landed with a crash right on the spot as planned. There was the usual "boom," followed by a loud, cracking sound. I felt the ring give under me. I was frozen in fear for a moment as I waited to see if I was going through the mat and onto the floor, or to feel the sharp edge of a broken board piercing my back. The floor shuddered and I only sank in about three to four inches. There was dead silence in the building. Bobby picked me up and asked if I was okay. I assured him that I was fine and we finished the match on the other side of the ring. Of course, the fans ate it up.

As I headed back to the dressing room, I looked back to see the referee gingerly pushing his foot into the soft hole in the corner of the ring. A short time later, the promoter was running around the dressing room, looking for help to get a quick repair job done. He never said a word to us and I don't think he ever had a clue as to what really happened. They had to call an intermission which lasted more than an hour while they found the materials to "jury rig" the hole so they could finish the show.

A few weeks later, we worked for him again. He didn't have a new ring, but he had replaced the flooring and had replaced the old, worn-out mat. The mat was used, but the flooring was smooth and there was a noticeable absence of lumps and duct tape. It still looked like it had never been cleaned, though. The ropes weren't replaced or even fixed, but we could live with that.

Only a few of our closest confidants from the gym knew what really happened that night. They were too grateful to snitch on us.

Homer Miller had a small ring that folded up and could be loaded into a trailer. Due to the heavy beam that hinged so the ring could fold in the middle, the flooring was as hard as concrete. That same beam also meant that the ring had a slight slope to the sides, making it far from an even surface. At least Miller had enough sense to know that the ring was small and a real pain to work with, so he rarely used it. It only came out when we had a small venue where the larger rings weren't practical. We often teased Miller about his ingenious folding ring, but we never would have thought about destroying it.

On the other hand, we felt the only way to convince the other promoter was to force his hand. His ring was far from being safe. If OSHA supervised wrestling events, they probably would have shut him down long before we did what we did. Bobby and I did all the guys a favor by risking our necks to put that ring out of commission. Each time we crashed into the mat that night, we were prepared for the ring to give way. If someone else had it happen unexpectedly, they might have been seriously hurt.

That was just another adventure in the lives of a couple of professional wrestlers. We didn't always just mess with each other. Revenge was sweet, especially on the promoters who hated to open up their wallets.

Chapter 11

It's a Long Way to Minnesota (and back)

Working a full-time job and being a weekend warrior in the ring could be a grueling task. It seemed like the more bookings I got, the further away from home they were. On most of the long trips, we didn't make enough money to get a motel room (or fly), so we would spend the whole weekend in our cars. Bobby's collection of Richard Pryor tapes, the jokes and pranks, and switching off of driving duties eased the grind a little. And yet, there were many times when I got home with only enough time to roll across the bed and get up to make a six o'clock shift. Those were mighty long work days. By the time the afternoon rolled around, I didn't always demonstrate a sunny disposition. That was especially true if I was a little banged up and nursing a bruise or two from a bad bump.

One weekend trip in 1975 turned out to be a quite an experience, and it was the beginning of the end for my wrestling days. We were booked on a Friday night show in Chicago, and then we were back on the road to Minneapolis for a Saturday afternoon TV match for promoter Verne Gagne. Two guys who had hooked up with Bobby were going to meet us in Chicago and would ride with us to Minneapolis. I had never met them before and I never saw them again after that weekend. I suppose they had been working some of the smaller Chicago shows and worked the AWA on occasion as "hamburger." Since I had the newer and roomier car (and we were heading west), it was decided that I would pick up Bobby and drive to Chicago. Of course, I was assured that between the four of us, the drive from Chicago to Minneapolis could be split up so nobody had to drive too far. In those days, there was no such thing as a GPS device, and we didn't have Internet websites from which we could get directions. We relied solely on maps for directions to the towns. When we got there, we had to ask for directions to the arenas and TV stations.

We didn't know for sure how long it would take to get from Chicago to Minneapolis, and once we got there, we didn't know how to find the TV station where the matches were being taped. We decided to drive all night, find the studio, and hang out in Minneapolis until the show. Of course, I would begin driving and let them know when I wanted someone else to take over.

Before we reached the outskirts of Chicago, I was the only one in the car who wasn't snoring. Three hours later, I was beginning to get sleepy. I tried to wake up the guys up, but nobody would budge. I rolled down my window, cranked up the radio, and still couldn't get any response. Finally, I reached over and poked Bobby in the ribs. He managed to open his eyes and glare at me. *"Hey, I need someone to take over. I'm bushed."* Bobby held up his hand and said, *"Give me another fifteen minutes and I'll drive the rest of the way."* A quarter of an hour later, he was still snoring loudly and refused to budge. I decided to push through and drive the whole trip. Thirty miles outside Minneapolis, I pulled into a rest area and went right to sleep. Two hours later, Bobby began poking me in the ribs. *"Hey, West! Where the hell are we?"*

"I don't know and I don't care. What I do know is that I'm done driving and one of you assholes needs to drive!"

Bobby grunted and gave me the finger, but we traded places and he took the wheel. The next thing I knew, we were in downtown Minneapolis with time to kill. We got something to eat and walked around for a while before heading to the studio for the matches. Back then, we encountered the "Moonies" selling flowers on every corner. Three of us managed to duck them, but our fourth passenger was a little slow on the uptake.

He was a super nice guy who worked out in Tommy Lynch's gym in South Bend. We told him to ignore the flower peddlers and follow us. After a bit, we noticed that he was gone. We turned around and began re-tracing our steps, only to see him emerge from a crowd which was crossing the street about a half a block behind us. Sure enough, he held a bouquet of flowers in his hand. He told us they were really nice people and he had given them a few bucks. He just couldn't understand why we were avoiding them. After we thoroughly chewed him out, we teased him about it for the remainder of the trip.

Thankfully, I brought along some extra ring gear on this trip. When we arrived at the studios, I discovered that they had not booked the Canadian Rose. In fact, they wanted a couple of babyfaces they could throw in against Black Jack Lanza and Bobby Duncum, who worked as the "Blackjacks." Bobby Heenan was their manager at the time. I had to change to my other ring outfit and wait for further instructions. Before I knew it, I was being called to the ring. I never saw my partner, the Blackjacks, or Heenan until I got to the ring. All I was told was that they wanted the Blackjacks to "look good" against us. Boy, did they ever get what they wanted.

My partner was a local kid and he volunteered to start out the tag match. I soon discovered how glad I was that he did. They tossed him around like a rag doll for a good five to seven minutes, while I stood outside the ring wondering what they were going to do with me. I soon found out. While I was leaning over the top rope in an attempt to tag my partner, who was about to pass out from exhaustion, Lanza spotted me. He grabbed the back of my neck and hair and snapped me over the top rope. It happened so quickly that I was caught totally off guard. I tried to grab the middle rope as I fell, but my fingers slipped off. My right shoulder hit the mat first, causing me to snap around and twist my back. My shoulder felt like it was on fire.

The rest of the match was a complete blur. I remember very little about it, other than the fact that my shoulder was killing me and I wanted the match to be over. I think we made them look good enough. I remember that when it was over, my partner and I were both lying on the mat. I saw Heenan coming into the ring with a cane or something in his hand. I fully expected he would either wind up kicking me or hitting me with whatever it was, and at some point, he would probably hit my shoulder. While Heenan stood in the middle of the ring raising Lanza's and Duncum's hands in victory, I crawled out under the nearest ropes and left my partner to fend for himself.

Back in the dressing room, the pain in my shoulder went from a burning sensation to numbness and tingling. My back never hurt, but I felt a pressure in my lower back like someone was pushing in on it with their fist. To make matters worse, a few minutes later, Jack Lanza strolled into our dressing room to thank me ... and slapped me right on the shoulder. I just shook my head in acknowledgment. I knew that if I opened my mouth to speak, I would probably scream.

It was a really good payday, though. It was around $300, which was a good payoff back then. In fact, it was the most money I ever made for a single match. Unfortunately, I paid for that trip with many years of pain and suffering.

We were still a little gun shy about getting checks from promoters. Even though the checks were from Verne Gagne himself, we decided the smart thing to do was to cash them before we left town. We wandered around until we found a liquor store where the owner knew the promoter (now that's a surprise) and agreed to cash our checks for us. By that time, it was almost six o'clock in the afternoon and we had a 573-mile trip ahead of us. When we got back to my car, no one offered to drive, and they all jumped into the car in the same positions as the trip up. I probably should have insisted that someone else drive, but the only one I knew enough to trust was Bobby. At any rate, I just wanted to get on the road, get home, and get to sleep.

We didn't get too far down the road before everyone else was sound asleep ... again. By that time, my right arm was useless, and it felt like someone was pushing their knee into my lower spine. I was really concerned about the damage I might have done to my body when Lanza pulled me over the ropes. Not only that, but I was going to get home on Sunday morning and I had to report for my regular job at five-thirty on Monday morning. I couldn't afford to be hurt. I was getting some good bookings and I was scheduled to wrestle again the following Saturday night. Besides, if the little bit of extra money I picked up that weekend was eaten up by medical bills, things might get a little uncomfortable on the home front.

When we reached Chicago, I woke everyone up and I dropped off our "guests" at their cars. I don't know how he did it, but Bobby managed to stay awake until we made it to his house near Etna Green. After that, I still had another hour or so drive ahead of me, so with the air conditioning and radio on full blast, and the windows rolled down, I somehow managed to get home without driving into a ditch.

I didn't want my wife to know that I was hurt, so I flashed the cash I had earned and told her what a fun trip it had been. She clearly was not impressed. She had been alone with our two girls since Thursday night and made it pretty clear to me that I was not going to sleep all day. When I woke up from a short nap, we were going to some things together. Or, I could watch the girls while she did something on her own. I was right. I would get only two or three hours sleep.

When I got up, I decided my wisest course of action was to take out my wife and use some of my money I had made to buy the new clothes dryer she had been wanting. It wasn't what I wanted, but in order to have a chance of ever wrestling again, I knew I had to make the sacrifice. Otherwise, I would never be allowed out of the house again on weekends.

I managed to survive the week and wrestle the next Saturday as scheduled. My shoulder healed up quickly, but my back problems got progressively worse. A few weeks later, I came back from Michigan with a concussion. When my doctor told me I would feel better in a few days, I told him that was good because I had to get back on the road the following weekend. He was not happy with my response, and more or less told me if that I wouldn't listen to his advice, I need not bother to come back. I didn't take his advice, and yet, I still went back to him from time to time. Each time he saw me walk into his office, he would roll his eyes and lecture me.

The Minnesota event wasn't the first time I hurt up my back during a match. I worked a battle royal in Lima, Ohio. There were ten wrestlers in the ring with the last man standing being the winner. To be eliminated, you had to get thrown out over the top rope. I had hurt my leg in my earlier match that night and tried to beg out of the battle royal. I was especially concerned because the one thing I was not proficient at was going over the top rope. I even sucked going out between the ropes. Big Jim Lancaster, the promoter of the show, said there was absolutely no way was I getting out of the battle royal. Everybody was going to participate. Promoters were never known for their sympathy or caring. When the promoter left the room, I selected the biggest guy there and told him to put me over the top rope as soon as the bell rang. He told me not to worry. He would take care of it. I learned a lesson that night. Never, ever, believe a wrestler when he tells you not to worry.

When the bell rang, I looked around desperately for my friend. I spotted him all the way over on the other side of the ring. He looked at me and grinned as he grabbed one of the other wrestlers. I tried to work my way in his direction, but suddenly found myself being grabbed by two guys who promptly tossed me over the top. I grabbed the top rope as I went over, but I lost my grip before I could flip myself over so I could land on the apron of the ring. Instead, my back landed on the edge of the ring and I bounced off, landing on one of the guys already on the floor. Luckily, he broke my fall and probably prevented further damage. When I asked him if he was okay, he said he was fine. I said, *"Let's get the hell out of here,"* and we limped off to the dressing room.

My back was sore for several days and the pain just never went away completely. It did, however, cause me to forget about my sore leg. At least twice a year, I would be laid up for two or three days with severe pain. The doctor would give me pain medications and send me home. They never seemed to get to the root of the problem. The Minneapolis match was around 1975 or 1976 and it was many years before I found a doctor who got me straightened out. It brought an end to my wrestling and almost stopped my law enforcement career. Do I regret the time I spent in the squared circle?

No. Would I go through it again? I would still consider it. I'm not sure I would be willing to go through the same thing again, though, for the money we made back then. Of course, there are even fewer opportunities today for guys like me.

The wrestlers of today are a completely different breed. We had fun and never took things, or ourselves, too seriously. There were plenty of regional promotions out there, too. If you ticked off one promoter, you could go work for another one for a while. No matter who we worked for, though, none of us were going to get rich. I never heard talk in the dressing rooms about steroids or any other kind of drugs, either. On the other hand, I didn't pick up the newspapers to read a tragic headline about how one of the young wrestlers overdosed or "whacked out" and hurt himself or someone else.

The guys who get a spot with the national promotions make big money. However, when the promotions finish with them, they are pretty much done. When they get used up and tossed aside, there's just no place for them to work. Some of them can't handle it. The competition for those big money jobs is brutal and I think that leads to drug abuse, especially steroids. They all know their careers are short-lived and they want to do all they can to stay on top. Sometimes, the things they have to do can be a big price to pay.

I recently watched some shows on television put on by the Pro Wrestling Ohio promotion. It is supposedly the most successful regional promotion in business today. They have a combination of "old school" and modern day wrestling. Occasionally, some of the "old timers" make an appearance. It is heartbreaking to see some of them who are now quite out of shape and move much more slowly. Their timing is way off, too. I don't think they have any idea how bad it looks.

If that is what the wrestling business is today, I'm glad I did what I did when I did it! I have no delusions about still being able to wrestle. I'm glad I have a life outside the ring and don't have to live off the past. I really feel sorry for the guys who are trying to live in that world that left them a long time ago. I pray they learn that their value as human beings is not in what they once were — but in what they are today.

Chapter 12

Mr. No Emotion

I always tried to work with the newer guys that came along. I never wanted to forget what it was like when I was a new kid. We all have that experience of starting a new job and the apprehension that often goes with it. If a new kid showed up at the gym and showed some real talent and desire, I took the time to offer whatever help I could. I tried to treat them and accept them the way Bobby and Miller did me.

One young man came along who seemed to have some real talent. He was kind of quiet and did not have a lot to say. In fact, we told him whatever gimmick he came up with would require some personality that he just didn't show. He was good at the basics in the ring, but he would never be able to do a good interview or sell himself. Most of the time, he had a blank expression on his face. He would sell some of the moves you put on him, but he rarely showed any emotion. We repeatedly told him that if he went over in a match, he should be happy. If he lost, he should be pissed off, or at the very least, disappointed.

The Warsaw, Indiana armory became the home for a series of shows that were taped for local TV. A lot of the guys from Miller's gym worked the shows and Big Jim Lancaster would bring in some of the guys from his Midwest Championship Wrestling promotion. We had some pretty good shows. Bo worked a few of them, along with a few other guys, like Tommy Lynch, Moose Cholak, and Paul Christy, who had been big in the Indianapolis promotion, so we drew some good houses.

As the series of shows in Warsaw progressed, the Canadian Rose became a regular and gained some real fan recognition. When the announcer would read off the night's card for the television taping, the mention of the Canadian Rose got a large chorus of "boos" from the audience. It was a good feeling to know the people came to see me get my ass handed to me by one of their favorite wrestlers. In the past, my name being announced got no real response. Here in Warsaw, finally, was something that made me feel like, *"I've made it."*

On some of those shows, I worked with Bobo, Tommy Lynch, Jim and Rick Lancaster, the Flying Tigers, and Al Snow. It was great to work for an ongoing operation where I could build up my name and develop a following. Working with and on shows with guys who were already big names, both in the Midwest and nationally, made me feel like I was a part of a big promotion. It was nice to know that we were going to work with guys we knew and who knew us. And while it lasted, it was steady work.

Warsaw was only a 44-mile trip for me, so it was actually quite convenient, as it was for all the other guys who trained at Miller's gym. Unfortunately, it was also an easy drive for the new guy who had shown no personality at the gym. Someone, in their infinite wisdom, decided Warsaw would be a good place and time for his first live match ... and I got the nod to work with him.

I was going to go over, but I consented to make him look good in the process. The promoters hoped to make a strong babyface out of him. I had no problem with that. I sat down with him and told him what my high spots would be. I explained how he was expected to let me do my thing, and in turn, I would give him an opportunity to work his stuff. He agreed and seemed to be ready to go. There was no indication that he had something else in mind.

Since he was making his debut, he brought along Mom, Dad, and his girlfriend. He wanted to be sure he made a good impression. "Mr. No Emotion," the quiet guy who never said much, showed his ass that night. He was an absolute jerk. He decided he was going to look really good and make me out to be a real loser.

I began my routine by carefully removing my jacket and sunglasses. He knew that was when I would strut around the ring and work the crowd. As soon as I turned my back on him, he ran across the ring and leaped up onto my back. From that point on, he wanted it to be "his show." He wouldn't let me do anything. I guess he wanted Mommy, Daddy, and his main squeeze to be proud of him. I was of the opinion that he assumed I would just roll over and play dead.

At first, I gave him the benefit of the doubt. I thought perhaps he was just nervous and worked up. I am a very patient person. As I have said, I always tried to work with the new guys and help them along. I kept telling him to relax and loosen up, but it soon became obvious that he wasn't going to listen. When it came time for me to do one of my moves, he pretended like he had no idea of what was going on. We had gone through everything at the gym, but he was like a man possessed.

For a second time, I told him to lighten up, and then threw him into the ropes. When he came off, I got way up in the air and planted a solid dropkick on his upper chest. When I rolled over and jumped up to go for the cover, I saw him standing in the middle of the ring with his chest puffed out like he was Yukon Eric or Moose Cholak. He never even left his feet. I was a lot bigger than the guy, and one of my high spots was my ability to get up in the air and land a good dropkick. And yet, the guy just stood there like he was Superman.

The Canadian Rose was used to getting booed. This time, however, when the booing began, I knew it wasn't because I was building heat. It was because the match was looking really, really bad! Not only were some folks booing us, but there were snickers and laughter. The fans knew full well that he should be reacting to the pounding he was getting from me. If I tried to give him a hip toss or an arm drag, he would resist and refuse to go along with it. It looked like crap! Anybody who ever worked with me will tell you that I sold every move they made. I never screwed anybody over by trying to make myself look good at their expense. For that matter, I had never been booed by the audience for poor performance.

For a few seconds, I flashed back to the days of my old friend, Rick. However, this time, I was really hot. It was no longer a matter of teaching him a lesson. I was ready to kill him. I had a good thing going with the Warsaw shows and I wasn't going to let that jerk screw it up for me. He was making me look bad, and I wasn't going to take it sitting down, so I decided the "shoot" was on. I pushed him into one corner of the ring and began pounding him with some solid shots to his chest and gut. I let him know that I was taking over and that we were going home [end the match]. I bodyslammed him in the middle of the ring and dared him to move or try to get up. I hit the ropes and went into my flying rollover — my big finish. I made sure I landed square in the middle of his chest. I knew it had to hurt and, with my size, there was a possibility that I would break a few ribs. At the very least, I heard the air rush out of him.

Normally, I would flop over on the guy and that would be the finish. However, I was pissed off. I wasn't through with the guy. I hit the ropes and did my finish again. After the third rollover, I decided it might not be a good idea to actually kill him. I knew he was hurting and was not going to get up on his own. Still, on the fourth rollover, I flopped down hard on him and the referee counted the kid out, which was the planned finish. The kid did a great job of selling it, but I don't give him any credit for doing such a great sell job. He sold it because it was real. He didn't have any choice *but* to sell it. I could see in his face that he was really hurting. The kid rolled around on the mat for several minutes before he stood up. The crowd yelled and screamed obscenities at me as I strutted around the ring in victory. This time, however, the boos and catcalls were directed at the Canadian Rose, and not at the match itself. If only the crowd knew that the Canadian Rose really *was* a bad guy that night.

When I got back to the dressing room, I was still furious. I immediately let the promoter know what had happened. *"I just beat the sh— out of your boy! That little son-of-a-bitch got exactly what he had coming to him."* I think that was the first time anyone in the dressing room had ever seen me angry. The whole room fell dead silent as I continued. *"If you want another shoot, just put me in with that asshole again."* I finished by making it clear that he had better watch himself if he showed up in the dressing room anywhere near me. I know Bobby was shocked. He was seated on one of the benches. His eyes got wide and he kind of rocked back, as if he was getting ready to run for it. He just stared at me until my little tirade was over.

Normally after a match, we would get together in the dressing room and critique the match, or apologize if there was something we screwed up, or congratulate each other on a good job. I wasn't in the mood to see the guy again. I paced back and forth, looking for something to hit or throw. It was one of those rare occasions when I really lost control.

As a cop, I worked one time with a female officer that was on our shift. We went to pick up a young kid who was not being cooperative. There were three of us there and I was the senior officer. I tried to talk the kid into cooperating, but nothing I said seemed to get through to him. I decided it was time to just snatch him and get it over with. As I stepped into the room, he lunged and tried to tackle me. When he slammed into me, the impact knocked me back into the frame of the steel door. As I wrestled around with the kid, I realized my arm had a funny feeling to it. I looked down and noticed a huge knot on my forearm where I had hit the door frame. I was sure he had broken my arm. The other two officers were trying to get through the door to help me subdue the kid. I lost control and began to scream and curse. I picked him up and bodyslammed him to the floor. I slapped the cuffs on him and drug him out of the room by his collar, bouncing his head off the walls as we went. The two officers wisely stepped back and just stared.

A few days later, someone asked the female officer if she wanted to partner with me when we had to go after a suspect. She declined. She told the Lieutenant that she had only seen me angry once … and she never wanted to see it again. I think everyone who heard me in the dressing room that night felt the same way. No one said a word to me and they all acted as if they wished they could be someplace else.

After the show, I heard the kid complaining to the promoter. The promoter blew him off and told him he had it coming. The kid never worked any of the Warsaw shows again. I did, so I guess I won the war … and the battle.

Later, when I had calmed down, I told Bobby I felt kind of bad about it and probably should apologize to the kid. That was when Bobby told me about the parents and the girlfriend being there, and how he had been trying to impress them. I decided there would be no apology forthcoming. Maybe another ass kicking — but no apology. I never saw the guy again. It's a good bet that he never did anything else in the business.

The incident took my mind back to my brief amateur wrestling career at Wilson Junior High School. I rarely got into trouble at school because I knew I would be in even more trouble when I got home. Whenever I did something wrong at school, it seemed as if my parents knew about it before I did. On one particular occasion, the gym floor was being used when we had a practice scheduled, so the mats were up on the stage at one end of the gym. The curtains were closed because one of the girls' teams was usually down on the floor and we were more interested in watching them than practicing. For practice, we usually broke up into pairs and wrestled each other. Most of the time, we could pick our own partner, and we would choose someone close to our experience and skill level.

One kid on the team was into judo. He liked to slip up on guys who were working together, grab one of them, and give them a flip. One minute you were wrestling with your buddy, and the next thing you know, you were flying through the air. It seemed that he managed to make his way over to me and my partner and slamming one of us to the mat at nearly every practice.

Complaining to the coach had about the same effect as when we would complain to Homer Miller when he began "crowbarring up" on us. Coach would just grin and tell us to learn to deal with it. We couldn't do anything about Homer Miller because we were playing in "his house." However, I wasn't nearly as concerned about getting kicked off the wrestling team. Amateur wrestling wasn't like the "real" wrestling that I wanted to be in, anyway, so we plotted a scheme to take out our vengeance on the creep. I even forewarned my Dad that coach had ignored our complaints and more or less told us to "deal with it." I let him know we were going to do just that. Dad didn't say much, but I really don't think he had seen his little boy's dark side yet, either.

One of my buddies back then (and still is to this day) was a kid named Don Eplin. Don, who was on the team, had also been the victim of one of the sneak attacks. At the next practice, Don and I hooked up as partners and strategically picked a mat as far away from the coach's usual observation spot as possible. Our game plan was simple. While we were "working together," we would actually be keeping an eye out for "Mr. Judo." If either of us spotted him heading in our direction, we would warn the other guy and get the jump on him for a change.

Sure enough, within a few minutes we spotted the guy slipping around and grabbing unsuspecting kids, and slamming them to the mat. The coach must have seen that crap going on, but he chose to ignore it. Now I was really getting mad! It didn't take long for "Mr. Judo" to head in our direction. We pretended like we didn't see him, all the while keeping each other advised as to his exact whereabouts and what he was doing. Pretty soon, like a lion on the prowl, this guy began creeping up on us. This time, we were ready. As soon as he got close enough, we pounced, catching him unawares. I picked up the kid and bodyslammed him. However, I chose to slam him, not on the mat, but through the curtain and onto the gym floor. Of course, the coach, who previously had been blind, suddenly had his vision miraculously restored. He walked over, glared at me, and told me to hit the showers. I reminded him that both he and the kid had been warned that this would happen if the kid continued to harass us. Later, he told me he was going to call my parents and have a little chat with them. I told him that was fine because my Dad was fully aware of what was going on, and that I had complained to him and warned him that we were going to take care of things if he didn't. Now in those days, kids didn't talk to teachers or an adult like that. However, the coach was a jerk, and so was the judo kid. I guess the coach knew he was wrong. I wasn't known as a troublemaker in school, so my story would have some credibility. Regardless, I never heard any more about it. I didn't return to the wrestling team that year. One good thing was that the kid came out of it unscathed. He only had the wind knocked out of him. On a positive note, nobody at school screwed with me for a while.

There were a lot of similarities between the incidents at the junior high school and at the show in Warsaw. I never had any desire to hurt anybody. However, I have my limits, and if you push the wrong buttons, you will pay.

My oldest daughter often accompanied me on trips out of town, and other friends occasionally rode along. I never changed up what I did to make an impression. Most of them were aware of what my gimmick was. My daughter picked up a lot of the lingo and often critiqued the matches. She would look over the card and say, *"Wow. It looks like Bobby is babyfacing against Bobo!"* Or, *"Dad, you ought to use that finish again. You got a lot of heat."* As soon as she was old enough to go with me, I smartened her up about the business. I know the old-school way of thinking was to keep the family in the dark, but can you imagine the shock of her being at a match for the first time and seeing her usually mild-mannered dad stomping on the hero? That guy should have done the same for his family, or at least worked the match like he was supposed to. What shame does a babyface ever get from losing a match against a heel? He would have lost the match in the end, but I would have made him look good. I always believed that is what a good heel should do.

I paid my dues and had been "hamburger" for some of the well-known wrestlers, but I had reached a point in time where nobody was going to make a fool out of me before they had paid their dues. From that point on, when I worked with new guys at the gym, I told them they had better respect the more experienced wrestlers. If you want to work and survive in the wrestling business, you had better know your place. There is a pecking order in the business. You can call it a chain of command or a seniority rule, but you had better know it. You don't mess with another guy's gimmick and you sure as hell don't try to make a veteran of the mat look like a fool.

Chapter 13

Row 9, Seat 11

There were so many people in those days who thought all professional wrestlers lived a glorious lifestyle. Most folks thought we traveled the country by air (first class, of course) and lived a life of luxury. They would have been shocked to have known the reality.

I previously discussed the Horse Palace, where we actually dressed in horse stalls. Believe it or not, that was quite pleasant compared to other places. There was nothing quite like working a match at one of those outdoor shows in the dead of summer, toweling off the sweat, and then bouncing down the road in a car with four or five other guys who had also been deprived of a shower facility. Even with all four windows rolled down and the air conditioning running full blast, you just couldn't shake the smell of perspiration and cheap cologne. It could make a three-hour car ride seem like six.

A "deluxe" dressing room came with a shower and a locker. You never worried about your things getting stolen, but you never knew what someone might do to your stuff when you were out of sight. I will never forget the story one of the "old-timers" told us. Bobby, Chief, and I had a tradition of lighting up a cigar when we arrived at the venue. When we strolled into the locker room one night, Moose Cholak began chuckling. He told us to either finish or get rid of our stogies before our match. He recalled a time when Freddie Blassie lit up a big cigar in the dressing room. He was still enjoying it when the time came for him to hit the ring. He carefully tamped it out and put the remainder on top of a locker so he could retrieve it when he returned.

One of the wrestlers sharing the dressing room that night was none other than Dick the Bruiser. Bruiser had quietly watched Freddie's ritual. As soon as Freddie was out of the room, Bruiser strolled over and grabbed the cigar. He then dropped his trunks, methodically twirled the end of it in his butt crack, and placed it back on top of the locker where Blassie had left it. Bruiser calmly sat back down, not having said one word the entire time.

When Blassie returned, he retrieved the cigar and sat down on the bench. After going on and on about the match, he lit the cigar and took several puffs. Suddenly, with a puzzled look on his face, he held the cigar out in front of him and said, *"This tastes like sh—!"* Of course, the entire dressing room broke out in laughter.

Now, we knew that a lot of those guys were "B.S.ers," but that story was too good to have been made up.

At any rate, many of us carried a padlock in our bag. If we were fortunate enough to get a locker, we could lock up anything we didn't want the guys to mess with.

It wasn't often that guys who wrestled at my level got a deluxe dressing room. We dressed in tents, bathrooms, cars, houses, sheds, and a few times in the back of Bobby's TV repair truck. I always hated that because I never knew when Bobby might fling open the back or side doors. He would stand outside to "guard" for me, and after giving me enough time to remove my clothes, he would bang on the side of the truck and say something like, *"Hey! Do you girls want to peek at some of the little tools I keep in here?"* He would laugh like a fool while his victim in the truck thrashed around trying to get himself covered up. I only fell for it once.

There were some promoters who actually segregated us "low-life" card fillers to separate dressing rooms from the big names. I once worked a show which featured Bobby Heenan and never saw him until we were leaving the arena. He had built a lot of heat that night and was concerned about getting out of there in one piece. As we walked past one of the rooms, he stuck his head out the door and asked, *"Are any of the cops still here?"* We told him the cops who were our security had probably been the first ones out the door. He asked us to send a cop to his dressing room to escort him to his car. We looked around for a while, but we never found one. By the time we returned to his room to offer to walk out with him, Heenan was already gone.

The next time I saw Heenan was in Minnesota. I never got to speak to him there, either. I must say I felt somewhat slighted by him. In neither instance did he come into our dressing rooms to say "hello." I'm sure he's a great guy, but I was disappointed that he never acknowledged our presence, other than to ask for help. It was important for us "little guys" to at least get some recognition for our contribution to the business. I know it was the promoter who segregated us by putting him in a different dressing room, but it would have been nice to have had our egos stroked once in a while.

At one Ohio show, we changed clothes in a small motel room. After we dressed, we were shuttled by car to the match site, which was about a half mile away. After the show, we were driven back to the motel. However, since the promoter only rented one or two small rooms, we had to go in shifts. There was no time to shower or relax in the room afterwards. We went into the room, got dressed, came back out, and headed home. Dressing rooms were like cheap motel rooms. We never knew what it was going to be like until we got there. In fact, we learned not to judge it by the way the building looked on the outside. And, if any of the amenities (toilets, shower, etc.) actually existed and worked, we were grateful.

Most of our paydays back then were insufficient to even cover our gas, let alone a motel room. If we had to drive all night to get back home, or sleep in the back of the car, that's what we did. Sometimes, a couple of guys would rent a motel room, and five or six other guys would crash in there with them. In most cases, they got caught and the extra guys were thrown out. Knowing that was the norm, we usually decided to just get on the road and drive home after our matches.

With all of the time spent behind the wheel, and some of the guys having a bit of a lead foot, we heard a lot of stories about their dealings with the police. A lot of great "advice" was thrown around in the dressing rooms about how to avoid speeding tickets. A lot of it was just BS and old wives' tales that had been floating around for years. I usually just listened and smiled. Most of the guys didn't know they were talking to a cop. I figured, why spoil the moment for them?

One of the guys we regularly worked with was always late. The reason was that he always left late and raced as fast as he could to get to the show. He got his fair share of speeding tickets. One night, he announced that he had found the secret for getting out of the tickets, especially in Ohio. He bragged that he kept a $20 bill clipped to his driver's license. He said that if he got stopped, he would get the license back (minus the twenty) and they would tell him to be on his way.

A few months later, we were at another show in Ohio. Our friend stormed into the dressing room late (as usual). He was obviously upset and threw down his bag in disgust. As he undressed, each article of clothing was thrown to the floor with increasing force. When someone summoned up the courage to ask him what was wrong, he said he had been stopped on the way there. He got his license back, minus the twenty ... with a ticket clipped to the license! We decided not to laugh at him. At least ... not right away.

Johnny Dillinger made several of those road trips with Bobby and me. He was also a lot of fun to be on the road with. We drove many miles, so we all tried to entertain each other. One of the great things about being on the road with those guys was that we were able to get in "sync" when it came to our bladders. After a while, we had it all timed out so that when the gas tank was almost empty, our bladders were almost full. Pity the fool who would ride along with us and even think about a "potty break" before we needed to stop for gas. We had miles to cover, and getting to our destination meant coordinating everything. We pretty much had it down to a science. If you were going to ride with us, you had better plan on leaving early, arriving early, and following our rules of the road.

The driver usually brought the cigars and the passenger(s) brought along beverages and snacks if it was to be a long trip. The first time Johnny went with us on a long ride, he made the mistake of requesting a bathroom stop about an hour into our journey. Bobby slammed on the brakes and pulled over to the side of the road. He pointed out a tree in the field and told him to hurry up. Johnny was sitting in the back seat right behind me. He just sat there with a stunned look on his face, so I got out and opened the door for him. *"You have two minutes. After that, we are heading on down the road ... whether or not you are back in the car!"* He decided he could wait. He had been told about the rules, but he needed to be shown that we were serious and we made no exceptions. If you didn't like our rules, then it would be best if you drove yourself. It was that simple.

One time, we had several guys ask about riding with us to a show that was about three hours away. I drove, but Bobby took the time to write down the rules and present them to our guests. I can't remember all of them but I know it went something like this:

Don't fu— with the radio.
Don't ask "how much further."
Don't bitch because we left too early.
No farting in the car (unless Bobby starts it).
You can wait to pee until the rest of us are ready.
Don't complain about the driving.
Don't whine about being hungry, cold, hot, etc.
And, most of all, no talking while the Richard Pryor tape is playing!

Johnny could attest to the fact that Bobby wasn't kidding

Likewise, when we stopped for gas, you had better hit the bathroom. Everyone in the car was warned that when we pulled up to the pumps, that was the time to go to the bathroom. We would make no unscheduled stops. Of course, usually, everyone was good and ready by the time we stopped. Being ready to go was probably a good thing because standing around in a men's room at a truck stop while waiting for the urge was *not* a good thing (especially if you are like me and tap your feet when you get impatient). We might have had a truck driver offer to take us out back and show us his "big rig." That would not have been a good thing. After all, I am not gay. I just used to play one on television. I certainly didn't want to leave anyone with that impression outside the ring.

Then came the gas crisis of 1973. The first gas crisis was a time when not only did the prices go up, but there was a shortage. Finding gas was a challenge and it was rationed in many places. News reports claimed it was supposed to keep getting worse, and the word spread that there would be no more gasoline at all by the year 2012. That was not good news for people in businesses that required them to constantly be on the road. We had to car pool and plan our routes carefully, not only to find the shortest or fastest route, but the route where we were most likely to find gasoline. When we found it, we knew we had better fill up because we never knew where our next gas stop might be.

On one trip in 1974, at the peak of the gas shortage, I had a fairly new, full-size sedan, so I was selected to haul Bobby and three other guys. It was a good trip, but on the return home, we had such a blast that I totally forgot to keep an eye on the gas gauge. Bobby lived about an hour or so west of me, so he was my last drop off. As I pulled into his drive, I noticed my fuel gauge was almost on "E." By now, it was the middle of the night and I knew that the big hog I was driving was not going to make it back to Fort Wayne. I told Bobby about my dilemma and he told me about an all-night gas station just up the road. He said he never had a problem getting gas there.

Of course, he wasn't me. If odds are one in a thousand that something could go wrong, I would be the "one." I found the station and, as soon as I pulled in, I saw that all-too-common sign in those days: "Sorry. No Gas." I decided to go in and call Golden to see if I could stay at his place, or have him drive me the rest of the way home. Before making the call, I explained the situation to the night manager and he told me he would fix me up. I was directed to an older pump in the back that "they don't use much." I was tired and wanted to get home, but I should have known better. I filled up the car and was only about ten minutes down the road when the car began to act up. The car began spitting and sputtering. By that time, I was in no man's land with a long way to go before I hit another town. Somehow, I coaxed that baby home and breathed a deep sigh of relief when I pulled the car into my driveway.

I took the car to my mechanic and left it with him. A few days later, he called and asked me where I was getting my gasoline. It seems that old gas pump had accumulated a lot of water and gunk, and had pumped it right into my engine. They had to flush all the fuel lines, pull the gas tank, and clean it all out. Needless to say, when we were wrestling for $35 to $50 a night, it took a long time to cover the mechanic's bill and fuel for that trip.

After that incident, we began traveling with CB radios. Most of the time, we could get help, directions, or find out what gas stations were open by chatting with the truck drivers. Of course, with Bobby, just chatting was never good enough. His father-in-law owned a trucking business and Bobby had gone out on the road with him several times as a co-driver. Bobby knew the jargon and liked to act as if we were in a big rig, rather than a sedan. Some truckers just didn't appreciate Bobby's sense of humor, and there was many a time that we were threatened by an irate trucker.

On one occasion, Golden got into one of his conversations with three truckers. They were traveling together and there was a driver and co-driver in each truck. That was six against two. Bobby got them all fired up by telling them we were wrestlers and we would be glad to kick their asses if we caught up with them. I told Bobby that with my luck, those guys were all fans who were going to pull off the road that night to take in the match. Bobby just grinned, picked up the microphone, and said, *"This here is the Canadian Rose. I'll be lookin' for you sonofabitches tonight!"* I just shook my head and reminded him that he would be with me. Well, he kind of batted his eyes and said, *"Yes, but I am baby facing tonight."* I'm thankful we didn't run out of gas along that highway, and that the match didn't turn out to be a highlight of some truckers' convention.

We also never knew what kind of a ring we would be working in when we worked for a new promoter. Miller spoiled us in that regard. With the exception of the "trailer ring" that was too small and too uneven, his rings were all top shelf. If we were working an unfamiliar ring, we always tried to check it out before the show. I would ask the ring crew about it and then had a look for myself. I think some of the rings we worked in had been fished out of the junk yard and put back into service. In some, the ropes wouldn't stay tight. The ring crew would tighten them after each match, but before the next match was halfway through, they would be sagging again. I worked in one ring that was so lumpy, and the pads were so thick, that we had to worry about tripping when we moved around the ring.

Then there was the show in southern Michigan. About five or six minutes into the match, my opponent (who I believe was Red Ryan) whipped me into the corner. I held onto the top rope as he ran over and delivered a couple of shots to my head. That was a spot where the Canadian Rose would drop down and take a knee, and signal the referee for a time out. While I would argue with the ref over why there were no timeouts in wrestling, the babyface would get too close and I would deliver a shot to his groin. He would go down and I would take the advantage. The "time out" gimmick was one of my regular high spots.

On that particular night, my head rocked back as I took his punches. As I went to take a knee, I leaned forward with my hands remaining on the top rope. When I leaned forward, the whole turnbuckle came out and I almost fell flat on my face. I learned that when something like that happens, you might as well take advantage of it. That was one of those times when the ad lib training I got as a kid in drama school paid off. I acted as if I had physically ripped the turnbuckle off and used it to pound on my opponent. The match progressed from there without either of us losing a beat. When the babyface took the turnbuckle away from me and gained the advantage, I still got to do my "time out" gimmick to regain the advantage and take the match home.

There was another time when I was working with Fred Curry, one of popular babyfaces in Ohio at the time. He had a "Dick the Bruiser" type of high spot he liked to do when he was working outside the ring. He would grab the back of your neck and lead you through the aisle, pushing over the empty ringside seats as the people scattered. He would then slam your head into a pole, the bleachers, a wall, or any other immovable object he might find in the back of the arena. He would then stroll back to the ring while you "recovered." Of course, he got back into the ring and distracted the ref long enough to keep him from counting you out. It usually went over pretty good and became somewhat of a trademark for him.

One night, we were having a really good match. He tossed me around the ring a few times with hip tosses and arm drags. I rolled out under the ropes and began storming around the ring, building a little heat, and stopping occasionally to slam my fists on the ring apron in disgust. He bailed out of the ring after me and gave me a few good shots. He grabbed the back of my neck and turned me toward the concrete wall at the back of the room. I knew what was coming. Or, at least, I thought I did.

As the guy led me up the aisle by the neck, the crowd cheered their approval. You could hear the metal folding chairs at ringside banging and clanging as people cleared the way, and the hero tossed the empty chairs aside. I was really selling it for the guy. I was flailing my arms around and taking exaggerated steps. Suddenly, I realized that his hand was no longer around my neck and we were still a good five feet away from the wall. When I turned to look back, I saw him on the floor with his foot tangled up in one of the folding chairs. He was kicking away at the chair, trying desperately to break free from the grip it had on his ankle. Apparently, he had tripped over one of the chairs that a fan knocked over as he scattered to get out of the way!

I'm pretty sure nobody noticed that I had taken two or three steps toward the wall without the assistance of Curry. I think the fans were all watching him engage in an impromptu wrestling match with the chair. I was able to keep my composure long enough to walk over, point at him and laugh, and plant a few boots to his back. I pulled the chair off his foot and gave him a shot with it. He quickly recovered, and within seconds, I was back on my way to the wall. As I rebounded off the wall, I buried my head in my arms because I didn't want anyone to see the tears in my eyes from holding back my laughter.

The poor referee was a young kid who had no idea of what to do. As I was pulling the chair off Curry, I looked up and saw the kid standing in the ring with his arms on the top rope. He had the words "what do I do now" written all over his face. By the time Fred got back to the ring, he could have counted us both out ten times. Later, when I had the opportunity, I gave him some pointers on what to do when something like that went wrong. It was bound to happen.

Curry came strolling through the dressing room after the match. I couldn't quite keep the smirk from my face as I recalled the image of him rolling around on the floor with the chair attached to his foot. He pointed his finger at me and said, *"Don't you say a word. Not one go—amn word."* Of course, that was all I needed to begin laughing again.

The next day, Bobby called. He hadn't been on the show and wanted to know how things went. After asking me who I worked with, he wanted to know who went over. I laughed and told him, *"I think it was row 9, seat 11."*

When we were on a road trip, we learned to expect the unexpected. It seemed like every time we pulled out of our driveway, we faced another adventure. Was it going to be an equipment failure? Would it be something we forgot? Maybe we would have car trouble. It might be a filthy rat hole of a dressing room, or being attacked by an errant folding chair. In the event that everything went without a hitch, one of your buddies would be obligated to screw with you. That's 'rasslin'.

Chapter 14

From "The Rose" to "The Ref"

By 1980, I had curtailed my wrestling somewhat. I soon learned that when you begin to turn down bookings, they get fewer and further between. I would call Bobby from time to time, but didn't ask about any shows that might be scheduled. I told him I wanted to get my back problems straightened out, but never mentioned that I had doubts about ever getting back into the ring. He would fill me in on what was going on and who was promoting shows.

Each time I had back pain, I thought about the years of abuse I had put my body through in the ring. I recalled the contests at Miller's gym where we would back flip each other as high as we could. I thought about my finishing move, the flying rollover. During my wrestling days, I weighed between 260 and 285 pounds. I was proud of myself for being able to do aerial moves at that size. And yet, there were times when I wouldn't get all the over, and would land on my butt instead of flat on my back, or sometimes, on my feet. That was a lot of weight for my spine and hips to absorb. I wasn't getting any younger and I had to consider my future.

I also had gotten busy in my real life and was torn between wrestling and law enforcement. If I watched wrestling on TV, I got the bug to get back into the ring. On the other side of the coin, I also enjoyed the fact that I wasn't away from home every weekend and on my days off. I thought about how much I enjoyed the time I was able to spend with my daughters. I also had come to the realization that I was never going to make a lot of money or be a superstar. I knew that wrestling would never be anything more than an expensive hobby.

On one warm summer evening in the early 1980s, I accepted a booking for a show at an armory in Mishawaka, Indiana. As I slowly made my way up the long drive, I could see a small group of people near the front door. It was a good sign. More than two hours remained until "bell time" and the people were already in line for tickets. It looked like there would be a good "house" tonight.

When I got closer to the building, a few of the folks walked toward the sidewalk and leaned over to peek into my car. A few of them booed and I got the "thumbs down" sign as I rolled by. That was another good sign. I was known here, so I was going to get some instant "heat" when I made my appearance. I made my way around to the back of the building and parked close to the back door. I wanted my car to be safe from any fans that might want a little vengeance. I knew that now they all would know what car I was driving.

I grabbed the bag which contained my wrestling gear from the back seat and made my way through the rear door of the armory. A couple of guys were setting up the ringside seats and the ring crew was finishing the setup of the ring. They were putting up the ropes while a couple of others were attaching the apron around the outside of the ring. Others were preparing the concession stands for business. Out of the corner of my eye, I could see them stop and stare as I walked through. They whispered amongst themselves and nodded their heads in agreement. Once again, it was a sign that I was recognized here. In the wrestling business, that is a good thing.

I found my way to the locker room and threw my bag down onto the bench. Several of the other wrestlers were already in the room. We exchanged the usual greetings and I sat down on the bench and leaned back against the lockers to finish my traditional cigar. Bobby Golden and I, who often traveled together, had gotten into the routine of lighting up cigars when we arrived at the towns where we were wrestling. After the matches, when we were on our way home or on our way to the next venue, we would light up another stogie. It became a regular practice, and even though Bobby and I were traveling separately on that night, I carried on the tradition.

The promoter walked in and gave me the rundown of the card the night. I was scheduled for the fourth match of the evening, the one that followed the intermission. I would be going over [winning] against one of the up-and-coming babyfaces. He wanted me to stretch it out and make the kid look good. They were planning to build up the kid for a feud against one of the top heels in the area. No sweat. If the kid would make me look good and sell my high spots, I would be glad to reciprocate. I had worked with him before with no problem.

It should have been like another day at the office for me. However, something was different. Normally, I would be excited and ready to go. Tonight, a dark cloud covered my usual enthusiasm. I couldn't put my finger on it.

I never worked a show that began exactly on time. I also never knew a 15-minute intermission that was only fifteen minutes long. As long as there was a line at the concession stands and they had people queuing up to buy hot dogs, sodas, and popcorn the matches could wait. I didn't dress right away. I knew it was going to be a while. That gave me time to ponder the unusual, sober mood I was in. This was always supposed to be fun. Each show gave me another fifteen minutes of fame. Why would this night be any different?

Bobby Golden finally arrived and, as usual, was getting the dressing room all fired up with his jokes and antics. Bobby had arrived earlier, but he had been scouting the area for food or beer. Bobby was like a brother to me, but even his teasing and joking with me did nothing to lift my spirits. In fact, for the first time in all the years we had traveled and worked together, I was getting slightly annoyed with him. He seemed to realize that something was up, so he quickly moved on to someone else.

I decided that suiting up might change my disposition. I pulled on my tights and the pink trunks. When I sat down and bent over to slip on my boots, it hit me. I felt a slight "pull" in my lower back. I quickly sat upright and waited to see what was going to happen. I sat motionless for a few minutes and felt the beads of cold sweat pop out on my forehead. In the back of my mind, I realized that this would be my last show.

I already mentioned the bad bump I took during a match in Minneapolis. Since that time, I had experienced several bouts of severe back pain. A sudden move would result in a flash of pain that shot through my spine and out my legs like a lightning strike. During the two or three days that followed, I would be in constant pain. Several trips to various doctors and to the emergency room resulted in nothing more than pain medication and ordered bed rest. The symptoms were treated, but no one could find the source. It was a condition I would be forced to live with for many years. Every day since Minneapolis, I woke up with a stiff back. It took a few minutes to stretch out my back and begin to feel normal. On the mornings following a match, it took hours to loosen up. I kept my troubles to myself. I didn't even tell Bobby, in whom I confided almost everything. When I was stiff or in pain after a show, I would do whatever I could to act as if everything was normal. I didn't want anyone to tell me that I should quit wrestling. To be honest, I knew that I should, but I didn't want anyone else to tell me that.

Two weeks before the match in Mishawaka, I had suffered another episode of the pain. Usually, my back would return to normal after I took it easy for a couple of days, and I would forget about it. However, on that night, I couldn't banish the dark thoughts from the back of my mind. I had been recuperating at home when I got the call from the promoter. I had been sure I would be fine by the time the show was scheduled, however, I was in pain and I was a little concerned that it might be too soon to get back into the ring. I avoided going to the gym because I didn't want to risk injuring my back again and missing the match. Smart, huh?

The "pull" I felt in my back was a reminder that, no matter how much I loved the wrestling business, it wasn't worth the pounding my back was taking. None of the doctors had given me any hope that my back would ever be any better. Now, for the first time, I feared the pain more than I loved the game. In spite of the expected sprain, bumps, and bruises that happened, I always finished my matches, but I knew that if my back went out during a match — it would all be over! I began to think about what would happen if I wasn't able to communicate the seriousness of the situation to my opponent and he did something to me that would make it worse. I knew that I could be crippled, or that I would have to live with agonizing pain for the rest of my life.

I felt sick to my stomach. It was as though my very heart was being ripped out. I hoped none of the guys would notice the tears that were welling in my eyes. I looked around at the guys. They were smiling, laughing, and talking about matches of the past and present. Deep down, I knew I would never experience that again. The dreams I had of some day being a "main event" wrestler were gone forever.

Then and there, I decided I would finish that night without saying anything to anyone about my decision. I just wanted to leave the arena and fade into the sunset. For that matter, I don't think I could have gotten the words "I'm done" to come out of my mouth that evening.

I decided that the Canadian Rose would bow out gracefully and I would go with no regrets. I would not be afraid. I would take whatever bump or move was dished out that night, and I would land every bump as if my back was normal. I might pay for it the next day, but I would deal with it then. No one would ever know that it was my "swan song." I would finish my opponent with my "flying rollover," just as I had done so many times before.

When the time came, I made my usual grand entrance. The heat came as soon as I left the dressing room. With my sunglasses on, I strutted to the ring with an arrogant look on my face. I stopped occasionally to tell the fans who were heckling me to sit down. I jumped up into the ring and grabbed the microphone from the announcer. *"You people should be grateful I even came to this hick town! Now, sit down and shut up!"* The fans in the building exploded. Paper cups and other debris flew into the ring and onto me as I stood there with my hands on my hips and my nose in the air. The ref just looked at me and shook his head as he began to clear out the debris so we could begin the match.

After slowly removing my sunglasses and wiping them off on my tights, I turned and handed them to the ring attendant, saying loudly, *"You better take good care of my shades."* All the fans within earshot went wild again. I intended to build all the heat I could. I wanted the fans in Mishawaka to remember the night the way I would.

The match went off without a hitch, and surprisingly, my back actually felt pretty good. I took all the bumps without any problem. We went back and forth until, after giving him a good working-over, I bodyslammed him and came off the ropes for my flying rollover. I was pretty proud of that move. After placing my opponent on his back in the middle of the ring, I would come off the ropes, do a front flip and roll myself across the opponent's body. This flying rollover would be my last, so I went way up in the air, flipped, and came over his chest. My opponent was considerably smaller than me, so it looked like I was crushing him. You could hear some of the fans go "oooh" as I landed on their hero. I flipped over and made the pin. 1-2-3 and the match was over. The debris began to fly back into the ring as I arrogantly raised my hands and pranced around the ring. I even stopped to plant a farewell boot to the chest of my opponent.

I didn't feel any pain, but as I dodged the paper cups and cigarettes during my walk back to the dressing room, I felt the pressure in the small of my back. It was like someone was pushing the knuckles of their fist onto my lower spine. That feeling of pressure became a regular companion, and after that match, it stayed with me for more than a week. I knew that getting out of the wrestling business had been the right decision to make.

When I worked for the promoter in Mishawaka, he always promised me more than I ever got. For the most part, he was no different than other promoters. In my experience, they were all alike. He promised me $75 the first couple of times I worked for him, but I always wound up with $25 to $50, and each time, he said it would be better the "next time." Either the house was too small, or he had to pay extra to bring one of the big names in, or it was some other reason. That last night, he had promised he would give me at least $150. He couldn't say we didn't have a good house because there were only a few empty seats, and all the guys on the card were the regulars. There was no one from Dick the Bruiser's World Wrestling Association [WWA], Verne Gagne's American Wrestling Association [AWA], or any other major promotion. Still, I really wasn't too surprised when I opened my envelope and found $75. I didn't even bother to ask about the $25 he had promised to help cover travel expenses. Not that I could have asked him. After he handed me the envelope, he made like Houdini and disappeared, which was his standard MO every time I worked for him.

That was the early '80s, and since 1974, I had dealt with a number of promoters. Most of them never paid off the way they said they would. It usually wasn't worth complaining about. We were concerned that if we did, we might not get bookings, and if we didn't get bookings, we didn't get the exposure we needed to move up the business. The promoters had all the control, and at my level in the game, it just wasn't worth it.

My back problems were what convinced me make the decision to quit, but the short pay envelope reinforced my decision. It just wasn't worth it. I was sad, but I still had to chuckle as I thought about him scurrying out of the dressing room as soon as he handed out the envelopes.

The drive home was only about two hours, but it seemed like eight. I didn't have Bobby with me to keep the jokes flowing, the music blasting, or the Richard Pryor tapes playing. I did smoke my obligatory cigar (and, my last). I argued with myself a bit. I told myself that it wasn't so bad. I got through the match and it was one of my best ever, and there was no back pain — at least not yet. Maybe, if I really messed up my back, the doctors would actually discover the source of the problem and treat that instead of the symptoms. Common sense won out and I came to the conclusion that I was doing the right thing by quitting.

Sad to say, it took sixteen years to find relief for my back problem. I had one episode that was so painful that my wife had to call an ambulance to get me to the hospital. That time, the pain went on continuously for weeks with no relief. I didn't believe in chiropractors at the time, but there was one in a civic club I belonged to. I had been squirming around in pain and grimacing with every move I made during one of the meetings. When one of the guys there insisted I go talk to him, I decided that I would try a witch doctor if there was any chance he could help.

After the meeting, while everyone was standing around talking, the guy took me over to Dr. Victor Fitch. Dr. Fitch said, *"I've been waiting for you to talk to me. Be in my office at 8:30 in the morning."*

After a month of treatment, I remained virtually pain free for the last eleven years, with the exception of one episode. That would probably have been avoided had I continued with regular treatments as the Doc had suggested. I make all of my appointments now. I highly recommend to any new guys in the business that they find a good chiropractor and see him (or her) at least twice a year. Perhaps, if I had found Doc Fitch in 1978 or 1979, I could have had a longer run in the business. However, that is water under the bridge.

When I got home after the matches that night, I actually thought about throwing my ring gear into the trash to remove any further temptations. However, I couldn't bring myself to do it. I washed them and tucked them away in a closet. Out of sight, out of mind. I am glad that I held onto them. In fact, the outfit became a hit as a Halloween costume for my stepson last year. The Canadian Rose was revived ever so briefly. Still, it was "cool."

One day, a few weeks after the match in Mishawaka, Bobby called to tell me about a show he was helping promote in the Warsaw area, and asked if I would be interested in wrestling on the card. I was no Dick the Bruiser or Wilbur Snyder, but Bobby knew that I could put on a good show and that I was somebody on whom he could depend. I told him I had to think it over and would call him back. I knew if Bobby was involved, I would get paid. Even when the two of us went through the Sylvania fiasco, I believe we both knew we would never get paid for all those matches we worked. Regardless, we were both driven by our love of the business. The Sylvania shows were not the first ones we came away from with little or no money in our pockets. There was no shortage of promoters in that day that threw together shows and failed to keep their promise when payday came around. Still, when the promoters called, we answered. And yet, when Bobby called, I wasn't sure if I really wanted to jump back in. After thinking about it for a day or two, I decided to make a clean break. I called Bobby to let him know. I told him I just didn't think the Canadian Rose would ever come back. Bobby knew how much I loved wrestling. I think he also knew how badly he would feel if he had to make that decision.

Two days later, Bobby called me again. *"Hey, West. We could use a referee for this show, and you would be good. You know the business. You wrestled so you know more than a lot of refs know ... and you don't have to take any bumps!"* I told him I would have to think about it. I knew it wouldn't be the same, and yet, I was tempted because it might be a chance for me to stay involved in the business and not have to worry about my back. I finally agreed to do it, but told him I was not going to be out there "*sweating my ass off for five or six matches for twenty-five bucks.*" Suddenly, Duke West, aka the Canadian Rose, was now Duke West the referee. The guy who spent his last match going out of his way to be the heel of all heels was now going to be the guy trying to keep order in the ring. Oh, by the way. That thing about me not having to take a bump again? That was BS, too!

Things worked out pretty good for me as a referee, and as it turned out, I actually made more money as a ref than I did as a wrestler working one of the prelims. I think the promoters kicked in a little more because I could take an occasional bump and I had a good handle on what a ref should be doing to work with the wrestlers without getting in the way.

Being a good ref wasn't as easy as I thought. Working five or six matches in one night, one right after the other, was hard work. It was also a bit awkward at first, especially when I worked with guys who didn't know me. When we met, it was usually cordial, but they obviously reserved judgment until they could see what I was all about in the ring. It was also awkward for me to be in the ring and that close to the action without being involved in it. In the heat of the action, I was tempted to get my shots in. I guess you could say I was fighting off flashbacks. And yet, I was determined to be the kind of referee that I wanted when I was wrestling. I tried to keep the match moving, help communicate between the wrestlers, keep them advised of the time the match was running, and let them work their gimmicks and angles without interference.

My style was inspired by one of the great referees I watched growing up: Connie Marker. Marker was a referee for the Dick the Bruiser/Wilbur Snyder operation in Indianapolis. He had the ability to look like he was in control of the match the whole time, and yet, both the heels and the babyfaces got to "do their thing." The results and substance of the matches he worked were no different than the ones worked by Johnny Shorn or one of the other refs who worked for Bruiser, but Connie Marker was respected and loved by the fans. It was all a matter of the fans' perception.

If Connie Marker was the ref of a match in which a heel pummeled a babyface and used a dastardly deed to win the match, the wrestling fans would say Marker was overwhelmed and not able to handle what went on. If they took that same gimmick someplace else with Johnny Shorn or one of the other guys as the ref, the fans would come away saying that the ref was "bought off" or "blind." The other refs just kind of stumbled around the ring and stayed back until it was time to count somebody out. Connie Marker wore you out just watching him. He worked harder than the wrestlers. He jogged around the ring throughout the entire match. His eyes were always fixed on the wrestlers, and he would stop, backpedal, or change directions on a dime. He was a non-stop dynamo from bell to bell. When it came time for him to get in there and take action, he was always there, and he helped sell whatever gimmick or angle they were working on. The fans placed the other refs in that promotion into the same category as the heels. Connie Marker, however, was the babyface of the referees.

When I was in high school, I attended a Golden Gloves boxing tournament in Muncie, Indiana. Connie Marker was one of the referees. He was just the same during the boxing matches as he was with the wrestling. During one of the intermissions, I actually caught up with him and asked him for his autograph as he climbed out of the ring. He seemed surprised, but politely obliged. I, too, classified Marker as "one of the good guys." Anybody who stood up to those bad guys I saw on TV every Saturday was a hero in my book!

Later, when I got into the wrestling business, I really appreciated a good ref like Marker. Fans like to see action. When guys were locked up or just taking a break in the action, Connie Marker's constant movement gave the impression that there was a lot more going on than there really was. A good ref has the ability to cover mistakes and help sell the match. I think most of the guys appreciate that. When I refereed, I tried to help the guys out, and rarely did I get a complaint. There were a few who didn't like it when I tried to get them to move on when their gimmick was getting no reaction from the crowd, or when they were beating it to death. I loved the business too much to let some of the stuff go by. I'll be the first to admit that I wasn't the greatest wrestler in the world. However, I did my very best to see that the fans got their money's worth. That wasn't going to change because I was now wearing the striped shirt.

During that time, I actually dreamed of owning my own wrestling school. Having been a fan, a wrestler, and a ref for many years, I felt I had a good perspective on what worked and what didn't. I saw many of the common mistakes, and I learned ways to avoid them or make them less noticeable. To this day, when I see a young guy blow a move, I want to go up and say, *"This is how you make this work better. This is what it looked like to the fans."* As I said earlier, I was involved in many of the debates between fans and non-fans about whether professional wrestling was "all fake" or not. I know what the critics of old-school wrestling were pointing out as obviously staged or scripted moves, so I did everything I could as a wrestler to make sure that our fans had the upper hand if there was any debate over my matches.

At any rate, that was the backdrop for Duke West the referee. I soon got over being awkward about it. In fact, I was happy to remain connected to the business. I wound up going full circle. My first contact to try to get into the business was with the World Wrestling Federation [WWF] when it was still just the big northeast promotion. One of my last contacts in the business was when I just missed getting a shot at being a referee for the WWF.

My "putting wrestling behind me" sure didn't last long after I began to referee. At one show, I was called in on one of those dressing room conferences to discuss how a particular finish for the main event might go down. Someone talked about a "run in" where one of the guys would charge out of the dressing room to interfere with the match. While I was distracted, the heel would use some dastardly deed to get the advantage over the good guy. Of course, by the time I turned back to the action, the hero would be pinned to the mat and I would have to count him out. That sounded like a good plan to me.

Before I could excuse myself and leave the conference, the promoter looked at me and said, *"Hey! West there knows how to take a bump. Let's work out something where he gets knocked out for a minute and then comes around in time to make the count!"* I wound up that night getting flattened between the "run in" and the "babyface." From then on, Duke West the ref had the reputation of being the guy who would take a bump. If someone called and said they "really needed me," I knew they had plans for some big finish that would wind up with me on my back inside or outside of the ring. That helped me get a lot of work as a ref, but I had to set my limits. I was still concerned about my back. Going over the top rope was out of the question, and if I went through the ropes, I stopped at the apron and slid onto the floor. I was adamant that I would take no direct bumps from the ring to the floor. Most of the time, it was just a matter of taking an errant punch or getting knocked down. That was not a problem.

I refereed a few matches with some female wrestlers who were thrilled to death that they could work me into their gimmick. Throughout the match, the babyface would duck or move as the heel was throwing a punch or going to yank her legs out from under her, and I would be right there to catch the brunt of the move. While the heel was picking me up, dusting me off, and profusely apologizing, the babyface would sneak up behind her and take the advantage.

We worked that scenario several times during the matches, and for the finish, the gals would be on the mat after the heel caught the babyface in a sleeper hold. I would move around to check for a choke (at the direction of the babyface who was frantically pointing at her throat), and as I moved around them, the babyface would sweep my legs out from under me. Of course, I would get up and blame the heel and tell her that I had enough of her abuse. While she was trying to explain that the babyface did it, she would get swept down and rolled up into a pin. I would count her out and she would be furious. We would wind up nose to nose in the middle of the ring and I would wind up threatening to deck her if she didn't leave. The fans ate it up.

The girls thanked me repeatedly for selling their gimmick and for working with them so well. They told me I was the best ref they had worked with in a long time. I was happy because they had been in the business a long time.

During one show in South Bend, Indiana, I was getting pretty worn down by the time intermission rolled around. During the break, I was enjoying a cold drink and trying to relax before going out for the rest of the show. The promoter came into the dressing room and said a friend of his wanted to be a ref, and he wanted him to work the next match. At first, I was a little upset, and thought that perhaps I had done something wrong. He assured me that the guy was just trying out and that I would still be paid the full amount to which we had agreed. I was sure that since the guy was a friend of the promoter, I was going to be replaced or lose work. At any rate, I came to the conclusion that it was hot and I was tired. If that was the way the promoter wanted it to be, then I would just relax in the comfort of the dressing room.

Several of the guys assured me that they were going to insist that I referee their matches. It felt good to know they had that much confidence in me. When I wrestled, I didn't give a lot of thought to the referee (as long as he didn't screw things up). Now that my circumstances had changed, I had a deep appreciation for the role the ref played in the ring. About ten minutes after the match began, four of the guys came into the dressing room ... carrying the new ref. They told me to get to the ring and finish the evening. I thought the guy was taking part in some angle the promoter had cooked up, or that he was a well-known local and the "getting hurt" storyline was being used to build some heat.

When the last match was over, I went back to the dressing room. I was told that the new ref had been taken to the hospital with a broken leg. It seems he didn't know enough to get out of the way when the wrestlers were criss-crossing each other in the ring, and he got sandwiched between the two combatants when they collided.

As far as I know, the guy never refereed again. My job with that promotion was secure. When the action began moving, I knew what to expect and was smart enough to get out of the way until they were done flying around. I think that should be "Refereeing 101." The poor guy just didn't get it. He should have been sent to work with the guys at Miller's gym for training and experience before being thrown to the wolves.

It was also during my time as a ref that I had an encounter with a snake. Bobby Golden had a friend who owned an eight-foot snake called Monty. Bobby decided to borrow Monty and make him a part of his gimmick. Of course, with my luck, I wound up being the referee for one of the matches in which he brought along Monty. Before the match, Bobby asked me if I was afraid of snakes. Now I knew Golden, and I knew that the dumbest thing I could do was to let on that I had any fear of snakes whatsoever. I told him I wasn't afraid of them, but I wasn't a snake lover, either. I figured that answer would put an end to any ideas he had about pulling something on me. Of course, that wasn't good enough for Bobby. He had to test me.

As I waited in the ring for the wrestlers to arrive, Bobby walked out with a huge snake wrapped around his shoulders. I simply backed up into a corner of the ring and tried to act as nonchalant as possible. Bobby strolled around ringside, leaning in now and then towards the female fans, which naturally brought on a lot of screams. Several people, both male and female, jumped up and ran off.

When Bobby stepped into the ring, I avoided making eye contact with him and tried to appear as unconcerned as possible. However, when I looked up, I was eyeball to eyeball with Monty! Golden was pushing the snake's head toward my face and saying, *"Give him a little kissy-kissy."* Thankfully, I was able to keep my composure until Bobby and the snake moved on.

A few months later, I walked into a dressing room to get ready for a show. The wrestlers were all standing around looking into the shower. I was sure that whatever was going on, I really didn't want to know. When the group finally broke up, Bobby strolled out of the shower and greeted me. When my curiosity got the best of me, I asked him what had been going on in the shower room. Bobby explained, *"Monty was taking a sh— in there. He was sh—in' squares. I never knew snakes sh— squares!"* I told him I couldn't say I ever cared to know that information. I couldn't believe that watching a snake take a dump was something all those big, tough wrestlers would find so fascinating.

I don't think I ever sold Bobby on the fact that I wasn't too terribly afraid of snakes. However, after the first night, he never brought Monty too close to me. On the other hand, he never asked me to make a big deal about the snake, either, or to run around the ring and act like I was terrified.

Monty got to be a lot of trouble for Bobby to travel with. His owner was very concerned about Monty being out in cold weather. When Monty's owner decided Bobby was going to have to ante up some money to rent Monty for the shows, Bobby gave up the gimmick. As soon as I was convinced that Monty was no longer around, I let Bobby know how badly I had wanted to kill him *"for sticking that damn snake in my face."* Of course, Bobby just laughed and shook his head.

Months later, with Monty nothing more than a distant memory, Bobby came by to pick me up for a show in Ohio. When I opened the back door of his car, he said, *"Watch where you throw your bag. I got Monty back there."* My immediate reaction was to jump backwards, but when I crept up to carefully examine the back seat for the large bag in which Monty traveled, I realized I had been had. I threw my bag into the back and climbed into the front seat beside Bobby. I just looked at Bobby and said *"Bastard."* He roared with laughter and took off down the road, looking over at me from time to time and hissing. Then he would begin laughing again. That scenario went on for the whole trip. It was a long time before I could be around Bobby Golden without having him hiss at me.

One of the last matches I refereed that Bobby Golden was in was one of the most memorable. It was a tag team match and the guys were working hard and fast. Bobby was in against one of the heels when they began a criss-cross. Bobby was hitting the ropes really hard. When he hit the ropes for the third time, I heard what sounded like a gun shot. I had never seen him scared of anything, but that time, he froze against the ropes and had a "deer in the headlights" look on his face. The ropes sagged and the corner posts leaned in toward the middle of the ring. One of the two steel cables that crossed under the ring to hold the posts upright had snapped. Somehow, Bobby had stopped himself from catapulting out of the ring and winding up about three rows back in the ringside seats.

I had seen ring floors break before. There was one tag team match where Bobby was my partner and we both got backdropped at the same time by the babyfaces. Both of us weighed more than 250 pounds. When we hit the mat at the same time, there was a loud crack and the floor bowed. It was one of Miller's rings. We figured he was really going to be hot. When Bobby got the ring back to the gym, he told Miller what happened. Miller just shrugged his shoulders and said he would dig up some more plywood for the floor. There were a couple of other times when I saw ring floors break or a turnbuckle pop off. That night, however, was the first time I had ever seen one of the under-the-ring steel cables snap.

I had never seen Bobby as shook up as he was that night. We stopped the show, but the ring crew didn't have spare cables with which to make the necessary repairs. Bobby insisted (after he recovered) that the show go on. They finished the match without using the ropes and still gave the fans their money's worth.

Being a ref kept me in the business a little longer than I otherwise could have hoped. I got to see friends like "Bo" and Bobby, and some of the other guys I had worked with over the years. Many of those folks are gone now. I'm thankful for that little extra time I got to spend with them.

I settled into a nice little niche as a referee. I got fairly steady work and, because promoters wanted me around to take the occasional bump, they made sure I got more bucks than some of the other guys. For a while, all was well with the world. One day, however, the writing was on the wall.

After a few years as a referee, the smaller, independent promotions began to dry up and give way to the bigger national companies like the WWF. Most of the territories and smaller independent promotions were held together by television exposure through independent and local stations. The house shows drew crowds through the legendary wrestlers of that era, but those legends were retiring or dying off, and the big, national promotions made it hard to sell a regional operation to a television station. The new "superstars" were getting nationwide exposure through the cable networks. They wouldn't be caught dead working in an armory or a high school gym in rural America.

Without the television exposure, or the big names of the day on the cards, the smaller promotions began to fade away. The folks who once poured into the gyms, armories, and small auditoriums to watch us wrestle would now wait to drive to Indianapolis, Detroit, Chicago, or Minneapolis to see the new superstars. As the old venues began to dry up, so did the opportunities for guys like me of that previous era. Most of the guys I knew from those days just faded away. Only a few of the guys I worked with got a shot at the WWF or one of the other cable promotions. Lanny Poffo, Al Snow, and Bobo Brazil made the move, along with Brian Costello. So did Bobby Golden, but things were just never to be the same.

It was completely out of the blue that I got a call one day from someone who worked with the WWF. They might need a referee for a show they had scheduled at Cobo Hall in Detroit and I had been recommended. Would it be possible for me to be on standby to fill in on the Detroit show? I was finally getting my shot at the "big time." Of course, I will be available. However, as I wasn't thrilled with the new direction the business was taking, my motivation was no longer the love of the business. My motivation now was plain greed. Get a piece of the big pie if you can.

I cleaned my referee shirts and slacks, polished my boots, and packed them in the trunk of my car so I would be ready to go when the call came. That call never happened and I never heard from them again.

Later, I saw parts of that Cobo Hall show on TV and I must say I was quite jealous of the referee who was working it. I was gritting my teeth and saying to myself, *"I could do better than that. They should have called me. Surely, they're going to call me for another show."*

Once I came to the realization that not only was I never going to get that call from the WWF, and that the promoters I had been working with were all but gone, I was somewhat ashamed of myself. I had been critical of the way things were going when those mega promotions began pushing out the little guys. And yet, when I got that phone call, I was as anxious as anyone to jump on the bandwagon. I had been willing to compromise my values for a price. I told myself then and there that even if Vince Jr. himself called me, I was done with the business. I never had to make that decision, but I like to believe that I would have stuck to that pledge. Still, I felt honored that someone had recommended me.

By 1984, I was all but out of the business and refereeing only occasionally, usually when a close friend needed some help. I hadn't seen Bobby for a while, and every time we talked on the phone, we talked about getting together. Many months passed, but we never scheduled a time to meet.

One day, Bobby called to tell me he was promoting a Saturday night show at a high school about 20 minutes from his house in Bourbon, Indiana. He told me he had plastered the town with posters and was expecting a huge crowd. He said he would pay me a minimum of $100 to ref for him. After working all morning on my regular job, I hopped into the car and raced to the high school. I left in time to be there about an hour before the show was scheduled to begin. When I pulled into the town, I saw no evidence of the posters Bobby said he had put out to promote the show. That was my first clue that something was amiss.

When I arrived at the high school, all I found was an empty parking lot. The doors of the school were locked and there wasn't a soul to be seen. With just an hour remaining before the scheduled bell time, I realized that I had been duped. I didn't have any change for the pay phone, so I headed in the direction of Bobby's house. I was hot! A rib is a rib, but Bobby had gone too far with this one. I was going to lay him out when I saw him. I had busted my butt to get off work so I could get to the show on time, only to discover that it was all BS.

When I pulled into Bobby's driveway, the wheels of my car had barely stopped turning before I bailed out and began banging on his door. When the door opened, Bobby was standing there with a grin on his face that stretched from ear to ear. *"I've been waiting for you to show up,"* he said. He pulled me inside, slapped me on the back, and escorted me into his living room. His dining table was set up with snacks and wrestling videos for us to watch while we caught up on old times. That was Bobby. At one moment, you want to kick his ass, and in the next, you're kicking back with him!

Shortly after that night, with the smaller independents all but extinct, I put wrestling behind me for good. The business as I knew it was dying and my heart was no longer in it. Unlike the last time I retired, this time, there would be no coming back. My striped referee shirts and slacks went back into the closet. My boots went back into the drawer with the Canadian Rose outfit. Maybe someday after I'm long gone, someone will pull my "Canadian Rose" outfit out of an old trunk. They can then read these stories and perhaps understand who I was. They may not be as enthusiastic about my past as a professional wrestler as I have been, but that's okay. At least, they might still get a good laugh from me.

Chapter 15

Old School

For a number of years after I quit the business, I rarely watched wrestling on TV ... until someone tipped me off that Bobby Golden was going to be on the WWF show. I made sure to watch that. I hadn't seen him in years. I was proud to watch him that night, and yet, I somehow had a sense that he was out of his element. He made a good showing, but like me, he was a big guy who didn't have the muscular, athletic type of build that the new era of wrestling favored. He was also close to my age. His opponent that night looked like he had just stepped out of a body building magazine and towered over him. Bobby, who once was "on top" in many of the independent circuits around the Midwest, was there only to do a "job." He was young enough that he should have had many good years ahead of him. It was my hope that he would hang in there, as he always had, and find himself a place in this new and much more profitable wrestling world. I don't know if Bobby got sick shortly after his appearance with the WWF, or if he just didn't fit into the scheme of things, but I never saw him on TV again.

My daughter called me when Al Snow came into the WWF. When I worked some shows with him in the Ohio area, my daughter was often there and enjoyed joining the chorus of folks yelling, *"Snowflake! Snowflake!"* Al would cover his ears and storm around the ring. It got a lot of laughs and good heat before the match even began. I wasn't at all surprised to see him have a good run with the WWF. He seemed to have a natural talent from the get-go.

I also watched for a while when Bobo Brazil made his appearances. I was happy to see him on TV, but I knew from my last time working with him that it was a struggle for him. Age was catching up with him and the end of his career was near. Like with Bobby Golden, it was the last time I saw him wrestle.

For a while, I would turn on the matches to see if anyone else from our old gang would make an appearance. I really expected some of the younger guys, like the Flying Tigers, to show up on television. They were small in stature, but very athletic, and the fans loved them. They did quite well in the Ohio and Indiana area. Lou Botka was another young guy I thought had a lot of talent. Lou came out of Tommy Lynch's bodybuilding gym in South Bend. He reminded me of a young Bronko Lubich. He was really easy to work with and he got a good reaction from the fans. I think his downfall was that he wasn't really enthusiastic about the business. He came to the gym long enough to learn the ropes and then seldom showed up. He also turned down a lot of bookings. He just sort of faded away and I never saw him again.

After awhile, there was no longer any reason for me to watch wrestling. On the other hand, there was still no way to completely divorce myself from the business. Since I was a police officer, as soon as the word got out about my wrestling, my nickname around the department became "Rose." I also got a lot of ribbing about the pink tights I wore to the ring. Whenever I met someone new, it wasn't long before the other officers filled them in and told them to ask me about the Canadian Rose or the pink tights. Of course, they had already heard the story from whoever they had spoken with.

Some of the guys enjoyed hearing the stories about my wrestling experiences. I was paired up with one guy, in particular, who insisted I tell him about wrestling. I told him about some of the humorous things that happened, and before the night was over, he was in tears from laughing. After that, he was always asking me to tell him some more stories, and insisting I share them with anyone who was around at the time. I really didn't mind, but it did remind me of how much I missed those days and the adventures I had. They say you never really stop being a cop, and I think you can never really stop being a wrestler. Many times, I dreamed about having an opportunity to once again suit up and jump into a ring. I've done nothing else in my life that compares to the rush I got while walking out of that dressing room, down the aisle, and stepping into that ring.

A few years ago, I ran into Tim Replogle. We crossed paths on several occasions when I was a referee and he worked as "The Golden Lion." Later, when he was a substitute teacher at my daughter's high school, we reconnected. Tim now runs the WWA Bruiser Wrestling promotion, which is based in Fort Wayne, Indiana. He bills himself as "Dick the Bruiser, Jr." and often works with Bobo Brazil, Jr. I caught one of his shows on a local independent TV channel and it got my attention because it was "old school" wrestling. Seeing him wrestle as the son of the great Dick the Bruiser, and seeing Bobo Brazil, Jr., brought back many memories of watching the Bruiser/ Snyder Indianapolis promotion when I was a youngster.

Tim ran his shows and tapings out of an old building near downtown Fort Wayne. They ran pretty regularly and drew decent crowds. When I ran into him at a local college football game, I told him I enjoyed watching his show. He invited me to come out to the next show, so I took him up on his offer.

When I arrived at the show, I was escorted back to the dressing room. At bell time, I was paraded out with some of the wrestlers on that night's card. For the first time in many years, I got to relive that thrill of stepping through the ropes. I got to feel the canvas under my feet. I couldn't resist leaning back against the ropes to get that feeling again. I was introduced as a former WWA referee and the former "number-two-ranked contender for the U.S. title." It was a bittersweet moment.

The thrill was there just as it had been many years before. However, I knew that once the National Anthem finished playing, I would climb down out of the ring and my part in the program would be over. I returned to my seat to watch the show. Like my grandfather before me, I had trouble sitting still. I was watching "rasslin'," just like it was in the good ol' days. I felt like this was wrestling as it should be.

As I looked around the crowd that night, I saw that many were older folks. They remembered Dick the Bruiser, Wilbur Snyder, Bobo Brazil, and all the other legends of that day. I'm sure, like me, many of them were reliving those old memories. Perhaps, like me, they weren't happy with the new era of wrestling. I was pleased for them because many of them looked like they wouldn't be able to afford the $30 or $40 to see the World Wrestling Entertainment [WWE, formerly the WWF] at the Fort Wayne Coliseum. When the show was over, however, I wondered if this promotion would be able to survive.

It wasn't that I just didn't like the direction the wrestling business had taken. It was that it left me and so many others like me behind. It brought back memories of a time that ended far too soon ... not just for me and the guys and gals I worked with, but for the fans like those who were there that night. There are very few places around today where hard-working, everyday people can plop down ten dollars for a ticket and get a good show.

I often attend the matches when the WWA has a show nearby. They have a small, but loyal, following, and they seem to do okay, considering they're competing against the big national promotions and their TV time is relegated to the wee hours of the morning. The shows give me my fix for old-school wrestling, and since they present them in much the same fashion we did, the shows brings back a lot of good memories. When I have an opportunity to talk to some of the talent, they all act very humble and pleasant. During the intermissions, the babyface wrestlers all come out and are available to the fans for autographs and photos.

Duke West and Dick the Bruiser Jr.

The Association of Retarded Citizens [ARC] usually brings a large group of people to the shows. Dick the Bruiser, Jr. makes sure they get good seats and spends time with them before, during, and after the show. The ARC group really gets into the matches. Since some of them live in group home settings, they have a curfew. As a result, on the night I was there, the ARC staff members who transported them made the whole group leave before the main event. As they trudged out of the building, they looked very disappointed that they didn't get to see Dick the Bruiser, Jr. wrestle. He was their hero. Carl, one of the ARC clients, works at the school where I now work in the security department. I saw Carl at one of the shows and saw him leave early with the others. Carl is fairly independent and lives on his own, so he was quite upset at being forced to leave. He had to pay for his ticket and felt he was entitled to see the whole show. Of course, like the rest of his friends, none of them are able to drive on their own.

While we were talking at the school, he was quite surprised to learn that I just happened to know Dick the Bruiser, Jr. I told him I would see what I could do about the situation. I contacted Tim and he told me they were aware of the problem. He said that on the next show, he would work two main events so the ARC clients could see his match. Can you imagine asking the WWE to modify one of their shows so twenty mentally disabled citizens could see the main event?

At the last show, my wife and I picked up Carl and took him along with us. We really enjoyed watching the reactions of Carl and the other ARC folks at the show. Carl got a kick out of telling the other ARC folks that he got to ride to the show with an ex-wrestler, and that he didn't have to leave with the rest of them. He brought along his digital camera, but he was so excited that his hands wouldn't stop shaking, and most of the pictures he took came out blurry. I had to take the pictures for him.

One young lady with the ARC group would occasionally yell at the heels, or begin clapping loudly for the good guys. When she realized what she was doing, she would immediately stop and look around, as if she was afraid someone had noticed. We wanted so badly to walk over to her and say, *"Honey, go right ahead and cheer. This is what this is all about."*

When the main event is over, Dick the Bruiser, Jr. has the youngsters in the crowd jump into the ring with him, and they all dance to the song *"Who Let the Dogs Out?"* It is quite a sight to see the ring full of kids enjoying their moment with Dick, and sometimes, Bobo, Jr. The joy on their faces, the excitement of the ARC clients, and of the other fans who attend the WWA shows, is what professional wrestling is really all about. Perhaps the WWA is building a fan base for a new generation of old-school professional wrestling.

I still go to Tim's shows when I can. Occasionally, my wife even asks me if there is a show coming up in the area. We both enjoy old-school wrestling as presented by groups like WWA Bruiser Wrestling. When she was a little girl, she made her grandfather watch wrestling with her, and apparently, they had their debates over whether or not it was "real." She told me she only watched the WWE when "The Rock" [Dwayne Johnson] was wrestling.

Go figure.

Chapter 16

Dancing with Danger

The stories I have shared are the adventures and misadventures of a small-time professional wrestler who plied his trade "back in the day." They took place during a different time and era. There was no cable, no Internet, and very few of the kind of wrestlers you see today. Most of them today have ridiculous muscle mass that, in my opinion, is artificially produced through the use of steroids. The transformation from old-school wrestlers to the new could be seen on cable TV as the WWF and other large regional promotions went nationwide. Yes, many of the wrestlers today make a lot of money, and many of them have achieved fame and fortune that was unthinkable in our day. However, in many cases, their fame is short-lived. When a wrestler's gimmick runs its course, there are no other promotions to move on to. How many of the "superstars" of five years ago are still around? Sure, a few manage to switch gimmicks and prolong the end of their careers. Some even go on to make it on TV or in Hollywood, but those guys are few and far between.

While Dick the Bruiser and Wilbur Snyder anchored the Indianapolis promotion, other wrestlers came and went. They would stay for anywhere from a few weeks to a year, but invariably, when their star began to fade, they would disappear from the area. They would move on to Minneapolis, Florida, Texas, or one of the many other territories in existence at the time. They might return to Indianapolis a few years later with a new gimmick, or they might flip from babyface to heel, or vice versa. Those changes afforded them an opportunity to continue their career and stay fresh. Bobby Heenan, Black Jack Lanza, and Blackjack Mulligan were a good example. They would work Indianapolis for a while, and then move on to Minneapolis or one of the other territories. The circuit allowed them to have some longevity to their careers.

Bobby Heenan had a successful and fairly long run with the WWE. When that ended, he disappeared. The same thing happened to Roddy Piper. They may have retired voluntarily, but when the WWF quit giving them bookings, they had nowhere left to go. There are still a few regional promotions left, but the options are greatly limited.

We never made a lot of money. We didn't live in big mansions. We didn't have bobble-head dolls built on our likeness on toy store shelves. And nobody had a reality TV show. On the other hand, we also didn't have issues with steroids or other illegal drugs. Yes, there was some alcohol abuse, but I never heard of steroids, crack, or even marijuana from the guys with whom I worked.

Most of us were in it for the love of the business, and not the love of money. We had fun, and for the most part, we all got along. We were all in the same boat. There was no time for bickering and petty competitions for attention. The guys who refused to play well with others didn't last long. Of course, we all had dreams of being headliners and working the main events. We all hoped to one day wear a championship belt. We also knew there were dues to pay and learning to be done. Having the looks and the body of a Greek god gave you a good jump start, but it took more than that to get recognition and success.

We didn't worry about blood-transmitted diseases like HIV. If we got juice or if somebody accidentally bled during a match, it was good for business. It seems like most promotions today avoid blood like the plague. Maybe OSHA is regulating the WWE these days, but I couldn't believe it when I saw the floor outside their rings covered with mats. If we got tossed out of the ring, we knew we were landing on concrete or wood. No one ever suggested putting mats on the floor. I sometimes wonder if the performance-enhancing drugs the guys today are into makes their bones too brittle to take a good bump on a little cement.

I don't begrudge for one minute the success of the national promotions. The powers that be jumped on the cable TV bandwagon at just the right time and have developed a huge fan base. When the WWE or one of the other national promotions appears at the Fort Wayne Coliseum, it is the only event where the fans show up in the middle of the day to try to catch a glimpse of the wrestlers as they arrive at the stage door. The arrival of the WWE resembles that of a big Hollywood movie premiere. They have security outside all day long. They set up barricades by the entranceways that extend all the way out to the street. Fans line up along those barricades and lean across them to check out every car that pulls into that back lot. Each time a wrestler emerges from one of the cars, the crowd screams and cheers. Some acknowledge the mob with a wave, some ignore them, and, a few will head to the barricade and sign autographs. It is unreal.

The WWE puts a lot more money into the set up for one of these big shows than I made in all my years of wrestling. The lights, music, staging, and sound equipment go far beyond anything we ever dreamed of. We ran with a ring and a public address system. The WWE comes to town with several tractor-trailer rigs. Our rings were hauled around on a trailer behind an old pickup truck, or in Homer Miller's case, an old bread truck he picked up at an auction. Sometimes, we had to hook up that old open trailer to the back of Bobby's car and haul it to wherever the next show was being held.

Many times, we had the duty of rounding up local kids to be the ring crew and help set up for that night's show. In return for being on the ring crew, they were given free tickets to the show, a hot dog, and a cold drink. Many of them didn't even care about the cold drinks and hot dogs. They were happy to get free tickets, but like us, most of them did it for the love of the business. They could tell their friends they were part of the show. Sometimes, I would hear them explaining to fans at ringside just how the ring was put together, and how much padding there really was underneath the mat. You could see the gleam in their eye. Wrestling meant something to them. Their participation was an experience they would not soon forget.

I remember one young man who was on the ring crews whenever we appeared in a small town in northwest Indiana. He appeared to have a slight mental impairment, but always showed up early and ready to work. He would carefully carry every piece of the ring from the trailer or the truck and made sure it was placed exactly where he was told to put it. After he assisted us two or three times, he actually supervised the operation. He would begin unloading the ring before the wheels on the truck stopped turning. With the proper placement of every piece of that ring committed to memory, he was able to direct the other helpers who showed up. I first met him when I went out to talk to Bobby and see how the set up was going. The young man immediately briefed me on the procedures of how the ring was being set up and how he had everything under control. He also had the job of helping pass out the flyers that served as programs for that night's card. As I turned to go back to the dressing room, he asked me to sign my autograph on one of the flyers. As a heel, I didn't normally sign autographs, but since he was a good helper, I agreed.

That night, as I did my slow strut out to the ring, the crowd stood up and booed me as usual. I slowly worked my away around ringside, building as much heat as I could. One group of fans at ringside all gave me the "thumbs down" sign as I strolled toward them. Suddenly, at the end of that row, our young ring crew member jumped to his feet and gave me a thumbs up! He nodded and winked at me like we were old pals and he was showing me his support as I went out on a mission. He then turned around and showed the flyer I had just signed to everybody around him. There I was, trying to build up some heat and sell myself as the bad guy, and the kid was telling everyone how nice I was to him, and how I had given him an autograph. That incident taught me to always stay in character when I was outside the dressing room.

I was involved in another autograph incident at a show in the Indianapolis area in Greenfield. I was going to be on one of the feature matches that night, so I didn't dress right away. I went outside the dressing room and stood in the opening between the stands to watch some of the prelims. A few of the babyfaces were there and a steady stream of kids were coming down and handing them things to autograph. They would sign a few autographs before heading back to the dressing room, giving up on the possibility of watching anything that might be going on in the ring. I was in my street clothes and rarely wrestled in the Indianapolis area, so I assumed I wouldn't be bothered.

After I watched the matches for a few minutes, two of the kids came down and leaned over the railing with paper and pen in their hands, *"Are you a wrestler?"*

"Yeah."

"Will you sign this, please?" I was trying to be as gruff as possible, but the kid was cute and he had said "please." How could you turn down a kid like that? What would it hurt for me to sign one autograph? I took his paper and signed it, "Big Duke West – The Canadian Rose." The kid looked at the

autograph carefully, looked back up at me, and suddenly shouted, *"Oh, I know who you are!"* He promptly tore the paper into pieces and threw it in my face as he and his buddy turned and ran up the steps. I was about to laugh when a paper cup full of cold soft drink sailed down from the stands and bounced off my head. I decided that was a good time to make my exit to the dressing room.

I don't think the wrestlers today can appreciate that kind of fan contact. Sure, they have almost a cult following, but they don't have the same relationship with the fans that we had. I also believe that those who came in on the tail end of the "old-school era" have forgotten what it was like. In fact, many of them seemed to have forgotten their roots. I won't mention any names, but there is one WWE "superstar" who started out at the same time I did. We wrestled on the same show and in the same high school gymnasium in front of (at the most) 300 fans. We had a nice chat before that show and later on at a party after the show. Several years later, when the WWE came to Fort Wayne, I was working the security detail at the Coliseum. He walked in and I went over to re-introduce myself. When I asked if he remembered me, he looked at me like I was nuts and blew by me without even a, *"Hello. How have you been?"* At the very least, he could have lied and said, *"Yeah, I remember. How are you doing?"* Well, his run as a "superstar" came to an end. Now that his fifteen minutes of fame are over, I wonder if he suddenly remembers that little high school gym in Indiana and us little "peons" who were there that night. I wonder if he now looks back and thinks, *"Those were the good times."*

Another wrestling phenomenon of sorts is the "backyard wrestling" thing, where kids with video cameras put on "shows" in a park or other public venue. They then air the tapes on the Internet or on a public access TV station. The first time I saw one of those shows on TV, I was hot. I thought they were mocking wrestling. I saw a group of snot-nosed teenagers in the middle of a park with no ring, no ring gear, and no training, and they were "playing" wrestling. I'm sure I looked like that when I was a seven-year-old playing wrestling in my backyard. The difference was that I was a little kid and nobody saw it.

It took a while before I came to the realization that they were really trying to start something. They had an "organizer" (I won't call him a promoter) and were really trying to build up a following. Supposedly, their organizer had been in the business and was training them. Well, it didn't show. He also claimed a ring, house shows, and paydays were all "in the works." Of course, none of those things ever happened.

It would be easy for me to dismiss them as a bunch of stupid kids. However, I began to see a little of me in their faces. They were chasing the same dream I had chased. I can remember a lot of empty promises from fly-by-night promoters I worked for in my day. The only difference was that we had the rings and equipment, and those kids have nothing but Internet and public access television.

Looking back, I would be financially comfortable if I had a dollar for every time a promoter handed me a skinny pay envelope with the promise that he would be able to take care of me the next time. There was always some excuse for why "the next time" never came.

"The house was smaller than we expected."

"We had to pay one of the name guys a lot of money so he would come and build up the promotion."

"The receipts from the advance ticket sales won't be deposited until next week."

And, of course, there was the old standby: *"We don't have the gate counted yet. Here is a little to get you by until we figure up how much we have to work with. I'll send you a check or give it to you at the next show."*

Yep, the check's in the mail. After a while, we just laughed to ourselves, took our pay, and asked when and where he wanted us next.

So, I kind of feel sorry for some of those kids who just haven't caught on to the reality of the business. Unfortunately, the organizer makes some of those guys think they are pretty good. Most of them don't have a clue. Many of the young guys in the small, independent promotions have problems with timing and selling moves, but those problems are magnified ten times in the backyard kids. I always told the younger guys I worked with at Miller's, *"Don't sell it until you get it!"* I've seen the "recipient" of a clothesline move begin flopping two feet before he got to his opponent's arm. If you are afraid of getting a potato, a bump, or a bruise once in a while, you shouldn't be in the ring. I had an Internal Affairs Officer at the police department tell me one time that if a cop didn't get a complaint filed against him about once a year or so, he probably wasn't doing his job. In wrestling, if you didn't have a few wounds and scars to show, you probably weren't doing it correctly.

I always tried to convince trainees that a forearm shot to the chest needs to be planted. They need to feel it before they begin to sell it. I really think one of the problems is that the new guys today don't get the proper amount of ring time necessary to develop trust in their fellow wrestlers. I still see backdrops where the guy taking the bump barely touches the guy handing it out. My mind goes back to Miller's gym where you timed backdrops, and worked it so the guy taking the bump could try to get high enough to kick the ring lights. Sure, it sometimes made for some hard landings, but that was real good for business at a house show.

When I go to shows today, I see those rookie mistakes. I want to grab them and share some of my experience with them. If old school wrestling is going to survive (some say it's already extinct), the rookies are the ones who must carry the torch.

I recently discovered great videos of classic wrestling on the Internet. I found videos which featured Dick the Bruiser, The Sheik, Cowboy Bob Ellis, and others from "my day." The videos not only brought back great memories, but some gave me food for thought.

When I did a search on "wrestling gone wrong" or "wrestling accidents," I found things that made me cringe. And being a cop, I've seen a lot. I think those things upset me because I can envision those things happening to me or one of my friends. I'm lucky to be able to say that we never had a serious ring accident at any of the shows on which I was a participant. There was one incident where Johnny Dillinger bladed himself too deeply and went to the hospital for stitches, but I don't remember anyone suffering extremely serious issues. However, we all realized that the possibilities were there.

Most of the accident videos seem to involve props or stunts. In my day, we cut our foreheads with razor blades and hit each other with folding chairs. We hid "foreign objects" in our trunks, which we used on our "unsuspecting" opponents. Most of the time, the foreign object was nothing more than a tongue depressor wrapped heavily with gauze tape. That was a standard item carried by most heels from show to show.

Today, the wrestlers use ladders, tables, florescent tubes, and all sorts of external devices. Many of the videos of wrestling accidents revolve around one of those devices. In 1999, Owen Hart lost his life when a cable broke as he was being lowered into the ring from the rafters of the Kemper Arena in Kansas City. One video shows Mick Foley (as Mankind) and Undertaker wrestling on top of a cage in the 1999 King of the Ring show in Pittsburgh, Pennsylvania. When Foley is bodyslammed, he and part of the cage crash to the mat twelve feet below. In another, when a wrestler lands on a metal ladder, it flips up into the face of his opponent and splits him wide open. Other videos show bones breaking and sticking out through the skin, and guys landing on their spines on metal steps. That's scary stuff.

Still, even without the props, we had our share of bad bumps that resulted in painful, but not permanent, injury. I had my nose broken several times. I became quite familiar with that during amateur wrestling in high school. We were practicing an escape from someone who applies a bear hug from behind. The coach was teaching us to drop down and force the guy to break his grip. When I applied the bear hug to my partner, he dropped down, but threw back his head in the process and smashed my nose. I never forgot what that felt like. Most of all, I never forgot what the treatment felt like. I decided that future broken noses were best taken care of by letting them heal naturally, rather than have a doctor shove a metal instrument up my nose and then spread it out. There were several times when I heard that cracking sound and felt the pain, but I just ignored it. As long as I could still breathe through my nose, I wasn't going to visit the doctor!

One of my early matches was in a small town near Detroit. I wanted to make a good impression because some of the wrestlers on the card were sent to the show by Louie Klein and the Sheik. I knew my best attribute was the high and hard bumps. I'm a big man, but I could get way up in the air and make a big bang when I hit the mat. Unfortunately, although I had my "take offs" down pat, my "landings" sucked. I mastered that part of the business the hard way.

My opponent that night was Rick Rogers. Rick liked my style and let me do my thing. During the match, he gave me an arm drag. I went way up, but overcompensated and turned over too far. Instead of landing flat on my back, I landed on my butt. I flipped backwards and my head slammed into the mat. The padding on the ring was simply thin furniture blankets over plywood flooring.

When my head hit the deck, I immediately felt like someone inflated it with an air compressor. The headache was unbelievable. I continued with the match, though, and even took some more big bumps. Of course, I was really careful to keep my head off the mat. Even so, each time I hit the mat, I felt like my head was going to explode. My neck also ached from the apparent whiplash. After the match, I stumbled back to the dressing room. I couldn't hold up my head in any position without my neck hurting, and my head hurt so bad that I was nauseous. I was a trooper, though, and was determined not to say anything about being hurt. It was a macho thing and I wanted to act as if it was just another day at the office.

When I left the venue, I was faced with a three-hour drive home by myself. The trip seemed to take much longer than the three hours as I focused on holding up my head in a position that didn't hurt too much. I also worried about getting sick and vomiting all over the inside of my car. When I arrived home, I did another not-so-bright thing. I took some aspirin and went straight to bed. My doctor later chastised me, telling me I had the classic signs of a concussion, and the last thing I should have done was to lie down and go to sleep. You would think that by this point in my life, he should have been used to the fact that I never listened to him.

I had several more concussions during my career and I suffered cracked bones in my feet. I rarely brought those ailments to the attention of my doctor because I didn't want to hear the lectures about why I shouldn't work the next show. I always did, anyway!

Things like that made me think about why we went through all we did for a few bucks and a little excitement. Of course, I loved the business from the time I first saw a wrestling show on black-and-white TV. I liked all of the guys I worked with, and I enjoyed visiting different communities, but there were a lot of risks involved. Besides potential wrestling injuries, we worried about auto accidents, some of which claimed the careers and some of the lives of wrestlers like Larry Chene. Regardless of the possible dangers, we still got in the car and went on the road, week after week. But there was a time when I began to ask myself, *"Why am I doing this?"*

Certainly, there was the lure of getting a nightly "fifteen minutes of fame." When I strolled up to the ring and made eye contact with the fans, I saw the anger of knowing I was there to do harm to their hero. However, I also saw the respect they had for me. Whether I was a "good guy" or a "bad guy," they respected me. Even when I was in the company of "non-believers," who made fun of me and said they knew it was "all fake," they readily admitted that professional wrestlers were good athletes. In either case, that helped feed my often-bruised ego. None of the fans would have ever guessed that the Canadian Rose was lacking in self-confidence. Actually, that isn't exactly true. Harold West lacked self-confidence, but as his alter ego, the Canadian Rose, he was quite comfortable with himself. I went into the wrestling world with the assumption that I could be whoever I needed to be. As long as I was a good worker and was accepted by my peers, I had a confidence that I often lacked in the other areas of my life. I could face the challenges of the ring by being someone other than myself … someone other than Harold West, the fat kid from Muncie, Indiana. I could be whatever a promoter wanted me to be: Duke West, Mean Duke West, or the Canadian Rose. And, even when I lost a match, I could walk away with respect and a sense of accomplishment. I danced with danger and usually won.

I also find there is a parallel between the bond between wrestlers and the bond I experienced with my fellow police officers. In law enforcement, we had to depend on each other and trust that we had each others' backs. When things went bad, we depended on one another to make sure we all went home at the end of our shift. In wrestling, we also had to depend on our buddies. If I was going to lay prone on the mat while a 250-pound guy dropping onto me from the top rope, I had to trust he wasn't going to land with full force and do serious damage. I had to believe that everyone I got into the ring with was a pro, and they were going to trust me in the same way.

Likewise, we hoped our opponents would sell our moves for us so we didn't look like a complete boob out there. A really decent match always involved two pros who went back and forth and made each other look good. Even if we knew we were doing a job for somebody, and we were going to get soundly trounced, we expected them to let us have a few high spots of our own and to sell some of our stuff before that happened. I believe that's why wrestlers have a special bond that isn't found in many other occupations. That's why the reunions are so special. The friendships forged on that kind of trust lasts forever. A rogue cop in law enforcement soon loses the respect of his peers, and eventually finds himself very lonely. If he gets into trouble on the street, he may find his help is a step slower getting to him. A cop who is trusted and respected by his (or her) fellow officers knows they will bust their humps to get to them when the brown stuff hits the fan.

A wrestler who was a pro and worked well with his peers knew they would treat him (or her) the same. If you wanted to be a crowbar or a showboat, you could expect to get some potatoes and be roughed up by your opponents. They could be as stiff or as rough as you were. Most of the time, the guys who didn't return favors or who were unwilling to work properly, didn't have lasting careers in the wrestling business.

I think one of the other allures of the business was that we danced with danger. Every move had the potential of serious injury. Wrestlers did get hurt and sometimes died in the ring. That was always in the back of our minds. And yet, we always pushed the envelope to see how hard a bump we could take, how close we could come to actually having our head slam into the ring post, or how high we could go over the top rope to the floor. I believe that's why wrestling has evolved to what it has today. There is always that macho thing of trying to do one better than the next guy. The wrestlers want to fly higher and land harder than anyone else.

I can remember when the Beatles began the whole long-hair thing back in the '60s. A lot of the adults threw a fit about the Beatle's hair style. A few years later, the Beatle's hair was short. It seems like each group that followed had to have hair a little longer and a little wilder. When you look at early photos of the Beatles, you will see that their haircuts were very, very conservative compared to what we see today. The music also evolved into something besides the ballads and love songs they began with.

Likewise, wrestling has gotten crazier and crazier, and they push the limits to where they are "dancing with danger" on a nightly basis.

Putting all of that aside, wrestling was a good gig for an adrenaline junkie. Every match we walked away from without a serious injury was another conquest. It was exciting to go to the edge and come back. We were left with a good feeling when we would walk away after flying over the top rope and landing on the concrete floor. The danger was real, but we kept it in the back of our minds. We couldn't wait to get in the ring and meet it face to face.

All things considered, it was quite a ride.

Chapter 17

Good Guys, Bad Guys

I have said that a good wrestling match needs three components: a good babyface, a good heel, and a good ref. However, there is a fourth component that is the most important, and probably the least respected — the fans.

Over the years, I have taken quite a bit of ribbing about my experience in professional wrestling. I have heard all the talk about how fake it is, and how the fans are "trailer trash" and "rednecks." I was always amazed at how many people would go on and on with snide remarks about wrestling, only to finish up by asking if it really was all staged. I would simply smile and tell them the old saying: *"If you are a fan, no explanation is needed. If you are not, no explanation will do."* I have also had to laugh when folks trash the wrestling business in front of me, only to have someone in our party point out to them that I was a wrestler. It's funny how quickly the conversation changes.

Even today, there are a lot of people who think wrestling is a complete joke. They don't have any respect for anyone who is (or has been) involved in it. They view it as a glorified carnival act, a modern day medicine show put on by con men who try to bilk money out of the more ignorant souls in our society. If that were true, I would be ashamed and embarrassed for my participation in the wrestling game. I am not. I am thankful for those days when I was the Canadian Rose.

I had been a fan for many, many years, and a wrestler for several years, before I had my first opportunity to actually touch a championship belt. And yet, when I held that belt in my hands, it was as if there was something sacred about it. People can say the belts are just a sham and not real trophies. They can claim they aren't really earned in a true, competitive sport. They can say whatever they want, but I know what the belts represent: the history, the personalities, and the stories that are a part of everyone who ever wore that belt. They represent the elation felt by the grandparents, parents, and the youngsters when they saw the good guys lift the belt in victory. And, even as a hack wrestler who worked the "little" shows, I never lost my childlike dream of one day finding myself wearing one of those belts. I would have worn it with the thought of knowing how Grandpa and Dad would have been so proud. In what way could that be a sham?

Some folks would say that professional wrestlers are not athletes. In my day, I would challenge anyone who made such a claim to spend some time in the ring with us at Miller's gym. Not many of them could do what we did. How many 250- to 280-pound men can get themselves up in the air and plant a dropkick in the face and jaw of an opponent who stands six-feet tall? My finishing move, the flying rollover, required me to front flip or somersault, roll across my opponent's chest, and wind up back on my feet. One day a week at Miller's place, we spent hours wrestling each other in match after match and in scenario after scenario. That experience came in handy when we wrestled in Sylvania, Ohio, where we taped a whole month's worth of television shows in one day. Most of the moves and holds required precise timing, and the matches often ran from ten to twenty minutes with non-stop action. If you don't think that's a real workout, then try it for yourself. And when you wake up the next morning, go to your regular job and work an eight-hour shift, after which you can drive 100-plus miles to the next show. In most sports the coaches would have you sit out if you had a sore shoulder or sprained ankle. In the wrestling business, promoters expected you to be ready for the next show. They didn't want to hear about your problems. The only concern they had was to fill the card and make sure everybody showed up and worked as scheduled.

I can recall a few matches where the promoter would appear in the dressing room after a match and say, *"Are you okay? That was one hell of a bump you took out there!"*

When I said, *"Well, I twisted my ankle and it looks like it's starting to swell up,"* he would come back with, *"Well, you did good. Don't forget I need you in Parma by five thirty for tomorrow nights show."* That was the most sympathy we would get. I would take a few aspirins and be in Parma, or wherever I was scheduled to be, the next night.

I sometimes smile to myself when I hear someone talk about having gone to a wrestling match and seeing a wrestler limping down the aisle after a match. They would then recall seeing the guy stop limping when he went through the door or the curtain. They would use it as their proof that wrestling was "all fake." I never argued with them, but inside, I was thinking about the scenarios they never saw. There were times when, after beating my opponent, I would do my strut down the aisle. I would jeer at the fans and laugh about having beaten their hero. However, when I got inside the dressing room, I would flop onto the bench, or the floor, and writhe in pain, holding onto whatever part of my body I had strained or sprained. You can say I wasn't "a real athlete" if you want. However, I know that I, and many others like me in that day, often wrestled in spite of pain, total exhaustion, and illnesses that would have put a lot of other folks off work for weeks.

I owe my law enforcement career to the endurance and perseverance I learned in wrestling. When I went to the police academy in 1983, one of the drill instructors looked at my medical jacket and told me I would never make it through the training. I was 34 years old and competing against 21 to 30-year-old young men. I had been a Special Deputy, Reserve Officer, and Confinement Officer for many years, so I wasn't concerned about the academics. I knew the physical training was going to be tough. I had to get through twelve weeks of basic training with a bad back and occasional knee pain. To top it off, when

I was running to get ready for the academy, I sprained my ankle just one week before I reported to the academy.

Twelve weeks later, we were standing in formation, waiting to march in for graduation. That same D.I. shook my hand and told me that when the class began, he never thought I would be graduating. My other D.I. came along behind him and said, *"I knew you would make it. I saw you were determined to not let me or anyone else stop you."* I graduated fifth out of that class of 72 cadets. I know I made it in great part because of the lessons I had learned in the squared circle. My family and my extended family (my wrestling buddies) encouraged me and pushed me to succeed. How do you repay that? All I could do was try to be the best cop I could be ... just like I always tried to be the best wrestler I could be.

For those of you who say that wrestling fans are ignorant, then you are including me and my family, along with a lot of hard-working, honest, blue-collar Americans. My grandfather, a huge wrestling fan, never graduated from high school. And yet, I learned so much from him about life, especially how to treat my fellow man. He always told me to try to leave this world a little better off than the way I found it. He didn't just tell me that. He showed me. He was a kind, gentle, loving soul who never knew a stranger. If you visited my grandparent's home, you would be expected to stay for a meal. If you didn't stay, they would be very disappointed.

During the depression years, Grandpa was able to keep his job. He was one of only a few in our neighborhood that did. He and my Grandmother made sure they shared what they had. Leftovers were distributed from every meal to the neighborhood children. Every hobo that passed through the area knew that the West household would have a pot of soup, a sandwich, and a pot of coffee on for them. The two great sources of entertainment and enjoyment for my Grandparents were watching westerns and professional wrestling on TV. If they were ignorant or less than normal for that, I only wish this world was full of ignorant people.

Other than our fear that he was going to have a heart attack, we all got a kick out of seeing Grandpa rocking back and forth and side to side in his chair. Grandma would sit beside him with her arms folded, glaring at the bad guys and talking how something should be done about them. My mother would shake her head and complain about how awful the violence was, and how she couldn't stand to watch it. For some reason, however, whenever wrestling was on, she was right there in front of the TV with the rest of us. From time to time, when there was a conversation about wrestling, Grandpa would admit that he thought it had to be "put on," but that never swayed him from his Saturday routine of watching wrestling on TV.

Wrestling was a great outlet for folks of that era. World War II and the Great Depression left them with a lot of frustrations and uncertainties. They needed their heroes ... guys who would fight the good fight for them. Wrestling provided that for them, on TV and in the arenas, coliseums, and high school gyms. They shared the pain of the "good guys" when they were defeated by the dastardly machinations of the "bad guys." They rejoiced when the foreign menace, wrestlers like Fritz von Erich and Mitsu Arakawa, were defeated by good guys like Cowboy Bob Ellis and Pepper Gomez. Ordinary people relived for a moment the joy they felt when our country won World War II and they were told their loved ones would be coming home. Week after week, they would see the bad guys win their matches, until Wilbur Snyder, Bobo Brazil, or Dick the Bruiser came along to defeat them and administer justice to the evildoers. I know that people often felt there was no justice in their world. It left them with a good feeling to see something made right, and that the good guys do finish first. For one hour every week, my grandfather, my father, and countless others like them could put their daily struggles out of their minds and let the wrestlers fight their battles. They could sit one out. I'm sure many of them secretly envisioned their boss, or some other person who had brought grief, being pounded by one of their heroes. Perhaps all wasn't right with the world, but they could see a ray of hope when the good guys prevailed against the bad guys.

I have to admit that it's very likely that many of the fans never finished high school, and you would be hard pressed to find many of them who had ever seen the inside of a college. I'm sure they never had to make a choice of whether to attend the opera or the wrestling matches. I doubt they missed the TV matches because they were having an afternoon tea with the mayor. And yet, they were the folks who were the backbone of our country. They deserved a little rest and relaxation, and we tried our best to give that to them.

I continued to be a fan even after I got into wrestling. I loved to watch a good match even when I wasn't on the card. We often would try to slip out of the dressing room to find a quiet place where we could watch our buddies work. Years later, when I got out of wrestling, I continued to watch it on TV. At least, I did until the big promotions began putting on outlandish, soap-opera-type stuff that was too ridiculous for me to stomach. The old-school wrestling we did backed up the values my family taught me. The good guys were good guys and the bad guys were bad guys ... and the good guys eventually won. The battles we fought were pretty much black and white. A good guy took on the bad guy. There were no grey areas and the fans always knew which one of the two wrestlers in the ring was the good guy. We lost that when the WWF became the WWE. Today, the good guys are the bad guys, and vice versa. Our heroes have been cheapened and the line between good and evil has been blurred.

I think there are still a lot of old-school wrestling fans who long for the bygone days. The days when they weren't separated from their heroes by steel barricades. The days when a good show didn't mean an outlandish production. A time when your favorite wrestler appeared to be human, and not some "super-human" cartoon character. The wrestlers of the past came across as being (and often were) approachable.

Most importantly, I think there is a fan base out there who just can't afford to be fans of the big promotions. I haven't looked in some time, but the last time I looked at ticket prices when the WWE came to town, "nosebleed seats" were more than 30 dollars a ticket! I recently dug out the poster from the show where I met Moose Cholak. Ticket prices were $5.00 and $3.50 if you bought them in advance. Today, tickets for WWA Bruiser Wrestling run about

$15.00 at the door and $10.00 in advance. Sure, the WWA shows don't have the fireworks and special effects, but the fans get their money's worth in action. Good, honest, decent, hard-working people like my family deserve the opportunity to have some fun. That is what wrestling was and should be — fun! If they had half as much fun watching wrestling as I did actually doing it, then they got their five dollars worth.

You can look down your nose at wrestling fans. You can make fun of them and call the whole thing a big put-on. But wrestling fans are out there in the millions. Many of them no longer attend the matches, but they are there.

You see, wrestling is a lot more that just cheap entertainment, a sport, or any combination thereof. If you have wrestling in your blood, as a fan or a wrestler, it stays with you forever. I have been blessed to have been both. I no longer watch the matches on TV. It was years between the end of my last wrestling match and the next time I attended a live show. And yet, many times, I would open my dresser drawer to look at my trunks and tights. Those sweet memories of family, friends, and fellow wrestlers of the past always seemed to make my day a little brighter. It doesn't matter what you call it ... wrestling or 'rasslin'. You can call it fake, a glorified carnival act, an athletic event, a violent and cruel sport, or just entertainment. Whatever the label, professional wrestling was all about having a good time and building memories with friends and family.

I know what it has been to me. That wonderful business brought my family closer together. When I was a kid, Roy Rogers was one of my heroes, but to see Roy Rogers in person was all but impossible for a kid from Muncie, Indiana. And yet, we could always look forward to hearing those words each Saturday on *Championship Wrestling, "You fans in the Muncie area — Friday night, May 10th, Championship Wrestling will be at the Delaware County Fairgrounds at 7:00 p.m. with all your favorite stars."* Cowboy Bob Ellis, Wilbur Snyder, Pepper Gomez, Bobo Brazil, and the other wrestling stars of that day became my Roy Rogers.

In some way, perhaps wrestling influenced me to become a cop. I wanted to be the guy who rushed in to save the day, and just maybe, when I slapped the cuffs on the bad guys, I was recapturing that feeling of euphoria we got when Cowboy Bob Ellis charged into the ring to save the day. Maybe, just maybe, being a cop made me feel like I was making a difference for the better in this world. The wall of my office is adorned with plaques, awards, and mementos of my law enforcement career. At one end of the wall, however, is a section of which I am just as proud. There hangs my Cauliflower Alley Club membership certificate, a photo of me as the Canadian Rose, and a recent photo of me with Dick the Bruiser, Jr.

Chapter 18

Life Lessons from the Squared Circle

My brief excursion into the world of professional wrestling is explained by all of the enjoyment I received in and out of the ring. And yet, how is it that a kid from Indiana, who was raised on the Hoosier values of hard work, Christian charity, and integrity, would wander into a sometimes less-than-honest profession. Some would say that the business is dishonest by its' very nature of deception. Certainly, on more than one occasion, I was victimized by promoters who promised money that never appeared or promised a push that never happened. There was also a fair share of wrestlers who were of the type that I prayed my daughters would never date when they got older. Still, I was drawn to it like a bug to the light.

My parents raised me to be a Christian. I accepted Christ at an early age. In fact, I believed I had a calling to the ministry. When I approached our pastor about my beliefs, he simply told me that he "didn't know what to do with me." He told me he would talk to his superiors in the church and get back to me. When I called several times to follow up, he put me off, and after a time, it was never mentioned again. I became frustrated and discouraged, especially as the national church continued to cite the shortage of pastors and talked about actively recruiting young people for their seminary.

I had also been raised to respect our political leaders. I saw that many of them were not worthy of respect. I saw "dirty" politics first hand and did not see how those people could then go out into public and claim to represent the morals and values that I wanted to believe in. So, I walked away from the church, I didn't vote, and generally became soured on much of life. I was let down by friends, dumped rather unceremoniously by my first "love," and found the institutions I was told I could trust, the church and the state, were not always trustworthy.

What was left for me to identify with? What was left for me to believe in and cling to in this world? So, in this rebellion, venturing into the wrestling business was not an issue. Even if it wasn't "real," what in this life was? If I enjoyed it, the fans enjoyed it, and it gave me some identity, why not?

After leaving wrestling, I was able to throw myself into my work as a police detective. Of course, in that business, you did not see much to give you much faith in your fellow man. That is why cops tend to hang out with each other. They often struggle with trusting anyone outside of the profession.

Like kayfabe in wrestling, we were careful when we talked to a stranger, unless they had a uniform or a badge. I sometimes saw this mistrust lead to bitterness, and even abuse, against citizens. I never wanted to get to that point. I became a cop to help others. I worked to include folks from all walks of life in my circle of friends.

I never quit believing in God or country either. However, my jaded view of life led me to feel that man had so screwed up these institutions that they were best to be avoided. And, during my time of rebellion, I came to believe that because of the things I have done, I wasn't worthy. Maybe my belief that I was called to the ministry wasn't real. Perhaps the reason why the church didn't immediately guide me toward the seminary was that God was rejecting me. Or maybe I was more like the heel than the baby face that I want to be.

I had associated myself with some pretty "seedy" people in both the wrestling business and law enforcement. It took a great deal of time before I learned to accept who I was and work on being better, rather than worrying about what I have been. If the church is screwed up, it's not God's fault. He turned it over to us! Am I unworthy? Yes, but who isn't? I also remembered what I had learned about Jesus. The people he chose to hang out with were characters, too. He picked fishermen. I don't think the commercial fishermen of his day were much different than those of today. They weren't exactly choir boys. Tax collectors were not considered high moral leaders in that day, either.

I somehow believe that Jesus would be comfortable today in the dressing room of an arena talking to a bunch of rough and tough wrestlers. After all, wrestling imitates life. And, no matter where we are in this life, God is there. The life lessons from the squared circle somewhat parallel the lessons of the Bible.

At a time when the greatest heel ever known was beating the babyfaces into submission, God sent Jesus as a "run in" to save the day. Even when the heel thought he had put Jesus away, he came back and claimed the victory. In wrestling, the good guys eventually wind up on top. The Bible tells us that the good guys will inherit the earth.

Sometimes, when promoters and others we trusted in the wrestling business let us down, we still did our best to go out and put on a good show. If we trust in people or in ourselves alone, we will be disappointed. If we trust in God and believe that he will help us in all we do, we will be happy.

In 1998, my wife died of brain cancer. I saw her life change in that last year as God worked to prepare her for what only He knew was ahead. She only had to trust and believe. In the year before that, I went through the loss of two of my fellow officers in the line of duty. I had been living under threats against my life. I had to reexamine my faith and my own beliefs. Life is precious and short.

I was never a great success as a wrestler. I sometimes let myself and others down in the business, in law enforcement, and in life. However, I know that as long as I have Christ for a tag team partner, he'll be there to bail me out when I am on the ropes. He will stand by me when I screw up. He will coach me when I struggle. When I need correction, he will be the referee who warns me to change my behavior. And, most of all, someday when this battle called life is over — when I get the final three count — he will put that gold belt around my waist and no one can take it from me.

I loved the wrestling business. I sometimes think that if I had only done this or that I might have been more successful in the ring, and maybe got in on some of the big money. However, would that have been worth the price I would have paid.

God is the greatest promoter. He is honest and always does for us what we really need done. He knows what will put us over. He will give us the big push. And, when the show is over, we will get the fat pay envelope!

Most of all, when we let him down, he doesn't cast us aside. He doesn't "blackball" us, and he is ready to put us right back on the card.

What more could a "rassler" ask for?

Chapter 19

The Kayfabe Generation

I hope I have been able to keep the names and dates straight. My memory isn't what it once was. It is also important to keep in mind my role in the business. Most of the shows I worked were small promotions. Often, they were one-time shots where I never crossed paths with the promoter or the other wrestlers again.

I wrestled during the time near the end of the TV era when the regional promotions, like WWA, were no longer drawing big houses. The Bruiser/Snyder shows, which once sold out venues like the Allen County War Memorial Coliseum in Fort Wayne, or the grandstands at the Indiana State Fair, were now seeing about half of those seats being empty. More often, their house shows were held in smaller venues like armories or high school gyms.

With few regional promotions still in business, the regulars were getting fewer bookings and were firmly entrenched in the Chicago/Indianapolis area. At some point, many of them tried their hand at promoting or booking shows. They booked some shows as vehicles to raise money for charities, while others were just looking to make a few extra bucks. Homer Miller became the "one-stop shopping" location for the ring and wrestlers to fill out their cards. They would, of course, book themselves and some of their buddies on the top of the show and we would fill in the rest. The guys who ran more than one show usually rented the ring from Miller and then booked us directly. That really began when the guys complained about Miller's short pay envelopes. Nobody wanted to complain directly to Miller for fear of being cut out of the gym. We figured we had a better chance of getting paid if we could arrange to work a deal directly with the promoters of the shows.

During the run I had working shows in the Warsaw area, I can't remember who the actual promoter(s) were. Originally, Homer Miller ran the shows. Later, Paul Christy and (maybe) Moose Cholak ran the shows in that area. Eventually, Bobby Golden became the promoter and ran several shows in the Warsaw, Elkhart, and South Bend areas.

My bookings often came with a phone call from Homer Miller or Bobby Golden. They would ask if I was available on such and such a night. If I was, all they had to say was where to be and when, or Bobby would say, *"Be at my place at two o'clock."* Usually, Bobby would fill me in on at least some of the details, but often, I just showed up not knowing who I was working with, who

I was working for, or how much I was supposed to get paid. If, at the end of the night, I got a pay envelope that I didn't have to put my shoes on to keep it from floating away, I was happy.

I wish I had kept better records, but I just didn't. Remember, after a time, I came to the realization that wrestling was never going to be more than an expensive hobby for me. After awhile, one show just seemed to blend into another. Usually, I wrestled guys who were in the same boat I was. I had never heard of them and they had not heard of me.

That being said, I apologize if I left out someone who remembers those days, and if I mixed up a location or date, I'm sorry. I hope they will read this book, smile, and then look me up and say, *"Don't you remember when we ... ?"* If Bobby were still with us, this would not have been an issue. He would have been sitting right beside me recalling the names, dates, and places. He also would have recalled many stories that probably aren't suitable for print. It would have been a Bobby Golden–Duke West tag team event.

As it is, you have the memories of an old man about a magical time in the lives of some fellows who loved wrestling and every moment we spent in the ring or on the road. I hope this humble effort to share that experience with the readers will bring them even a few moments of joy, such as we had in living that life. I hope it brings some readers the smiles I saw on the faces of those fans at ringside. If so, it has been worth every hour spent at the computer.

Several things have happened since I first began putting this book together. A few years ago, while surfing the Internet, I stumbled across an organization called the Cauliflower Alley Club, an organization of wrestlers and boxers (mostly retired) and their fans. Their motto is "The Ring of Friendship." As I looked through the photos and the names on their website, I was taken back to the good old days of wrestling that I grew up watching, and the days in which I wrestled. I signed up for that group right away.

Someday, I hope to get the opportunity to attend the annual reunion they have in Las Vegas. I don't think anyone there will remember a Midwest hack wrestler who called himself the Canadian Rose. However, I am told that I will be just as welcome at that gathering as any of the old-time legends who will be in attendance.

Scott Teal, the wrestling historian who writes, edits, and publishes books through his company, *Crowbar Press*, encouraged me to head down to the Gulf Coast Wrestler's Reunion in Mobile, Alabama. I was hesitant at first. I had heard about the reunion being a get-together of true wrestling legends. Having never worked the south, I was sure that nobody there would have heard of me, much less worked with me, and I wasn't too sure that a part-time, no-name wrestler like me would be welcome. Scott assured me that I would fit right in, and described the gathering as a family reunion. I decided that since I was planning to attend a Cauliflower Alley Club reunion in the near future, the Gulf Coast get-together might be a good "warm up" to that event. If I felt uncomfortable, I could cancel my plans for attending the Cauliflower Alley event. Besides, if we didn't feel welcome at the reunion, my wife and I could leave and spend time with one of her friends in Pensacola, Florida, which was less than an hour from Mobile.

Before we left for Mobile, my wife called from work to ask me to bring a picture of the Canadian Rose. One of her co-workers had a grandson who was a huge wrestling fan. He was ten or eleven years old and he was thrilled to find out that his grandmother knew an ex-wrestler. I autographed one of the photos and took it to my wife. The next day, she called to tell me how excited the boy had been to receive the photo. She decided that the next time Dick the Bruiser, Jr. had a show in the area, we would take the young man with us. Sure enough, a few weeks after we returned home from Mobile, he had a show in Lima, Ohio.

With the boy and his grandmother in tow, we made the one-hour trip to Lima. Dick the Bruiser, Jr. was at the front door and greeted us when we arrived. When I introduced him to our young friend, he invited him to stop by his table at intermission so he could give him an autographed photo.

When we entered the main theater, I was sure it was the same place in which I had wrestled many years before. It was one of those old, ornate structures that were common for the movie houses of years gone by. The main floor had been converted into a reception hall. The seats were gone and there was a few round tables scattered about. The ring was up against the stage. They managed to find us some seats in the second row and we settled in for some old fashion 'rasslin'.

I don't know for sure that it was the same building in which I had once worked, but the feeling was still there. My mind flashed back many years to a day when I, Bobby Golden, Jim Lancaster, and many others, were in that ring. On that night, we watched a new generation of wrestlers in a resurrected version of the old WWA. Somehow, they managed to recapture much of the feel that Dick the Bruiser, Wilbur Snyder, and Bobo Brazil gave to that era. It was an evening replete with nostalgia.

During intermission, I took our young friend up to the gimmick table, where he collected autographs and photos from the babyfaces on the card. One of them, a big guy who worked under a mask, gave the youngster a souvenir that he'll cherish for years. He picked up the boy and held him upside down, like he was going to bodyslam him, and told us to take a picture. At first, I thought the boy might be scared and upset, but when he was back on his feet, he looked over at me with a huge grin on his face.

The previous show I had attended was in Auburn, Indiana. I had given a copy of my chapter on Bobo Brazil to "Jr.'s" wife. She read it during the show and told me she would give it to him. Bobo, Jr. and his wife were both there that night in Lima. She recognized me right away and pointed me out to him. He thanked me and told me he had really enjoyed it.

A few days later, my wife brought home a handwritten thank-you note from my little friend. I guess you could say that, after all of these years, the Canadian Rose finally got a fan letter that wasn't threatening. He told his grandmother that he liked the show a lot better than the shows he saw on television. Thinking back on that, it gives me hope that there may be a new generation of fans out there who will keep the small promotions alive. In fact, in Lima, I saw a whole new generation of fans who came to see live wrestling in a venue the larger promotions wouldn't touch.

During the Lima show, an announcement was made that WWA Bruiser Wrestling would be broadcast on a television station in Toledo. Perhaps I was too quick to write off the smaller operations as a dying breed. When you think about it, there may always be a market for those kinds of shows. That being the case, the national promotions should not see them as a threat. In fact, I believe they should embrace and encourage them.

Back in those old days, if a guy wore out his gimmick, or didn't like what a promoter was doing with him, he would just move on to another territory. I remembered Moose Cholak coming into the Indianapolis territory as a heel. He called himself "Golden Moose Cholak." After a time, he disappeared, but later returned as a babyface and wrestled as "Yukon Moose" Cholak. There was a core of wrestlers who stayed in the territory, but many big names moved in and out. When they returned, they were fresh again, and would begin or rekindle feuds with former opponents in the area.

Today, movement from place to place is impossible as there is no place for talent to go. That's sad because there are very few places where a young wrestler can learn his craft. The NBA has the developmental league. Major League Baseball has the minor league system. Several minor leagues in hockey feed into the NHL. I think outfits like the WWE could take a lesson from them by encouraging and helping independent promotions. The independents would give them a new talent base from which to create future "superstars." When a wrestlers' star begins to fade, they could return to the independent groups and work, until the appropriate time when the WWE felt like they could bring them back.

Mobile turned out to be a great experience. We were greeted at the door like long-lost friends and made to feel quite welcome. Bill Bowman, Cowboy Bob Kelly, and many others went out of their way to be sure we were comfortable. Several times, we were approached by one of the regulars, who asked if we needed anything. When they introduced us to the other attendees, not one of them asked about what status I had as a wrestler. I would tell them where I was from and they would ask about some of the guys who worked that area. Several of them shared war stories from the days when they had wrestled in Indiana, Michigan, and Ohio. They were all quite willing to have their pictures taken, and many of them asked to have their photo taken with me. The event was exactly as Scott had said it would be — a family reunion. And even I, a distant cousin several times removed, was made to feel like a part of that family.

The wrestling business was our common bond. No matter at what level we participated, our experiences were all much the same. The older folks like me, who were part of what I call the "kayfabe generation," all shared the secrets of the business. That alone made us a brotherhood and sisterhood. The young wrestlers who were there really seemed to appreciate the trails us old farts blazed for them. I was glad to hear Bill Moody (aka Percy Pringle, aka Paul Bearer) step up to the microphone and tell the young guys to quit calling themselves "jobbers" or "workers." *"You are wrestlers,"* he said. *"Hold your heads up and be proud of it."* It felt good to hear that from a man who (if he isn't already) is probably going to be in wrestling's hall of fame. I could

Scott Teal and Duke West in Mobile, Alabama at the 2009 Gulf Coast Wrestlers Reunion

relate to what he said. There were times in the business when I became discouraged, or put myself down as just a "jobber." When I was wrestling, it would have meant a lot to me to hear that from someone like Bill.

That event, which I had envisioned as a small gathering, actually drew more than 200 people, and the number of young people who attended came as a real surprise to me. I met members of a whole new generation of wrestlers who love the business and are willing to give the fans what they want. Many of them were just like me, willing to leave home and drive hundreds of miles, regardless of how much money was in their pay envelope at the end of the day. One young man talked to me about how much he enjoyed working under the hood (wearing a mask). I told him that I had tried it, but didn't care for it. That led to a conversation about the advantages and disadvantages of the mask, and the various storylines and gimmicks that go with it. He was a young man who didn't look at all like a wrestler. However, his enthusiasm and interest in what I had to say reminded me of the hopefuls who showed up at Miller's gym. Those of us who kept the passion and enthusiasm stayed, while the others drifted away.

I talked to some young people who were working for independent promotions in the south, and it seems that some of those promotions are doing quite well. It made me feel good to have one particular young man ask me about my experiences, and I felt even better when he asked me for any advice I might give him. Some of his questions took me back to a day when I was new in the business. I had asked many of those same question to the veterans I met. Of course, it also made me feel pretty damn old.

During the reunion, I was privileged to meet Dick Beyer, who was (and is) a big name in Japan as the Intelligent, Sensational Destroyer. He was a great guy who made me feel quite comfortable. Dick, a true legend of the sport, has been in the wrestling business since 1954. That's more than 55 years, and yet, he still had that spark in his eye when we talked about the business. Later, I saw him talking with a group of the young guys. I hope they appreciated him taking the time to speak with them as much as I did. I wondered how many of today's "superstars" would take the time to speak with "bush league" wrestlers.

Recently, I had occasion to be in Michigan and passed through the LaPorte area on my way home. I stopped to look through a phone book for the name Homer Miller. I found several listings for that name. I couldn't believe that in a small community like the LaPorte/Kingsford Heights area, there could have more than one Homer! One of the listings was for a Homer Miller in Kingsford Heights and I was sure it must be the Homer I knew. However, when I called the phone number, a recording informed me that the number was no longer in service.

I headed for home and drove south through town and down to Kingsford Heights. I hoped I would recognize the drive that led to the old gym. What I did find was a large building positioned on the highway with a lot of lumber, windows, doors, etc. on the lot behind a large fence. Right there on the sign in the front were the words, "Miller's Salvage." It did not appear that anyone was around and I had to get home, but I was sure it had to be Homer or some of his family.

On November 19, 2009, decided to make a run back up there to verify if it was indeed Homer Miller's place, or if someone there could give me some information on him. When I arrived, I was greeted by a gentleman named Charlie, who looked like he could have been an old wrestler. He was an older fellow with long, grey hair in a pony tail. He was a big guy, too. When I told him I was trying to locate a Homer Miller, he escorted me into an office and told me that it was Homer's place, but he wasn't there at the moment. Still, I wondered if this was the Homer Miller I knew. As soon as I stepped into the office, I saw an old poster on the wall advertising a wrestling match between Billy Goelz and Homer Miller. I had found him.

When I told Charlie who I was and why I was looking for Homer, he agreed to give him a call to see if he was at home. Charlie said, *"Homer, there's a Duke West here to see you."* After listening for a few seconds, Charlie looked at me and asked, *"Are you the Duke West from Fort Wayne?"* I shook my head yes and Charlie relayed that news to Homer. He hung up and said Homer was on his way.

While we waited, Charlie told me that Homer was now 82 years old. A few years ago, he had quadruple bypass surgery, and a month ago, he had a pacemaker installed. And yet, he still worked every day. That was the Homer I knew. Sitting still was never in his nature. As Charlie said, *"If he ever stopped working, it would kill him."* Charlie, a retired heavy-equipment operator who worked for Miller to have something to do, said he used to watch Miller wrestle.

When Homer arrived, there was no indication that he was now an 82-year-old man. He charged into the office and grabbed me by the hand. *"I've been thinking about you, Duke. I was wondering if you were still around and if you were okay."* He quickly introduced me to Charlie (the same way he introduced me to several others that day) as *"Duke West, who wuzz'a helluv'a 'rassler in his day."* Gee! Talk about making me feel old.

We sat and reminisced about days gone by. He rattled off the names of some of the old guys we knew and worked with. His eyes would dim as he would throw out a name and say, *"He's gone now. Died several years ago."* Or, *"I used to run into him now and then, but I don't know whatever happened to him."*

He said the "The Great Sobie" (I think his name was Rick Sobieski) stopped by once in a while. Tommy Lynch was still running his weightlifting gym in South Bend, but he didn't have a telephone. He said if I came back to visit again, we would drive over to South Bend and look him up. He also reminded me about Lou Botka, who I had forgotten about. I remembered Lou as a guy who used to come to the gym quite often. He showed a lot of potential, but he seemed to lose interest after a while. Homer reminded me about a Sunday when Lou didn't show up, even after he had told Homer and Bobby that he would be there. They later learned that while he was on his way, he struck and killed a child on a bicycle. He was never the same after that.

I gave Homer a bad time about his failure to tell Ted about my scheme to tear up the extra certificate from the Scouts. He just gave me that same old silly grin and chuckled in the same way that I remembered whenever we got something on him. We laughed together as he relayed how he had also been the victim of Bobby Golden's patented head scissors/gas attack hold. I wanted to ask him why he didn't go to Bobby's funeral, but as he talked about "the guys," I could see in his eyes that under that thick outer crust was a big heart. I don't think Homer wanted to take a chance that someone might see him cry. He was a 'rassler and he had to uphold that tough guy image. If he had been at Bobby's funeral, he would have seen a whole group of us tough guys tear up.

Homer Miller [2009]

Homer Miller and Duke West [2009]

The visit sure made me think. I wish I had told those guys back then what a pleasure it was to know them. I wondered, *"Why didn't we try harder to stay in touch?"* I wish I had thanked them all for being a part of my life, and for all of the pleasure they gave to me and to my family when we watched "'rasslin." Maybe that's what is so special about the wrestling reunions. The tough guys get a chance to share those memories and let each other know they are appreciated ... that there is a special bond between us. That was the first time I ever heard Homer Miller tell anyone that I was a "helluv'a 'rassler." It was great to hear that from a guy who had worked with Bruiser, Snyder, Lou Thesz, the Sheik, and all those guys I grew up watching. He never told me that when I worked with him. Of course, I never told him that I appreciated him, either. I guess that's a good lesson about life for all of us. Share your appreciation with the people who mean something in your life. Tomorrow is never promised to us.

When Homer asked if there was any wrestling shows going on in the Fort Wayne area, I told him about Tim Replogle's operation. Miller said, *"You can't make any money in the business these days. I tried to watch the 'rasslin that's on TV now, but there's nothing to it. It's all a bunch of talk. It's like a circus or something. You don't see the holds and moves like we used to do. Of course, they do some stuff that I would never have tried to do. The 'rasslers today make good money, but they don't last long. We did it for fun and not for the money, and we always gave the people a good show."*

Amazing. It was like I was hearing myself talking.

Homer gave me his telephone number and made me promise that I would stop and see him again. He said he had loaned all his old photos from the gym to Ted (Teddy Bear Ted) and never got them back. He said he didn't even have a picture of Bobby. I assured him I would give him copies of the few photos I have left.

I had to chuckle as he remembered all the promoters that he had trouble getting money out of. I also recalled some of the small shows he ran where he didn't exactly hand out fat pay envelopes. Still, when I left him that day, I really appreciated that conversation. It was a great time for all of us. The money wasn't as important as the business. Even Homer said he had no complaints, even though he "never made any money." We all sure did a lot of complaining back then. I guess time helps put all things into perspective.

I hope I do see Homer again soon. I hope we again share those memories. I hope he knows now that I do appreciate him.

I wish I had been given an opportunity to make the big money and wrestle in high-profile matches. I would have loved to have seen Canadian Rose action figures sold in department stores. I will never be in wrestling's Hall of Fame (unless I buy a ticket) and my name will never be listed among the legends of the sport. And yet, I take great pride in having been in the presence of those who are. During my lifetime, I have talked with hockey players and baseball players who never made it out of the minor leagues. They seldom talk of opportunities lost ... only of the pride of having taken the field or the ice and playing the game they loved. I felt much the same way. I had an opportunity that many people never had. I got to be a part of the game I loved.

Perhaps, if I had worked harder to build a better physique, if I had been willing to take steroids, or if I had been willing to go all out and sacrifice my regular job, I could have been more "successful" in the wrestling business. However, I have to say that I am quite satisfied with being who I was without compromising my values.

Going all the way in any trade does not always equate to success. Every time I worked a show, it was like a new adventure. I felt like a kid going to the circus for the first time. I never lost the excitement and thrill of it all.

I worked with and alongside some of the legends of the business. Some of them seemed to have kept their enthusiasm and passion for the game, but I met many others who looked at wrestling as just a job. They may have been at the top, but their spirits were down at the bottom. Without joy and a good spirit, there is no real success ... not just in wrestling, but in all of life. Looking back on things, I wouldn't give up a minute of what I experienced for what some of those guys had, but never seemed to appreciate.

I hope I'm right about the small regional promotions finding a niche in the wrestling market. I hope that some of the young guys I met in Mobile will someday look back with the same good feelings I have. I hope that more youngsters, like my little friend who went with us to Lima, will have shows to attend. I hope there will be more Tim Replogles out there to promote those shows and make them affordable and family friendly. I have to confess. You can call me old-fashioned, but if the wrestlers in the days of my youth did some of the things I've seen on cable, my parents would never have allowed me to watch wrestling. In fact, my parents wouldn't have watched it, either.

I also wonder if the "superstars" of today will ever be in an organization like the Cauliflower Alley Club, or will too many of them allow their oversized egos and fat wallets to cloud them from seeing what the wrestling business is really all about. We may not have much in common with the wrestlers of this modern era, but what we did have was a common passion that forged bonds, friendships, and memories that will last a lifetime. Not one of the "superstars" of today makes enough money to buy that.

It has been close to 30 years since I left the wrestling game. Even with all the time that has passed, I still get an occasional ribbing about my pink tights. Many times, I will meet someone, and the next time I see them, they will have met a mutual acquaintance who told them about the Canadian Rose. Unlike the past, however, I am no longer embarrassed by it.

I embrace it.

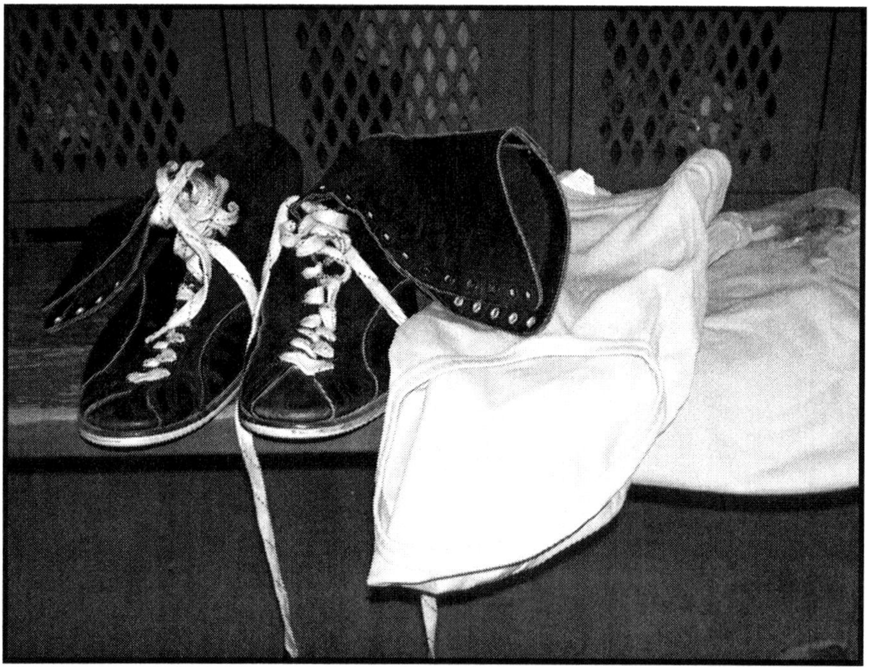

About the Author

A native of Muncie, Indiana, H.E. West moved to the Fort Wayne area as a young adult. He became involved with the Allen County Police Department, first as a reserve officer, and later became a civilian employee in the county jail before being commissioned as a sworn police officer in 1983.

Duke became involved in professional wrestling and spent seven years on various independent shows throughout the Midwest. He was best known as "The Canadian Rose," a flamboyant "bad guy" with pink trunks. A nagging back injury forced him to get out of the business as a wrestler, but he continued as a referee for several years before giving that up to concentrate on his law enforcement career.

As a police officer, West became known for his dogged pursuit of those who prey on the elderly and other at risk citizens. He has received numerous commendations and awards on the local and national level for his efforts. Duke is credited with helping draft and work for legislation that made certain crimes against the elderly a felony in the state of Indiana. He is still frequently called upon to speak for senior groups, police agencies, and other venues on senior safety and crime prevention. He also started a program called "Safe at Home" in Allen County, Indiana, which provides instant access to vital information on seniors and at risk citizens to emergency personnel.

West resides in New Haven, Indiana where he serves on the city council and is in his seventh term as president of that body. Still a fan, West continues to watch "old school" wrestling on T.V. and in person whenever he can. He credits the wrestling business with giving him many life lessons and confidence that made a difference in his career and his personal life. Even those who are not wrestling fans have commented on how they enjoy hearing his stories during his speaking engagements about his time as "The Canadian Rose." "Long Days and Short Pays" is an effort to put those stories in writing for others to enjoy.

INDEX

WELCOME GULF COAST
WRESTLER REUNION

— **Also from Crowbar Press** —

Is That Wrestling Fake?

The Bear Facts

by Ivan Koloff

with Scott Teal

ISBN: 978-0-9745545-4-9

6 x 9 Perfect Bound

208 pages, 205 B&W photographs

For decades, professional wrestling fans have asked the question – "Is that wrestling fake?"

However, they wouldn't have dared ask that question directly to Ivan Koloff, whose work in the ring made believers out of the most cynical viewers.

Growing up on a farm in Ontario, Ivan learned the meaning of hard work and discipline. Unfortunately, he made wrong choices and wound up in prison for cattle rustling. Upon his release, he enrolled in a wrestling school and began a career in pro wrestling as Red McNulty, the Irish Rogue.

Five years later, on January 18, 1971, he appeared in Madison Square Garden under the name Ivan Koloff and did what had never been done before. He pinned Bruno Sammartino's shoulders to the mat and won the WWWF heavyweight title. When the referee called for the bell, you could have heard a pin drop as the more than 21,000 screaming fans were instantly moved to a stunned, disbelieving silence.

That accomplishment made Ivan Koloff one of wrestling's biggest superstars until his retirement from the ring in the mid-1990s. Competing in virtually every major promotion throughout the world, he feuded with every top name in the wrestling business, including Andre the Giant, Ric Flair, Dick the Bruiser, Bob Backlund, Billy Robinson, Dusty Rhodes, and Ivan Putski.

Here for the first time, Ivan tells the story of his life: the highs and the lows; his admission of alcohol and drug abuse; reflections of a life spent on the road and the toll it took on his body and soul; and the event that took place in a small church in Kannapolis, North Carolina, that changed his life forever.

To schedule book signings, author interviews for print or online media, or personal appearances, or for more information about Crowbar Press, please contact **Scott Teal** at (615) 824-3347
or e-mail crowbarpress@1wrestlinglegends.com

— Also from Crowbar Press —

Wrestlers Are Like Seagulls: From McMcMahon to McMahon

by James J. Dillon

with Scott Teal and Philip Varriale

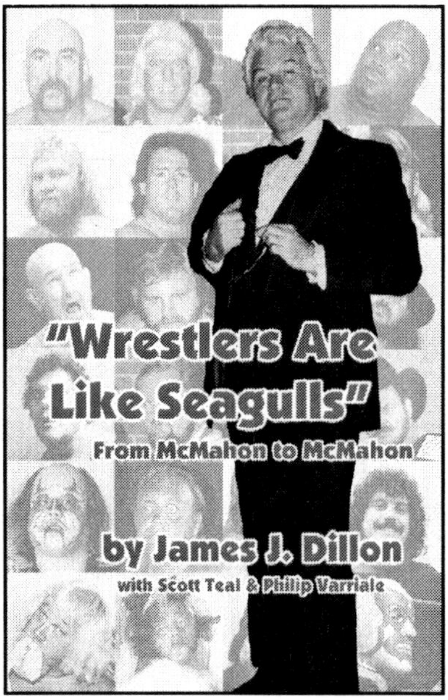

ISBN: 0-9745545-2-9
6 x 9 Hardcover
360 pages, 208 B&W photographs

For more than 40 years, James J. Dillon has been involved in the world of professional wrestling. Now he speaks candidly on all aspects of both his career and his personal life.

J.J. Dillon offers a first-hand account and detailed history of one of the most influential wrestling promotions in wrestling history — the World Wrestling Federation. For 7½ years, JJ served in the WWF as Vince McMahon's top lieutenant, right-hand man, and Vice President. Never before has someone from McMahon's inner circle written a book with an insider's perspective of the company.

JJ also gives a insider's perspective on the ludicrous business decisions made by executives who took World Championship Wrestling down a path that led to the company's destruction and eventual demise.

From the highs of making big money, winning championship titles, rubbing elbows with top celebrities, and appearing on television every week — to the lows of filing for bankruptcy, extramarital affairs, divorces, and drug use — no stone is left unturned when J.J. Dillon tells his story.

In this book, there are truly "no holds barred."

"There are a lot of good wrestling books out there. This is top of the line. I highly recommend this book."
— Dave Meltzer, editor, *Wrestling Observer*

"I've never read anything that even came close to describing how the business worked in those wonderful days of what are now, alas, yore — which is the added delight of the tome that J.J., Scott, and Philip have constructed."
— J Michael Kenyon

"Along with The Dynamite Kid's *Pure Dynamite*, Lou Thesz's autobiography, and yes, Mick Foley's *Have a Nice Day*, J.J. Dillon's *Wrestlers Are Like Seagulls: From McMahon to McMahon* stands proud at the top of the pile."
— Dan Lovranski, *The Fight Network*

— Available at crowbarpress.com —

— **Also from Crowbar Press** —

Assassin: The Man Behind the Mask

by Joe Hamilton
with Scott Teal

ISBN: 0-9745545-3-7
6 x 9 Perfect Bound
304 pages, 278 B&W photographs

This autobiography takes the reader behind the scenes for a personal glimpse behind the mask of one of pro wrestling's hottest attractions: The Assassin!

When Joe Hamilton was just 19 years old, he and his brother, Larry, headlined a show at Madison Square Garden, drawing a record 20,335 people to see them wrestle Antonino Rocca and Miguel Perez. To this day, Joe remains the youngest wrestler to ever headline a main event in the Garden.

In 1961, Joe hooked up with veteran wrestler Tom Renesto to form a team called the Assassins, and for the next eleven years, they were considered to be one of wrestling's hottest attractions, drawing sellout crowds to arenas in California, Georgia, Florida, Oklahoma, the Mid-Atlantic, and Washington, in addition to foreign countries like Japan and Australia.

Joe takes readers on a journey as he tells about life both in and out of the wrestling ring—being attacked, stabbed, and shot at by angry wrestling fans; wrestling under a mask and trying to keep his identity a secret; legitimate fights and confrontations behind the scenes in the dressing rooms; a war between two wrestling promotions in Atlanta, Georgia; and never-before-told stories about legends like Ric Flair, Andre the Giant, Giant Baba, Toyonobori, Pedro Morales, Bill Goldberg, Ray Gunkel, and their biggest rivals, the Kentuckians.

Excerpt from *Assassin: The Man Behind the Mask*—

When Barnett told (Ric) Flair that (Rick) Rude was really angry, Flair didn't want to go. He tried to talk his way out of it until Barnett just about pushed him into the dressing room. We were in the room next door and heard everything that was said. When the door shut behind him, we could hear Rick Rude cussing and calling Flair everything but a human being. *"Don't just sit there with your head down, you gutless &^#%$! Get up out of that chair and do something about it, you yellow *#&^$@!"*

The abuse went on for several minutes, with Rude relentlessly screaming at Flair, telling him to stand up. Flair just sat on the chair with his head down. Of course, if Flair had done as Rude asked, Rude would have killed him.

— **Available at crowbarpress.com** —

— Also from Crowbar Press —

The History of Professional Wrestling

This examination of professional wrestling is a continuing series. Each issue is filled with results for the matches during the years indicated.

The History of Professional Wrestling
#3 • Madison Square Garden
January 19, 1880 to December 4, 1999
$29 postpaid

The 3rd volume weighs in at a massive 128 pages. This book features reports on over 500 wrestling shows held in "The World's Most Famous Arena," along with reproductions of over 224 newspaper promotional ads originally published in the New York newspapers. Also included, when available, are attendance and gate figures, the time of each match, stipulations of the matches, title changes, aliases of wrestlers, and newspaper reports. One of the highlights of the book is a 9-page section devoted to the famous riot that broke out after a match on November 9, 1957 between the teams of Argentina Rocca and Edouard Carpentier and Dick the Bruiser and Dr. Jerry Graham.

The History of Professional Wrestling
#6-7 • St. Louis, Missouri: 1930-1985
$25 each, postpaid

The 6th and 7th editions of *The History of Professional Wrestling* features what many considered to be the wrestling capital of the world -- St. Louis, Missouri. Almost every show from 1930 through 1985 is included in the book. This encyclopedic work features reports on over 1,200 wrestling shows, plus reprints of 44 arena program covers and 65 - 3x5 publicity photos. Also included, when available, are attendance and gate figures, the time of each match, stipulations of the matches, and aliases of the wrestlers. The first volume opens with an introduction by wrestling historian J Michael Kenyon, who gives an overview of the high points of the St. Louis promotion.

— Available at crowbarpress.com —

Book Design and Illustration
by Tracy Sabin

Paperback version
ISBN-13: 978-1-951668-26-6
https://tharsheblowsbooks.com

Thar She Blows
BOOKS

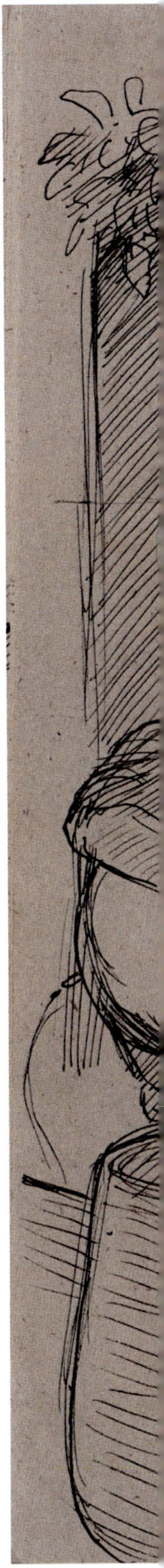

Tuesday Nights at the Calypso

A Decade of Inspired Entertainment by Jack Tempchin & the Rocket Science Band

FROM THE SKETCHBOOKS OF TRACY SABIN

6/8/2000
CAFE
TIPS
Rocket Science
@ Calypso Café

Thank you Bridget

—T

12/05/2000

Calypso 7-17-01

ROCKET SCIENCE

By 1995 I had written two songs for the Eagles that ended up on the biggest selling record of all time. I had recorded albums for Clive Davis and toured as an opening act for many major stars. I spent 14 years writing hit radio songs with my friend Glenn Frey for his albums.

What a wonderful ride!

Then I came up with what turned out to be my favorite creation... the band Rocket Science.

Rocket Science was not a career move, it was a lifestyle move. I wanted a real life outside of show business. So I figured out what I wanted.

My plan was:

1. A weekly gig in a great place where our friends could come and hang out. A real life scene.

2. I decided to choose the people I liked to spend time with to be in the band. They were great players but I did not choose them for that. They were friends who I wanted to see every week and hang out and play music and have fun with.

3. Instead of me singing all the songs and being the front man I decided we would rotate from one band member to the next all night and each guy would play whatever song he liked. Some of the guys had never been front men or singers before so it kept it exciting for everyone and over time we all got to grow and get better.

The Calypso had just opened and we got a gig playing every Tuesday. I told the audience we were on a world tour playing ten years in each town.

We actually played every Tuesday for 13 years!

The pay was not much, but we all would sit around and have a great free dinner together before the gig. It was a family thing. Just what our lives needed!

Looking back on it, I realize that every one of those Tuesdays for 13 years I had a really great time.

Tracy Sabin was always there quietly drawing, but I never got to see the drawings until recently. Drawings of real life are my favorite kind of art, and this captures a wonderful time in my life in a way that nothing else could.

Jack Tempchin and Rocket Science was:

Dean Smith, Warner Davis,
John Barnard and John Scott.

Jack Tempchin

Scan this QR code to play the Rocket Science album.

Calypso 4-17-01

CALYPSO CAFE

The Calypso Cafe opened in Leucadia, California in 1995, conceived as a place for good food, eccentric ambiance and nightly live entertainment. It quickly became a local favorite. In 2009 tragedy struck when a kitchen fire forced its closure. When it reopened two years later, Coast News Lick the Plate columnist David Boylan, celebrated its return. Unfortunately, the revival didn't last. It closed for good January 2013.

Like an old friend, Calypso Café is back and it's great to see

by David Boylan, November 3, 2011

There is really no place like Calypso in San Diego and when it was closed for renovations it left a huge void in the dining and entertainment scene.

It's good to have you back old friend.

Cool is hard to manufacture and I can smell it a mile away when a business is trying too hard. Proprietor Gilles Knafo has defined cool at his Calypso Cafe with a dose of soul thrown in to keep things real. Walking into Calypso, you immediately feel a sense of warmth and energy that makes it very easy to relax and lose yourself in the music and delicious food. There is also a very international feel. Knafo is French Moroccan, and you can hear several languages being spoken on any given night.

Live music fills the air seven nights a week at Calypso with a wide variety of genres represented. Songwriting legend Jack Tempchin, who wrote several hits for the Eagles, has a standing gig on Tuesday nights. If you ever want to treat an out-of-town guest to a pure California moment, take them to Calypso on that night and stick around until Jack breaks into "Peaceful Easy Feeling." It's a good thing. It's too bad there is not a dance floor at Calypso as many of the bands really inspire movement though people do tend to shake it around wherever they can.

Other nights feature jazz, classic rock, salsa and every Sunday night is reggae night. Local favorites the Mar Dels, Jeff Moore, John Bennett, Michael Tiernan, Triple Shot and the Peter Sprague Trio all have regular gigs. All this talent and regular full houses makes every night feel like a weekend at Calypso. It can be tough to get a table between 7 and 9 p.m., so if that is your desired time to eat I'd suggest a reservation.

Both indoor seating areas are fun though the tables in the bar and music area tend to be a bit more high energy. It's nice to sit outside on the sidewalk with the music in the background also and soak up the vibe of a Leucadia evening.

The new Calypso still retains its old-school charm but has some nice new touches including a much bigger bar area. One of my favorite things to do is pop into Calypso early, grab a seat at the bar, order a drink and some food and listen to some music. Easy conversation with new friends almost always ensues and the staff is always friendly.

I've tried just about everything on the menu at Calypso and have narrowed it down to my current top five… that tends to change weekly as Chef Ryan Adams whips up some amazing specials. My current top five starts with Denisa's Yellowfin Tuna Napoleon with sashimi grade tuna, crab, avocado and mango salsa. Next up would be the mussels. They offer them four ways and all of them are very nice. Henri's Coq a Vin transports me to a French bistro every time. The Poisson Au Sel is also named after Henri, who is Knafo's father, and is a whole sea bass baked in rock salt and stuffed with rosemary. If you are lucky and Henri is around, he will expertly fillet it tableside for you, though the servers are well trained in this procedure also.

I'm also a big fan of the St. Pierre, which is a John Dory with a light, crispy exterior covering a moist and flaky fillet. So that leaves me one more. Why did I limit myself to five? I'll have to go with Yvette's lobster ravioli. It's rich and decadent and very hearty.

Long live Calypso!

11 - 20 - 01
Sue Sheryl Bridget

THE DRAWINGS

The friendship of Susan Scott, Sheryl Tempchin and Bridget Salyer brought me to the Calypso Cafe Tuesday evenings. They golfed, dined, and went to shows together. When I started seeing Bridget, I tagged along on the Calypso runs. The appeal was immediate–the amazing songs of Jack Tempchin and the band wittily performed by Rocket Science, coupled with the funky ambiance and delicious food of the Calypso. It was irresistible!

For years, I had filled sketchbooks from life drawing sessions. When my sons were little, I briefly tried sketching people in a public setting–observing from the stands at little league practice. It was hard. Drawing a model in a static pose for minutes to hours differs considerably from drawing people in public spaces. Folks just don't sit still. Arms and heads are in constant motion. Torsos change less often, but a shift in weight or a tilt in response to someone's comment can change the whole configuration of the body.

When I resolved to sketch the lively scenes at the Calypso, I knew I had to be resourceful. I sat for a few minutes before starting, observing how a subject was moving about. If I saw a "home" position that would periodically repeat, I would rough it in quickly, then fill in details each time the subject returned to the position.

The greatest catastrophe occurred when the subject just up and moved away. Honestly, the nerve of some people! There were workarounds. Sometimes they would come back. It was just a bathroom break! If not, I would scan the room searching for a similar subject. Let's not get too worked up about the fact that Fred's head now lives on Wally's body.

As one continues to draw, one develops the skill of faking a head or hand or slouch, understanding general proportions and how features curve in space as angles change. But faked body parts can have a generic aspect that fights against the depiction of an authentic moment in time.

Except for those darkly-toned, the sketches are presented in chronological order and are shown actual size. I take some satisfaction from the fact that the tentative penwork of the first Calypso drawings gained confidence and depth as the years rolled by. Some days went better than others. On rare occasions, I felt I was creating the drawings I most strive for. Just as often, it was a struggle. Such is the nature of self-improvement of any skill. I suspect Jack has a similar relationship with his music. Despite his vast experience and success, he still strives to learn more, to get better, to achieve the unachievable. We are the lucky beneficiaries.

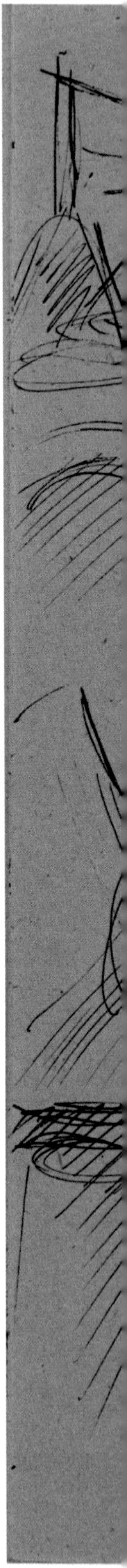

2/26/02

The Cap'n – Henri

Calypso 3.19.02

Calypso 5.26.02

Jerry McCann

Kyle Jester
6-11-02

2 Johns

Kyle

Calypso 7-16-02

Bridget & Sue

Henri & drunk patron

Calypso 7.30.0

8.27
Calypso

Calypso 10-8-02

Calypso 11-26-02

12-10-02
Calypso

12-17-03

Calypso
12/17/02

Calypso 3-18-03

ean

Calypso 4-22-03

Calypso
5-27-03

Calypso
9-9-03

9-30-03
Calypso

calypso

10-21-0

Calypso
12-9-03

Calypso
1-13-04

Rob Burke

Jason

Dean

Calypso
1. 20. 04
Jack

John

Dean Smith
Rocket Science
3.21.04

John Scott

John Barnard

Warner Davis

Calypso 3-30-04

Calypso 5·25·04

Calypso
6.22.0

Calypso

Calypso
8·10·04

Calypso
11.9.04

John B.

Calypso 12-14-04

Sheryl

Calypso 1 - 11 - 05

Calypso 4-12-05

Calypso

4 · 26 · 0

Calypso
6-21-05

Calypso 8·23-

Calypso 8.23-

Dean 9.29.05

Jack

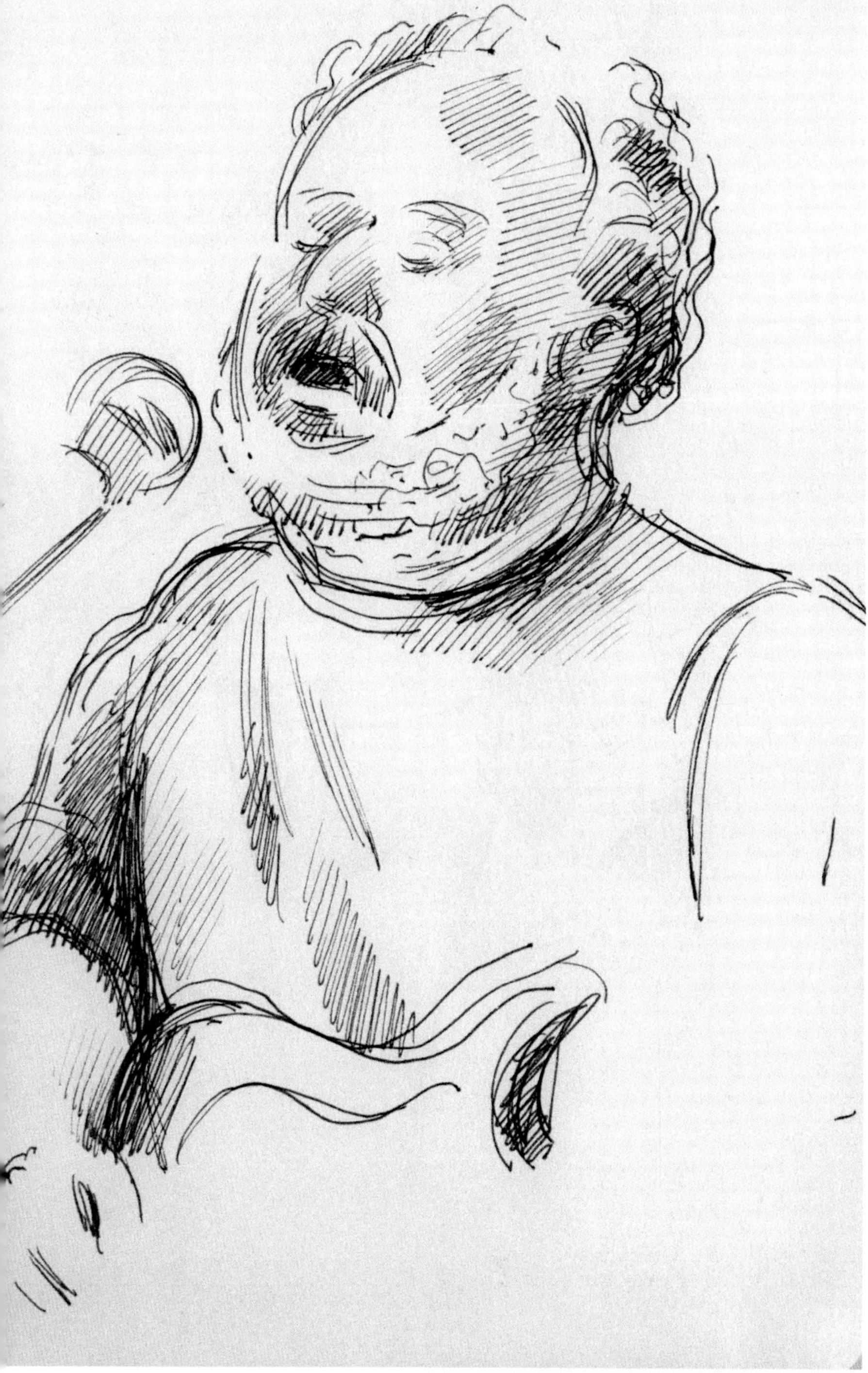

Calypso

10-25-05

Calypso
11.15.05

calypso 12.13.05

Calypso
12·20·05

Norm

Calypso
1-31-06

Jack 2-6-0

Jeff Moore

Sheryl

2 · 10 · 06

ach

Dean

warner

John Scott

Calypso
4-11-06
Ray Pierce

Jeff Moore

Calypso 4-25-06

8-66

Calypso
6-20-06

6-24-06

Calypso
8 · 22 · 0

Calypso
12.12.06

Calypso
1-16-07

Tony Dubow
Calypso 3.27.0

Jeff Moore

Calypso 4.17.0

Calypso.
5.22.07

Calypso
6-26-07

Calypso
7/24/0

Calypso 12-11-07

Calypso 1-22-08

Calypso
2.19.

Calypso 3.11.

Calypso
Tax day 2008

Rob Burke

8·12-08

Calypso 10-28-0

Rob

Yuni

Calyps
11/ 2/

Calypso 12-16-08

Calypso
1-13-09

Calypso
8/4/0

01/23/01